Edward Caswall: Newman's Brother and Friend

Edward Caswall: Newman's Brother and Friend

Nancy Marie de Flon

GRACEWING

First published in 2005

Gracewing
2 Southern Avenue
Leominster
Herefordshire HR6 0QF

ISBN 0 85244 607 1

Typesetting by
Action Publishing Technology Ltd, Gloucester, GL1 5SR

Dedicated, with gratitude, to the memory of Gerard Tracey,
Archivist of the Birmingham Oratory
and an ever-present help in time of research

Contents

Illustrations

With the exception of the photograph of the Church of St Lawrence, all photographs are courtesy of the Fathers of the Birmingham Oratory.

Foreword

John Henry Newman valued loyal friendship. Ever since his Oxford days as leader of the Tractarian Movement, he set enormous store on the value of spiritual 'amicitia'. Newman's own incipient breach with the Church of England was marked by a farewell sermon which was significantly entitled, *A Parting of Friends*, the phrase which the late David Newsome used as the title of his moving and evocative account of the Oxford Movement, published in 1966. For behind all the soul-searching over doctrine and ecclesiology, the human dimension of the loss and pain induced by inevitable breaches of contact was never far from the surface. Yet if Newman 'lost' or was separated from many former spiritual acolytes and disciples on becoming a Catholic, in time he was to gain many more, many of which, though converts like himself, he had never known personally while an Anglican, even if he had influenced them in varying degrees. Edward Caswall (1814–1878), the subject of this fascinating and highly scholarly biography, who converted to Catholicism at the age of thirty-two and upon his wife's sudden death at the age of twenty-eight joined Newman's Oratorian community in Birmingham, falls into this latter category.

The perennial historical tendency to categorize or 'pigeon-hole' can give a false impression that there was a unity or coherence to that body of individuals within the mid- and later nineteenth-century English Catholic Church to which the label 'converts' is commonly assigned. While the influence of the Oxford Movement was crucial in many cases (it certainly left its mark on Caswell's Anglican ministry in a Wiltshire parish, with his revival of daily services, fasting, and confession), there were instances of converts such as Richard Sibthorp whose path to Rome was made rather in spite of than because of the impact of Tractarianism. The work of Sheridan Gilley, Patrick Allitt and others should make us more sensitive to the wide varieties of converts in the period, varieties that encompassed personalities as diverse as Frederick

William Faber, William Maskell, Frederick Oakeley, William Dodsworth, Thomas William Allies, Richard Sibthorp, and Peter Le Page Renouf, all of whom have enjoyed recent scholarly attention (Renouf being the subject of a masterly four volume edition of his correspondence by Professor Kevin Cathcart). For some, questions of ecclesiology and issues of religious authority were paramount; for others, the attraction of Rome lay more in terms of her spirituality and devotional riches. In the case of Caswall, experiential spiritual and devotional factors seem to have rather outweighed the intellectual and ecclesiological (though like others influenced by the Oxford Movement, he gave due weight to the issue of apostolical continuity). Caswall's early sense of the mystical and inextricable linkeage of the visible and invisible worlds (a characteristic of the Tractarian *ethos*), which had found expression in his Anglican *Sermons on the Seen and Unseen*, were perhaps the crucial element.

Given the archival riches of material within the hallowed precincts of the Birmingham Oratory, it is surprising that Edward Caswall, especially in comparison with his fellow Oratorian and hymn writer Frederick Faber, has hitherto been so neglected, except for a 'biographical preface' to an edition of Caswall's *Hymns and Poems Original and Translated* by Edward Bellasis in 1908. This may not be surprising given that, unlike so many other mid-nineteenth-century Anglican converts to Rome, Caswall never published his conversion narrative or intellectual reasons for religious change. However, this fact makes the first book-length study of Caswall by Nancy de Flon all the more welcome, especially because it is grounded on the manuscript bedrock of Caswall's own unpublished 630-page journal. This journal, begun as a mere notebook in 1846 and charting Caswall's inner and exterior spiritual journey, is housed among Caswall's papers in the archives of Birmingham Oratory. It was one of the very many great services to scholarship bequeathed by the late and much lamented Gerard Tracey that he should have brought this neglected source to the author's attention and made it available to her. It is truly fitting that this volume should be dedicated to his memory.

One of the many merits of this work is that it recognizes the above temperamental as well as intellectual distinctions and nuances, and seeks to place Caswall's life, religious journey, theology and spirituality, in historical, religious, and family context. Many of the 'Oxford converts', such as Robert and Henry Wilberforce, Frederick William Faber, and Frederick Oakeley as well as notably Newman himself, came from an Anglican Evangelical family stable against which they reacted, though for many of them their Roman conversion might be viewed as a 'second' conversion which completed or supplemented an original

Evangelical conversion. Caswall had no such religious lineage, and his own 'Anglican death bed' while perpetual curate of Stratford-sub-Castle in the diocese of Salisbury, lacked the drama and poignancy of Newman's at Littlemore. Nonetheless, Caswall's path to Rome was not without much personal and family sacrifice. As de Flon shows, his maternal great-uncle the famous Bishop of St David's, Thomas Burgess (1756–1837), successively Bishop of St David's and Salisbury, was a learned Protestant controversialist whose 'penchant for polemics' helped 'to strengthen an anti-Catholic sentiment in the family that eventually proved a thorny (but, not in the end, insuperable) obstacle to Edward's conversion'. Edward Caswall's Catholicism was also to be a foil to the staunch Anglicanism of his brother Henry Caswall who would achieve fame as an Episcopalian churchman in the United States of America. De Flon shows that Caswall, perhaps reacting against his episcopal great-uncle's extreme emphasis on British Protestant apostolical continuity, readily came to doubt one of the main shibboleths of Tractarianism – the assumption that the apostolical succession of the Church of England was self-evident and a matter of pure faith.

Nancy de Flon steers the reader through the fascinating family background and Oxford years of her subject and does much to explain Caswall's own distinctive path to Rome before treating his fruitful Oratorian years when Caswall was the financial and administrative mainstay of Newman's community in Birmingham (he was Acting Superior for long periods when Newman was preoccupied in Dublin with the Catholic University of Ireland). Caswall's pastoral, evangelistic, and educational labours among the poor of Victorian Birmingham are also highlighted.

The particular strength of de Flon's study, however, is the extent to which she focuses on and draws out Caswall's outstanding literary, poetical and devotional genius. This literary dimension to Caswall was first vividly expressed in his flowering as a humorist during his time at Oxford in the 1830s (he was the author of that seminal work of Oxonian humour, *The Art of Pluck*) and in later works such as his *Sketches of Young Ladies* in which he satirized the Bridgewater Treatises and in a fanciful autobiography in which he imagined himself into the guise of an easy chair. The latter work was one of a series of quaint anthropomorphisms of inanimate objects and members of the animal kingdom of which Caswall was to be the author. This whimsical side of Caswall especially appealed to Newman's sister, Harriet Mozley who described him as the 'quaintest of men', and to her husband Thomas Mozley who (as he described in his *Reminiscences of Oriel College and the Oxford Movement*) was much entertained by Caswall's 'meditations of a toad' during a visit to Caswall's then home of Stratford-sub-Castle in the early 1840s.

Caswall's literary skill was exemplified in his authorship of several spiritual manuals for children, but found its fullest later expression in his emergence as an original and accomplished hymnologist (he was 'one of the great hymnologists of the nineteenth century', to be ranked alongside the Anglican John Mason Neale) – as de Flon modestly concedes, there is material here for another book. It was as an exemplary pastor, who in his leisure composed hymns and poems, rather than as an intellectual figure at the forefront of theological or ecclesiastical controversies of the day, that Caswall deserves to be remembered. As de Flon makes clear, Caswall's hymn translations provided invaluable service in making the Breviary and other Latin hymns accessible to an English readership. It is impossible to underestimate this unique devotional legacy, and de Flon herself movingly recounts her own early acquaintance with Caswall's hymns which formed a staple part of the devotional life of pre-Vatican II Catholicism. It is a legacy that cannot be too quickly recovered and restored.

Peter Nockles
Manchester, March 2005.

Introduction

Edward Caswall (1814–1878) first made his mark as an author of satire and humour while an undergraduate at Oxford. Ordained as an Anglican, he converted to Roman Catholicism at the age of thirty-two and, upon his wife's sudden death at the age of twenty-eight, joined John Henry Newman's Oratory of St Philip Neri at Birmingham, where he provided invaluable support to Newman for the rest of his life. Newman cherished Caswall for his loyalty and gentleness. Posterity knows and is indebted to Caswall for his hymn texts, some original and many translated from Latin and other sources, a number of which still appear in Roman Catholic and other Christian hymn collections.

Along with the Anglican John Mason Neale, Caswall was one of the most important hymnologists in the nineteenth-century English-speaking world. His hymn translations provided invaluable service in making breviary and other Latin hymns accessible to English-speaking Christians, while his original hymns enjoyed immense popularity during his lifetime, and several of them, along with many of Caswall's translations, still appear in modern Christian hymnals.

Caswall shares with Frederick William Faber not only the role of hymn writer but also the distinction of being one of the earliest members of Newman's Oratorian community in Birmingham. Caswall was a financial and administrative mainstay for Newman's Oratory for his twenty-eight years there. Indeed, it could possibly be claimed that without Caswall's assistance the Birmingham Oratory might not have survived its initial growing pains. His initial injection of money came just when the fledgling community was engaged in a search for a sorely-needed new base of activity, and his tenure as Rector during the years of Newman's absence in Dublin was marked by considerable growth in the Oratory's educational and pastoral apostolate, much of it made possible by his vision and gifts for organization as well as his financial contributions.

While Neale and Faber have both been the subjects of a number of biographical and critical studies, Caswall has had scarcely a scholarly article devoted to him. Meriol Trevor has drawn on Newman's *Letters and Diaries* to recount incidents about the Oratory that involved Caswall.[1] More recent books on Newman by Ian Ker[2] and Sheridan Gilley[3] give passing notice to Caswall. Hoxie Neale Fairchild[4] briefly discusses Caswall's poetry in a section on 'Catholic revival poets'; his attitude toward these poets tends, however, to be biased and dismissive. Thus far the most satisfactory account of Caswall as poet, but one not without its inaccuracies, is a very brief section on him in a chapter on 'Tractarian epigones' by G. B. Tennyson.[5] No one, however, has yet attempted either a systematic account of the life or a critique, literary or theological, of the hymns and poetry of this man whose spiritual journey from Anglicanism via Tractarianism to Roman Catholicism exemplifies the personal and theological dilemmas experienced by many during this era. Yet, as Tennyson has pointed out, Caswall 'would repay study in his own right'.[6]

It is this lacuna that I am attempting to fill with this book. Chapter one presents Caswall's early life up to and including his years as a student at Oxford. It discusses his family of origin, with particular focus on his influential great-uncle, Bishop Thomas Burgess, his youthful and university education, and the humorous articles and books that he published while still at Oxford, as well as his more important unpublished works. Chapter two discusses Caswall's career as an Anglican clergyman, his marriage, and the books he published in that period of his life.

1 Meriol Trevor, *Newman: The Pillar of the Cloud* (Garden City, NY: Doubleday, 1962); and *Newman: Light in Winter* (Garden City, NY: Doubleday, 1963).

2 Ian Ker, *John Henry Newman: A Biography* (Oxford and New York: Oxford University Press, 1988).

3 Sheridan Gilley, *Newman and His Age* (Westminster, MD: Christian Classics, 1990).

4 Hoxie Neale Fairchild, *Religious Trends in English Poetry*, vol. 4, *1830–1880, Christianity and Romanticism in the Victorian Era* (New York and London: Columbia University Press, 1957; repr. 1964).

5 G. B. Tennyson, *Victorian Devotional Poetry: The Tractarian Mode* (Cambridge, MA, and London: Harvard University Press, 1981).

6 Ibid., p. 185.

Chapter three is a central chapter, dealing as it does with Caswall's conversion journey. Beginning with his initial questions about the Established Church, it charts his investigations into the truth claims of the Church of Rome via his extensive reading, his discussions with other people, and his first-hand observation of Roman Catholicism in Ireland and on the Continent; and it explores his inner spiritual and emotional journey, particularly as it relates to his affinity with or irritation by certain Roman Catholic beliefs and practices, and to the attitudes of his family.

Not long after his reception into the Roman Catholic Church, Caswall's life changed in a most unforeseen way; chapter four relates this period of his life that spanned his early years as a convert up to his joining the Oratory. Caswall had not been ordained priest very long before Newman entrusted him with the responsibility of Rector of the Oratory. This forms the basis of chapter five, which discusses Caswall's contributions to the apostolate of the Birmingham Oratory, particularly in the area of education.

Chapter six deals with Caswall's hymns and poems. This could have been the subject of a book in itself, and so I have tried to limit the chapter to a discussion of those issues that illumine some of the broader themes connected with Victorian hymn publishing: Tractarian poetry, from which Caswall took much of his inspiration, and Catholic poetry, to which he made a significant contribution in his own time.

Once the Oratory really found its feet and became entrenched in serving the Catholics of Birmingham and the surrounding areas, Caswall had less time for translating or composing hymns or poems; the bulk (but not all) of this type of creative work took place by 1858. He did, however, produce some prose works, mainly of a devotional nature. The final chapter reviews these books and pamphlets, recounts his final illness and death, and provides a concluding summary of his life and work.

For assistance in researching and writing this book I have to thank, first of all, my dissertation committee at Union Theological Seminary: Dr David Lotz, my dissertation director, who kept me on track for the birthing process; Dr John McGuckin, whose perceptive comments saved numerous sections from mediocrity; Dr Janet Walton, whose interest in questions of liturgy inspired my investigations in this area; and, above all, the late Mr Gerard Tracey, archivist at the Birmingham Oratory, without whom this project would have been entirely impossible. He provided not only access to the incredible wealth of material housed at the Oratory but also a mind-boggling number of information bytes from his own encyclopaedic knowledge of everything to do with the Oratory. I hope he is enjoying eternity with John Henry Newman, whose cause he served so well.

I am grateful also to the librarians at the Burke Library, especially Seth Kasten for making available many materials from the Rare Books Collection, to the librarians at the Immaculate Conception Seminary library in Huntington, New York and at the British Library at St Pancras, London, as well as to the archivists at Brasenose College, Oxford and the Trowbridge (Wiltshire) Record Office, and the librarians at Salisbury Public Library; also to the parishioners at St Lawrence Church in Stratford-sub-Castle, descendants of the people to whom Caswall ministered in the 1840s, and particularly Patrick Coggan. I must also acknowledge and thank the Historical Society of the Episcopal Church for giving me a grant to travel to various spots in England to investigate Caswall's life and career as an Anglican. Thanks, too, to the Revd Peter I. Vaccari, Professor of Church History at Immaculate Conception Seminary, for starting me on my investigations of nineteenth-century Roman Catholic England by challenging me to make a case for sainthood for Gerard Manley Hopkins. And I warmly thank the Fathers of the Oratory community in Birmingham, who provided cheery help and hospitality during my numerous visits there, and especially Fr Dermot Fenlon for offering words of encouragement whenever they were most needed.

Finally, I thank Edward Caswall himself. In recent years he has become my soulmate as I have prayed with him, spoken to him, occasionally argued with and questioned him. But in the course of researching his hymns I have discovered that our acquaintance goes back much further than I had originally thought: during those many years of Catholic elementary and high school, at Mass, at Stations of the Cross, at various other devotions that punctuated the lives of pre-Vatican II Roman Catholics, it was he who provided the texts. From 'When morning gilds the skies' to the seemingly endless verses of 'At the cross', from 'My God, I love thee, not because' to 'O Jesus Christ, remember', from 'Come, Holy Ghost' to 'O hidden Godhead, humbly I adore thee', he supplied a hymn or prayer text for every occasion. If it is true, as St Paul claims, that the Spirit steps in and supplies the words for our prayers when we don't have our own, then on many occasions the Spirit has used Edward as – and I think he would have chuckled either heartily or quaintly at the pun – ghostwriter.

TO EDWARD CASWALL

Once, o'er a clear calm pool,
The fullness of an over-brimming spring,
I saw the hawthorn and the chestnut fling
Their willing arms, of vernal blossoms full
And light green leaves: the lilac too was there,
The prodigal laburnum, dropping gold,
While the rich gorse along the turf crept near,
Close to the fountain's margin, and made bold
To peep into that pool, so calm and clear:–
As if well pleased to see their image bright
Reflected back upon their innocent sight;
Each flower and blossom shy
Lingering the live-long day in still delight,
Yet without touch of pride, to view,
Yea, with a tender, holy sympathy,
What was itself, yet was another too.

So on my verse, my Brother and my Friend,
– The fresh upwelling of thy tranquil spirit,–
I see a many angel forms attend;
And gracious souls elect;
And thronging sacred shades, that shall inherit
One day the azure skies;
And peaceful saints, in whitest garments deck'd;
And happy infants of the second birth:–
These, and all other plants of paradise,
Thoughts from above, and visions that are sure,
And providences past, and memories dear,
In much content hang o'er that mirror pure,
And recognize each other's faces there,
And see a heaven on earth.

John Henry Newman

Chapter One

Family Background and Years at Oxford

It was typical of Edward Caswall that he would give his birthdate as 'St Swithin's Day':[1] typical of his wit and humour that he would, with that single allusion, both make a gentle play on the Tractarian custom of dating documents with the name of the saint of the day and acknowledge his own devotion to the Communion of Saints which had helped to confirm his acceptance of Roman Catholicism. And yet, ironically, what probably would have escaped Caswall's attention altogether, except for their shared geographical origins,[2] were certain parallels between his life and that of the saint on whose feast he was born: St Swithin built several churches,[3] while Edward Caswall contributed indispensable financial assistance to the establishment of John Henry Newman's Oratory and its related outreach

[1] Edward Bellasis, 'Biographical Preface', in Edward Caswall, *Hymns and Poems Original and Translated*, new edn (London: Burns & Oates, 1908), p. 5. In a footnote Bellasis discloses that '[f]or considerable portions of this sketch, a rough autobiographical summary of his life (occasionally quoted), written by Father Caswall's own hand, 23 April 1864, has been laid under contribution' (ibid.). Folklore held that if it rained on St Swithin's day it would continue to rain for forty days.

[2] Both St Swithin and the Caswalls came from Wessex (for St Swithin cf. John J. Delaney, *Pocket Dictionary of Saints*, abridged edn [New York: Doubleday Image, 1983], p. 468.) According to the *Memoirs of the Caswall Family*, 'The family of Caswall ... is said to have come from the county of Glamorgan and settled in the town of Leominster, county Hereford, as early as the 16th century' (p. 7). Perhaps Edward's Welsh genes help to account for his poetic gifts. Bellasis ('Biographical Preface', p. 5) records the West Country origins of the Caswalls; although Edward was born in Hampshire, it was to the dioceses of Bath and Wells and of Salisbury that he returned for his ministry as an Anglican clergyman.

[3] Delaney, *Saints*, p. 468.

at Birmingham; Swithin was known for his humility and his aid to the poor and needy,[4] as was Caswall – and that very humility would have caused Caswall to dismiss as a meaningless coincidence what others might well regard as prophetic.

Thus it was on 15 July, 1814 that Edward Caswall first saw the light of day, in Yately, Hants, where his father, the Revd Robert Clarke Caswall, was then Vicar of St Peter's Church. Service to God and the Crown ran like a red thread through the Caswall family's history. Edward's great-great-grandfather and great-grandfather Sir George Caswall and John Caswall were Members of Parliament for Leominster, Herefordshire, the home borough of the Caswall clan;[5] Edward, with his characteristic humour, recorded Sir George's distinction of having been 'summoned to the Bar of the House of Commons' in connection with his involvement in that notorious financial catastrophe known as the South Sea Bubble.[6]

Edward's grandfather, the Revd John Caswall, was Vicar of the Church of SS Peter and Paul in Swalcliffe, one of the largest parishes in north Oxfordshire, from 1761 until his death in 1808.[7] By the seventh year of his long incumbency he had increased the number of communion services from three to four a year, read prayers every saint's day and holyday, and catechized children both at Swalcliffe itself and at Epwell, where the parish maintained a chapel.[8] Swalcliffe was a prosperous parish that supported a flourishing church choir and band. In the 1780s three choir members undertook to organize a band and raise money to buy the instruments,[9] so that an oboe, a bassoon, a vox humana, a hautboy, and a bass viol were acquired over the space of two years[10] 'to be kept for the sole use of Swalcliffe Choir for the time being for ever'.[11] It is

4 Ibid.

5 Bellasis, 'Biographical Preface', p. 5.

6 The South Sea Company, founded in 1711 to trade with Spanish America, in 1720 'managed to outbid the Bank of England in an offer to purchase the whole national debt' (*Memoirs*, 10). Sir George Caswall was one of the company directors. When the entire scheme collapsed, a committee in the House of Commons ordered an investigation and summoned witnesses. Consequently, Sir George and his partners were sentenced to repay £250,000 to shareholders, and 'the Company being of unlimited liability, this loss mainly fell on Sir George, who with his partners was committed to the Tower [of London] until the whole sum was paid' (ibid.).

7 Alan Crossley, ed., *A History of the County of Oxford*, vol. 10: *Banbury Hundred* (London: Published for the Institute of Historical Research by Oxford University Press, 1962), p. 250.

8 Ibid.

9 Maurice Byrne, 'The Church Band at Swalcliffe', *Oxoniensia* 28 (1963): p. 79.

10 Crossley, ed., *History of the County of Oxford* vol. 10: p. 250.

11 Byrne, 'Church Band', pp. 79–80.

ironic that John Caswall's grandson became one of the most outstanding figures in the Victorian hymn tradition which ultimately sounded the death-knell of the church gallery bands.

The Revd Robert Clarke Caswall (1768–1846), Edward's father, matriculated at Balliol College, Oxford, in 1785[12] but obtained the degree of Bachelor of Civil Law from St John's College.[13] After a variety of livings he ended his days as Vicar of West Lavington in the Diocese of Salisbury. His first wife having died after barely a year of marriage, Robert Caswall married Mary Burgess at the age of forty-one.[14] His late marriage did not prevent him from fathering nine children,[15] but it did provide Edward with yet another distinguished ancestor: his maternal great-uncle was the Revd Dr Thomas Burgess (1756–1837), Bishop of St David's in Wales (1803–25) and later of Salisbury (1825–37).

Born the son of a grocer near Basingstoke, Hants,[16] Thomas Burgess was a diligent student who exhibited a 'love of books' and a 'taste for a studious and contemplative life'.[17] Already in his youth an inclination toward literature and a propensity for the poetic were apparent: he came to know personally the poet Thomas Warton (1728–90), for whose 'Sonnet to the River Lodon' (a river near Basingstoke, from which Warton, too, hailed) he 'ever reserved a special place of affection'.[18] Warton's sonnet was a typical example of the topographical poetry of that period; one wonders whether he ever recited it to his young great-nephew Edward, whose own poetry bears clear traces of the influence of such work. Here are a few lines from it:

[12] *Alumni Oxonienses: The Members of the University of Oxford, 1715–1886. Being the Matriculation Register of the University*, alphabetically arranged, revised, and annotated by Joseph Foster, vol. 1: Later Series (Oxford: James Parker & Co., 1891).

[13] *Memoirs*, p. 15.

[14] Ibid.

[15] Bellasis ('Biographical Preface', p. 5) reports that Edward was one of nine children, and the *Memoirs* give their dates.

[16] The sources of information for Thomas Burgess's life are: John S. Harford, Esq., DCL, FRS, *The Life of Thomas Burgess, D.D., F.R.S., F.A.S. &c. &c. &c., Late Lord Bishop of Salisbury*, 2nd edn. (London: Printed for Longman, Orme, Brown, Green, & Longmans, 1841), and the *Dictionary of National Biography* (hereafter *DNB*), s.u. 'Burgess, Thomas', pp. 313–14. Harford wrote 'from personal knowledge and authentic data, having been honoured with the friendship of the departed Prelate, and intrusted by him with the disposition of his papers and correspondence' (p. viii). The most recent information about Bishop Burgess relevant to Caswall's life can be found in Peter Nockles, 'Recreating the History of the Church of England: Bishop Burgess, the Oxford Movement and 19th-Century Constructions of Protestant and Anglican Identity', in *Bishop Burgess and His World*, ed. Nigel Yates (Lampeter: University of Wales Press, publication forthcoming).

[17] Harford, *Burgess*, p. 6.

[18] Ibid., p. 7.

> Ah! what a weary race my feet have run
> Since first I trod thy banks, with elders crown'd,
> And thought my way was all thro' fairy ground,
> Beneath thy azure sky and golden sun,
> Where first my Muse to lisp her notes begun![19]

While still an undergraduate in Classics at Corpus Christi College, Oxford,[20] Burgess himself published a poem, 'Bagley Wood', that immortalizes 'one of his favourite rural retreats' between Abingdon and Oxford[21] and could probably be considered to stand in the hallowed tradition of Oxford-honouring poetry, of which other exponents include John Keble's 'Oxford (From Bagley, at 8 A.M.)', 'Duns Scotus's Oxford' by Gerard Manley Hopkins, and his own great-nephew's 'Lines Written on Leaving Oxford'. A more prepossessing example of his literary precociousness can be seen in his scholarly achievements while yet a university student: he re-edited Burton's *Pentalogia* and published a new edition of Dawes's *Miscellanea Critica*.[22]

Late in his life, when his biographer Harford asked him about his motivation for the Anglican ministry, Burgess replied: 'At the time to which you refer, I was full of that ambition of literary distinction natural to a young scholar circumstanced as I was; but, after I had taken orders, and turned my attention to sacred studies, I gradually imbibed deep and serious views of Divine Truth.'[23]

Here is a striking parallel with Edward Caswall, who also had several publications to his credit before he had left Oxford, the success of one of which 'caused me at the time to think of turning my attention to writing as a profession. I had, indeed, gone so far as to prepare a companion to it, . . . but on calm deliberation, resolving to give myself up to the ministry, I put it aside'.[24]

Burgess's dedication to education and catechesis, such a prominent aspect of his career as bishop, emerged early in his ministry. In 1785 he was appointed chaplain to Bishop Barrington of Salisbury,

19 Quoted in ibid. That Burgess was in contact with his Caswall great-nephews and nieces is evident from a letter written 30 June 1831, and quoted in Harford, to Edward's brother Alfred, in reply to a letter that Alfred had written him from Bonn about his visit to a German scholar of Greek.

20 He matriculated in 1775, attained his BA in 1778 and his MA in 1782 (Harford, *Burgess*, p. 18).

21 Ibid., p. 9.

22 DNB, p. 313. Harford claims that Burgess was 'the most zealous, able, and successful promoter of Greek learning at Oxford, towards the close of the eighteenth century' (*Burgess*, p. 18).

23 Harford, *Burgess*, p. 73.

24 Bellasis, 'Biographical Preface', p. 7. The work to which he refers is *Sketches of Young Ladies* (see below).

who was then engaged in extending the system of Sunday schools throughout his diocese. Burgess proved a most able assistant, zealously exerting himself 'to promote the Christian education of the children of the labouring classes, and to train them up in provident principles and habits'.[25] To this end, because books for such schools were quite rare at that time (indeed, Sunday schools themselves were novelties then), Burgess compiled the *Salisbury Spelling-Book* which, in addition to the elements of spelling and reading, contained edifying stories 'in the simplest language; a series of scriptural lessons; and, finally, the church catechism'.[26] This was followed by a companion, a book of exercises. Then, perceiving the need for something even more basic, Burgess compiled *The Child's First Book* and *The Child's First Lessons in Religion,* 'with short prayers for children to learn by heart before they are taught to read'.[27]

As Bishop of St David's Burgess laboured assiduously to improve the education of clergy as well as laity. Finding, upon his arrival, 'no suitable establishments for clerical training'[28] and aware that a university education was a financial impossibility for most candidates for ordination, he licensed four grammar schools for the classical education of ordinands and required seven years of study instead of the one year that had been customary, instituting various prizes as a motivation toward study. He founded a 'Society for Promoting Christian Knowledge and Church Union in the Diocese of St David's' for the purpose of distributing Bibles, prayerbooks, and other religious literature in Welsh and English among the poor, and established libraries for the clergy as well as Sunday schools and English schools for the poor.[29] For the higher education of the clergy he also established St David's College in Lampeter, setting aside part of his own income for this purpose.[30] Harford depicts him as quite detached from money, which he regarded as a means to support noble ends:[31] 'His private charities were dispensed in the spirit of this noble sentiment. His applications were numerous, and were seldom unheeded ... He often said that avarice was the vice of old age, and that he was anxious to guard against its first approaches'.[32] His pastoral sense was shown in his refusal to 'induct

25 Harford, *Burgess*, p. 92.
26 Ibid., p. 93.
27 Ibid.
28 Ibid., p. 217.
29 Ibid.
30 *DNB*, p. 314.
31 Harford, *Burgess*, p. 302.
32 Ibid., pp. 302–3.

clergy ignorant of Welsh into Welsh-speaking parishes'.[33]

In 1825, needing a rest from such strenuous labours,[34] Burgess was translated to the Diocese of Salisbury where, despite his advancing age, he made his mark. There he established a Church Union Society similar to the one in St David's and 'showed great energy in visiting, confirming, educating, and ordaining'.[35] He died in February 1837, having never completely recovered from an apoplectic seizure suffered nearly two years previously.

In addition to his tireless pastoral work Burgess had one other consuming passion, and that was writing. His prodigious literary output included charges, sermons, devotional treatises, fragments of controversial theology, and attempts at ecclesiastical history.[36] And in all his writings, which numbered over one hundred published works, he was nothing if not polemical: 'In nearly all that he wrote Burgess had some cherished principle or opinion to defend, for the sake of which he threw away discretion and impartiality.'[37] Between 1814 and 1820 he wrote a series of tracts denouncing the Unitarian claim that Christ was 'a mere man',[38] adducing against their opinion 'Christ's declaration of himself, ... the attestation of his contemporaries, and ... the evidence of his trial', as well as 'the testimony of all the Christian Fathers of the three first centuries, who maintain, from the Scriptures, that Christ was God, God of God, the uncreated and eternal Son of God.'[39] But Burgess was also fervently anti-Catholic. In his *Tracts on the Origin and Independence of the ancient British Church; on the Supremacy of the Pope, and the Inconsistency of All Foreign Jurisdiction with the British Constitution; and on the Differences between the Churches of England and of Rome*[40] he set out to expose as 'deceptions'[41] the 'Roman Catholic claim for the *antiquity* of the Church of Rome, the *divine origin* of the Pope's supremacy, the *universality* of the Pope's authority over the Christian Church before the Reformation'[42] and to

[33] *DNB*, p. 314.

[34] The weakness of vision from which he suffered for several years (*DNB*, p. 314) must have been a family trait: Edward Caswall occasionally mentions the same complaint and records having acquired spectacles, e.g., in his journal of 1846–7. A letter to Edward from his brother Alfred (23 Oct. 1851) expresses Alfred's hope that Edward will 'call George Copeland's [a school friend and now a physician] attention to your state of blindness'.

[35] *DNB*, p. 314.

[36] Ibid.

[37] Ibid.

[38] Thomas Burgess, *Tracts on the Divinity of Christ, and on the Repeal of the Statute against Blasphemy* (London: Printed for J. Hatchard & Son, 1820, p. 434.)

[39] Ibid.

[40] 2nd edn, with additions (London: Printed for F.C. & J. Rivington, 1815).

[41] Burgess, 'Advertisement', in *Tracts*, p. v.

[42] Ibid.

> counteract these delusions, by shewing, that the Church (not of Rome, but) of Jerusalem, was the mother church of Christendom; that the British Church, founded by St Paul, was in its origin, and for many centuries, wholly independent of the Church of Rome, that the Pope's supremacy originated, not with St Peter, but with an unprincipled usurper, ... that the claims of the Roman Catholics are wholly inconsistent with the King's prerogative, and with the safety of the Established Church,[43]

and so forth. Burgess cites as authorities Gildas, 'our oldest native historian',[44] who records that the Gospel was preached in Britain before the year 61, and Eusebius, who reportedly claimed that 'the Gospel was preached in Britain by *some of the Apostles*'.[45] This, says Burgess, must have been St Paul;[46] we have the 'good historical evidence of ancient authorities, supported by the concurrence of very judicious modern writers',[47] that Paul preached the Gospel in Britain and appointed the first Bishop[48] and 'other Ministers of the Church'[49] in Britain, whereas we have 'no *credible* testimony that any other Apostle ever was in Britain'.[50] Since Linus, the first Bishop of Rome, was appointed by Peter and Paul only in the year of their martyrdom, then, Burgess contends, the British Church obviously predates the Roman.[51]

Burgess also takes on no less an authority than the great Roman Catholic bishop Richard Challoner (1691–1781), answering point by point the latter's tract 'A Roman Catholic's Reasons Why He Cannot Conform to the Protestant Religion'.[52] Burgess's claim in this tract that the Church of Rome has indeed 'greatly gone astray by idolatry in the invocation of Saints'[53] was to become a major issue in Edward Caswall's journey toward Roman Catholicism.

In the question of Catholic Emancipation Burgess was 'inflexibly opposed',[54] arguing that the 'fundamental principle of the British

[43] Ibid., pp. v–vi.
[44] Burgess, 'Apostolic Origin, Independence, and Protestantism, of the Ancient British Church', in *Tracts*, p. 188.
[45] Ibid.
[46] Ibid.
[47] 'Christ, and not St Peter, the Rock of the Christian Church: A Letter to the Clergy of the Diocese of St. David's', in *Tracts*, pp. 54–5.
[48] One Aristobulus, mentioned in the Letter to the Romans (ibid., p. 55).
[49] Ibid.
[50] Burgess, 'Apostolic Origin', p. 188.
[51] Burgess, 'Christ', p. 55.
[52] Burgess, 'A Roman Catholic's Reasons Examined and Answered', in *Tracts*, pp. 192–201.
[53] Ibid., p. 195.
[54] Harford, *Burgess*, p. 238.

Constitution ... was to support with the utmost tenacity the Protestant Established Church';[55] thus to admit Roman Catholics to legislative power would be both dangerous and inconsistent with the principles of the British Constitution. In 1820 he delivered a speech to the House of Lords in which he 'expose[d] the errors and corruptions of the Church of Rome; ... vindicate[d] the nationality and independence of that of England; and ... assert[ed] its claims as a branch of the Church Catholic'.[56] In a personal display of the 'utmost tenacity' he battled to the finish against Emancipation, via letters to the Duke of Wellington that were published in the newspapers and 'a violent harangue in the House of Lords'[57] that referred to 'the danger to be apprehended from the influence of that supreme spiritual authority by means of which the Pope extends his influence into foreign countries, and interferes with the temporal authority of sovereigns and states'.[58]

Burgess's indefatigable energy; his irresistible urge to take up his pen; his unstinting use of his own financial resources to further his pastoral work; his firm commitment to religious education and catechesis, especially of children and the poor; his deep piety – each of these attributes reproduced themselves in the personality of his great-nephew Edward Caswall.[59] The bishop's penchant for polemics helped, however, to strengthen an anti-Catholic sentiment in the family that eventually proved a thorny (but not, in the end, insuperable) obstacle to Edward's conversion and a source of deep pain and perplexity to parents, siblings, and other relations when first the younger brother Thomas and then Edward went over to Rome.

Of Edward's four brothers only Henry, the eldest (1810–1870), became a clergyman. Sent off to America at the age of eighteen because of Dr Burgess's interest in a theological school that Bishop Philander Chase proposed to establish in his diocese of Ohio, Henry married the bishop's niece and was ordained deacon and eventually priest. While in America he came to know and write books about Joseph Smith and the Mormons. In 1842 Henry

55 Ibid.
56 Ibid., p. 240.
57 *DNB*, p. 314.
58 Harford, *Burgess*, p. 369.
59 The *DNB* account of Caswall's life records that he became perpetual curate of Stratford-sub-Castle 'in the diocese of his uncle, Dr. Burgess, bishop of Salisbury' (s.u. 'Caswall, Edward', p. 1185). The implication of any direct family influence in Edward's appointment is misleading, however: Burgess died in 1837, two years before Edward was ordained priest and three years before his appointment to Stratford, having first experienced an ecclesiastical whirlwind tour of various minor posts.

returned to England with his family and was appointed curate, and later incumbent, of Figheldean in Wiltshire. He travelled back and forth to America a number of times and died and is buried there.

Of the other brothers only the second oldest, Alfred (1811–1855), who entered the legal profession, achieved any measure of professional success. Unfortunately he did not have long to live: he suffered from poor health and died at the age of only forty-four. Thomas (1816–1862), despite a promising start at Cambridge, appears to have suffered from mental illness and never followed a career; Frederick (1819–1900) went to America at the age of seventeen, settling first in Carrolton, Kentucky, and then in Akron, Ohio. Fred was constantly plagued by economic and other misfortunes. His first wife, Ellen, was mentally ill and died in 1856; in 1857 he was married again, to Catharine (Kate) Dawson. He had three children by his first wife and five by his second; the Caswall family in America today is descended from Fred's eldest son, Robert.

Edward had one sister older than himself: Jane, born in 1812 and married in 1833. She died in 1849. Maria (1817–1898) married Benjamin Dowding.[60] The two youngest sisters, Emma (1821–1903) and Olivia (1824–1882), never married.

A student at Oxford

Some time around 1820 the Revd Robert Caswall moved his family to Chigwell in Essex,[61] and there Edward attended the Chigwell School, where he met a fellow student named George Copeland who was to become his lifelong friend. After grammar school in Marlborough, Wiltshire, he matriculated at Brasenose College, Oxford, on 15 March 1832,[62] and is recorded as having kept terms there from Easter 1832 to Lent 1837.[63] Why he came to choose Brasenose is unknown. Although several Caswalls before and after Edward attended Oxford University, there was no family tradition connected with any particular college. George Caswall, a grandson of Sir George Caswall of South Sea Bubble fame, matriculated at

[60] Benjamin Dowding was the grandfather of Lord (Hugh) Dowding, hero of the Battle of Britain.

[61] Shortly after Edward's birth, in August 1814, Robert Caswall took over the living of Eglingham near Alnwick, where he remained for 'some six years' (*Memoirs*, p. 15).

[62] *Brasenose College Register 1509–1909*, 2 vols. (Oxford: B.H. Blackwell, 1909), p. 493.

[63] Brasenose College Archives, file MEM 2 F1: *Record of terms kept 1825–1901*.

Brasenose in 1738[64] but died shortly thereafter.[65] Edward's grandfather John matriculated at St Albans Hall,[66] and his father attended Balliol and then St John's College.[67] None of Edward's brothers studied at Oxford. Henry received a BA in America[68] and Tom, a mathematician by training if not ultimately by profession, attended Cambridge and became a Fellow of Clare College there.[69]

Although Edward was admitted to Brasenose as a 'Commoner', that is, not holding a scholarship, before 1832 was out he had been awarded the Somerset Thornhill Manor Scholarship.[70] This award, which reduced the college fees for the recipient, was open alternately to students from three different grammar schools, Marlborough among them, and the eligible school nominated one of their own old boys. As an old boy of Marlborough Edward was nominated and received this scholarship. In 1833 and 1834 he received the Dean's Prize,[71] and in 1835 he was named Hulme Exhibitioner.[72] Originally this award had been established to aid four of the 'poorest sort' of BA students at Brasenose, but by Edward's time it had very likely become merit- rather than need-based.

In his first 'quarter' at University[73] Edward occupied rooms in the Old Lodge Staircase, and in the next quarter he had moved to premises in the so-called New Building. Thereafter his name no longer appears in the Room Book;[74] that he occupied lodgings in a house run by a college-approved landlady is indicated by his 'Oxonian' articles (see below; the first one is dated March 1833),

64 *Memoirs*, p. 12.

65 Ibid.

66 *Brasenose College Register*, p. 14.

67 *Alumni Oxonienses* lists him as having matriculated at Balliol in 1785 at age sixteen and receiving the BCL in 1792 (*Alumni Oxonienses: The Members of the University of Oxford, 1715–1886. Being the Matriculation Register of the University*, alphabetically arranged, revised, and annotated by Joseph Foster, vol. 1, *Later Series* (Oxford: James Parker & Co., 1891).

68 *Memoirs*, p. 13.

69 Edward refers to Tom, his being a mathematician, and his connection with Clare College in several places in his 'Journal' of 1846–7. A contemporary of Edward's at Oxford who matriculated at Trinity College in 1831 and took his BA in 1834 and MA in 1838 was Benjamin Charles Dowding of Salisbury, who eventually married Edward's sister Maria and became a clergyman and the grandfather of Lord Hugh Dowding. Thus the RAF commander and hero of the Battle of Britain was Edward Caswall's great-nephew.

70 *Brasenose College Register*, p. 493.

71 Ibid. There is no information regarding qualifications for this award.

72 Ibid.

73 'Quarters' did not follow the calendar year; e.g., the third quarter, for which Edward is first entered, would have begun around May and the fourth quarter ended toward mid-November.

74 Brasenose College Archives, B 4 d. 4: *Room Book 1818–1867*, from which the above information is taken.

which he signed 'From my lodgings'.

Records in the Brasenose College Archives give some indication of what examinations the students took and of the students' relative standings. There is no book for before 1835; however, records from 1835[75] onward show that students were examined in Divinity and Classics (Latin and Greek literature) each time and that Edward underwent two such exams. In the first, which took place during the Lent Term which began on 30 March 1835, he was examined on the Gospel of John 1–11, Lucretius, and Sophocles, and placed second under the first-class students;[76] in the second, during the Easter Term of the same year, his subjects were Matthew 1–14, the *Odes* of Horace, and Aristotle's *Poetics*, and he was placed number one under first class. As of Michaelmas 1835 his name no longer appears among the examinees; it is likely that he took written exams instead for his BA. Edward officially took his BA on 9 June 1836, and his MA on 6 June 1838.[77]

Launching of a literary career

The humorist

In the autobiographical note written in 1864[78] Caswall disclosed that, although he read hard in 1836 for the BA, he 'gained but a second class ..., which is to be accounted for by the distraction of literary pursuits freely indulged in'.[79] The first of these 'distractions' was a regular series of papers entitled 'The Oxonian', which he contributed pseudonymously to a magazine called *The New Casket* between July and December 1833.[80] The majority of the

75 Brasenose College Archives, B 2 b. 3: *Collections 1835–1848* ('collections' was the term for oral examinations).

76 A student was grouped under first, second, third, or fourth class according to his standing, and then placed in rank within his class. At that time Honours degrees were rated first- to fourth-class.

77 Brasenose College Archives. B 1 c. 45: *Degrees 1807–1849*. A BA became MA by keeping his name on the College books (i.e. by paying his dues; he did not have to be in residence) a certain number of terms past the BA. There was no academic examination involved. We have seen above that Edward kept terms until the Lent term of 1837, in other words, nearly one year past his BA.

78 Bellasis, 'Biographical Preface'.

79 Ibid., p. 6. If Bellasis's paraphrase closely follows Caswall's actual wording, the position of the phrase 'in 1836' intimates that some last-minute cramming took place after three years of the 'literary distractions'.

80 The Biographical Preface in Bellasis names *The Metropolitan Magazine* as the publisher of 'The Oxonian', but either Caswall's memory was faulty or the series had more than one publisher, for the copies at my disposal from the Birmingham Oratory archives are all from *The New Casket*.

papers view some aspect of University life through a satirical lens. The first of these,[81] a tongue-in-cheek description of the members of a University club of which he is president, presents a Gentleman Commoner of Christ Church College who has studied 'a considerable portion' of English literature, 'having ranged through the whole series of Waverley Novels',[82] and gives a brief précis of an argument between two members concerning the relative merits of the Gothic shaft versus the Corinthian column.[83] The account of the complicated life-journey of one member who has just entered University at the age of thirty pokes fun at the expense of Edward's brother Henry: it recounts the man's sojourn in Ohio as a student and then clergyman and his learning that 'his Priest Orders were useless in his country'[84] when he returned to England.[85] An ironic coincidence occurs in paper no. 6, which, in spelling out the regulations of the Oxford Religious Society, satirizes those of a fundamentalist persuasion: it was being written precisely as John Keble was launching the Oxford Movement with his Assize Sermon.

'Oxonian' no. 7 uses an imaginary conversation with a surgeon who has made an extensive study of the brains of men who died from over-reading to poke fun at the overly studious – that is, those who devote their lives to scholarly pursuits to the exclusion of all else. As a corrective to a possible misconception that Oxford is 'little else than a large hospital of learned martyrs',[86] however, the sequel records a letter in which a French visitor to Oxford describes with the utmost seriousness what he observes to be the studies most zealously pursued in Oxford – rowing and riding – along with the minor studies of shooting, cricket, billiards, swearing, and drinking (the last is 'a very expensive study, although it may be self-taught'[87]). The humour softens the serious point Caswall wants to make: '... amusement in moderation is very necessary to keep up that tone of the spirits, which is so requisite to health and happiness. But to spend one's whole time in it, to a neglect of other duties, is equally unworthy of an Oxonian and a Christian.'[88]

Some of the 'Oxonian' papers are notable for containing the first

[81] No. 1, March 1833.
[82] These novels by Sir Walter Scott were highly popular at that time.
[83] *The New Casket*, p. 87. Succeeding issues were numbered continuously.
[84] Ibid., p. 86.
[85] This actually happened to Henry and is recorded in the *Memoirs* and other sources. Uncertainty regarding (the validity of) orders conferred outside the United Kingdom was eventually rectified with the passing of the Colonial Clergy Act in 1874.
[86] *The New Casket*, p. 365.
[87] Ibid., p. 366.
[88] Ibid., p. 374.

published appearance of themes and features of which Caswall makes use in subsequent works. For example, a fanciful autobiography of an easy chair as related by the chair to its present owner, the author, is the earliest published example of Caswall's talent for composing quaint and charming anthropomorphisms of inanimate objects and members of the animal kingdom. John Henry Newman's brother-in-law Tom Mozley recalled a visit to Caswall's home in Stratford-sub-Castle in the early 1840s, at which Caswall 'entertained me with the probable meditations of a toad that had been found under the pavement of the church, where it must have been, hearing though not seeing all 'that passed above for centuries'.[89] The Oxonian easy chair has conceived 'a settled hatred towards mankind'[90] because of the suffering and inconvenience it endured during its manufacturing ordeal and has resolved to take revenge on its successive owners through the only means at its disposal, that of sending the person to sleep, inevitably with at once disastrous (for the owner) and hilarious (for the reader) consequences. A University student who has allowed the chair to be mistreated at his endless parties is irresistibly lured to sleep when he must study for his final exams, and so he fails or (in Oxford slang) is 'plucked'. Later the chair sends the wife of a college scout to sleep while she is in the process of drying clothes by the fire; the entire house is thereby set ablaze, and the chair is rescued in the nick of time by a neighbour. In the course of its life the chair is owned and sat on by so many students and scholars, it claims that it 'can repeat the three first books of Euclid by heart'.[91] But one outstanding accomplishment on which the chair particularly prides itself is that it once sent to sleep 'his late Majesty when he paid a visit to Oxford; though some are unfair enough to take from me the honour of this grand action, by attributing it to the Vice-Chancellor'.[92]

Caswall made use of his gift for anthropomorphism again in *Morals from the Churchyard* (1838), a little book anticipated in an affectionate portrait of a seaside village in Dorsetshire[93] that singles out the churchyard for a detailed description and then depicts the author sitting under a tree and musing on the lives of those now buried there.

[89] T. Mozley, *Reminiscences, Chiefly of Oriel College and the Oxford Movement*, 2 vols. (London: Longmans, Green, 1882), vol. 1, p. 12.
[90] Ibid., p. 158.
[91] Ibid., p. 166.
[92] Ibid.
[93] Papers No. 5 and 6.

To the satire of the overly studious, Caswall appends a tale, supposedly of Persian origin, that supports the theme of the folly of over-reading and contains a device he used in a later, extensive manuscript entitled *Travels to Castles in the Air*, a supernatural figure who takes the protagonist (in the 'Persian' tale, an amazingly learned philosopher) to a vantage point above the earth from which he beholds persons in vain pursuits and thereby learns a lesson – in this case, that 'the wisdom of man is folly; the folly of Allah is wisdom'[94] – after which he is returned to his spot on earth a wiser man. This would also not be the last time that Caswall was to write on folly and vanity.

Finally, Caswall concludes the paper containing the letter from the Frenchman with a facetious 'Dissertation upon the Word "Pluck",' out of which his book *The Art of Pluck*[95] undoubtedly developed. The dissertation refutes some theories of 'persons whose opinions are of great weight'[96] and then offers the author's own ideas on the subject, in which he draws an analogy with the plucking of a bird's feathers, as unpleasant and uncomfortable an experience for the bird as it is for the hapless Oxford examinee.

Much of the material in the 'Oxonian' papers reached a wider audience when its author recycled and developed it in his first published book, *The Art of Pluck*. Written under the pseudonym 'Scriblerus Redivivus', the book apparently sold out its first edition in six days[97] and firmly established the still-undergraduate Caswall as a witty and incisive satirist. In a letter written in 1843 to Henry Formby, his friend and former fellow student at Brasenose, which he appended to the third and subsequent editions of *Pluck*, Caswall recalled 'the sudden popularity which it obtained, not only amongst the Undergraduates of that day, but even with the more sober Bachelors, and in part too at the very High Tables'.[98]

The aim of *Pluck* is, ostensibly, to teach the undergraduate how to

94 *The New Casket*, p. 309.

95 Edward Caswall [Scriblerus Redivivus], *A New Art teaching how to be Plucked, being a Treatise after the fashion of Aristotle; writ for the use of Students in the Universities. To which is added a Synopsis of Drinking*, 11th edn (Oxford: J. Vincent, 1864).

96 *The New Casket*, p. 374.

97 note re 2nd edn and its preface

98 This quote is from the 4th edn, p. iii. G.V. Cox, an Oxford alumnus whose *Recollections of Oxford* (London: Macmillan & Co., 1868), span the years from 1789 to 1868, records that 'November [1836] produced two singular works, 'The Art of Pluck' and 'Oxford Night-caps'!!' (p. 263). In the letter to Formby, Caswall also explains the omission of previously published passages that showed how to get plucked in Divinity, expressing profound regret for the sin he committed in 'investing certain passages of the Divine Word with ridiculous associations' (p. iv).

fail his examinations – or, in Oxford University slang, how to get 'plucked'. Observing that being plucked is industriously pursued by many students, Caswall sets down, in a detailed, systematic fashion in the manner of an Aristotelian treatise, advice on how to achieve this end.[99]

Originally the *Pluck Examination Papers* were published as a separate volume, but the fourth and subsequent editions of *The Art of Pluck* bound *Fragments from the Examination Papers* in the back of the book.[100] The purpose of the papers is to afford the reader an opportunity to put into practice the theory of getting plucked. The subjects covered included translation into and from Latin and Greek, history, logic and rhetoric, moral philosophy, and mathematics. For example, the student is asked to write an essay on the 'origin of boat races in the University, with a detailed account of the principal victories gained in them since their commencement; tracing their influence upon the morals and studies of the place, and comparing the Athenian navy at the death of Pericles with the navy of Oxford and Cambridge' (p. 48); to translate 'into your worst Latin prose, in the style of Cicero's Orations', a speech in the Debating Society against the admission of dogs into the Reading Room (pp. 48–9); and to answer a series of mathematical questions concerned with various aspects of drinking (e.g., rates of drinking and amounts drunk, velocity of a thrown bottle) (p. 61).

In his 1843 letter to Henry Formby Caswall emphasized what he now regarded as the chief purpose of the book:[101] to exhibit,

> in a plain and conclusive view, the essential absurdity and folly of that miserable course by which too many young men of our Universities is so studiously pursued, as though it were the end of their residence ... [L]et every person reflect for himself, what such a waste of time, opportunities, and energies must appear in the sight of God, and when judged by His Holy Law. (p. v)

99 In the Preface he asserts that the treatise really 'deserveth ... the name of a science', (p. ix) but then he concedes that he will be content with calling it an art, because, while the process of getting plucked has been around for a long time, its arrangement into 'the axioms of a true philosophy' is in its infancy (p. ix).

100 Another change, effective from the third edition onward, was that the book now addressed itself to Cambridge as well as Oxford students. This may have presented itself as a means of widening the readership and thereby increasing the revenues from the book; or it may have been brought about by the fact that Edward's younger brother Tom was by that time a student at Cambridge.

101 In this letter Caswall also explains the omission of previously published passages that showed how to get plucked in Divinity, expressing profound regret for the sin he committed in 'investing certain passages of the Divine Word with ridiculous associations' (p. iv).

Outline of *The Art of Pluck*

Book I: General advice on how to give wrong answers and how to avoid learning anything.

Rules, with examples, for answering wrongly in various examination subjects: e.g., Latin, Greek, Divinity, Science, Logic. In construing Latin or Greek, e.g., one could simply mistranslate the words, or, in some cases, actually 'improve the wrongness' (p. 4) by bad grammar. A sentence from Livy – *Hannibal Alpes transivit summa diligentia* ('Hannibal passed over the Alps as fast as he could') – can be construed by one desiring a Pluck as 'Hannibal passed over the Alps on the top of a diligence' (p. 3). Also, it is best to buy one's Euclid book second-hand, so that one can tell by the thumbing where the difficult problems are and thereby avoid mastering them (p. 6).

Book II: Description of various 'Idlenesses' (activities that can serve as a distraction to learning).

Smoking, falling in love, reading novels, riding and driving, billiards, rowing, playing a musical instrument, and drinking (to which is appended the Synopsis of Drinking). Things to be avoided include sober friends, owning a dictionary or lexicon, and attending lectures. The Idlenesses are arranged into various divisions and subdivisions. The various forms of some Idlenesses are assessed for their relative effectiveness at producing Pluck (e.g., port wine under 'Drinking', because it is imbibed most often), and places where one might avail oneself of necessary items are recommended (e.g., a certain Mrs Hall rents out such an excellent sailboat that it has already produced five Plucks).

Book III: Miscellaneous topics.

E.g., 'proper' deportment at examinations (wherein one must consider the examiner, the examinee, and types of questions and answers), types of persons most likely to be plucked, and examples of approved Plucks. Among the last are John F., who, known as a diligent student, accepted bets from his friends that he would certainly pass, whereupon he purposely got himself plucked and thereby won hundreds of pounds.

Not for the last time did Caswall write satire in order to convey a moral.[102] Two years after the initial publication of *The Art of Pluck* he teamed up with the illustrator Hablot K. Browne to produce *Sketches of Young Ladies*[103] under the pseudonyms of 'Quiz' and 'Phiz'. The following title-page sketch from an early notebook suggests that an

[102] Nor, indeed, for the first time, as we have seen from one of his Oxonian papers above. From this it can be reasonably assumed that the moralizing purpose of *Pluck* was present from the beginning, even though he did not state this explicitly until the letter to Formby was added to the third edition.

[103] London: Chapman & Hall, 1837.

incidental purpose of the book was to satirize the *Bridgewater Treatises*, the collection of writings being published between 1833 and 1840 for the purpose of reconciling religious presuppositions about creation with the new scientific discoveries.[104]

Anatomy of Young Ladies
being a philosophical enquiry into
the natural history, condition and
clarification of
this important part
of creation
which has never been examined
by naturalists.
Intended for one of the Bridgewater Treatises
by Sir Peter Grizzle.[105]

The chief purpose, however, as overtly stated, was to describe, 'to the best of our zoological powers, two dozen classes of young ladies'.[106] The author admits that this is by no means an exhaustive list; rather, for fear of tiring out the reader, he has 'selected the most striking and important classes at this present time existing in Great Britain'[107] and has thus not included several types all of which are, nonetheless, indeed greatly influential in the country 'and their own villages in particular'.[108] Among the classes described are 'The Young Lady Who Sings', 'The Romantic Young Lady', 'The Literary Young Lady', 'The Young Lady Who Is Engaged', 'The Natural Historian Young Lady', 'The Hyperbolical Young Lady', 'The Abstemious Young Lady', 'The Young Lady from School'. Particularly noteworthy is the sketch of 'The Evangelical Young Lady', whom he gently chides for eschewing any form of amusement[109] while acknowledging

[104] Around the same time he also considered writing *The Grammar of Philosophy: The Philosophy of Lies or Lying made easy to the Comprehension of the young. Being the last of the Bridgewater Treatises*, but never made anything of it beyond a list of contents and a sketch of the text.

[105] Edward Caswall, notebook now in the archives of the Birmingham Oratory. In the published version he moved the reference to the Bridgewater Treatises to the end of the brief introduction ('... all young ladies being Troglodites, and not Ichthyosauri, as Dr. Buckland hath erroneously observed in his late Bridgewater Treatise' [*Sketches*, 4th edn, p. v]) and retained the scientific flavour in the subtitle (*in which These Interesting Members of the Animal Kingdom Are Classified according to Their Several Instincts, Habits, and General Characteristics*).

[106] Sketches, p. 78.

[107] Ibid.

[108] Ibid., p. 79.

[109] To the recent proliferation of this type could be attributed 'the reduction of our county balls from four a year to one; the total abolition of our archery meeting, and the insolvency of the dancing-master' (p. 12).

that the other extreme, 'to waste heart, health, and energy, in a continual pursuit of irreclaimable frivolity' (p. 16), is even less acceptable. And here we come to the unstated but no less valid purpose of the *Sketches*, for their satire, far from betraying a concealed aversion to the opposite sex,[110] demonstrates a respect for them in pointing out to young ladies 'what it is that makes them sometimes to be ridiculous with all their good qualities' (p. 80).[111] Caswall concludes his scientific treatise on young ladies with the hope that they 'will forgive us for trying to serve them a good turn, especially as we engage ever after from this time to praise them up to the skies, and down again too, if they so desire' (p. 80). Once again, Caswall has employed satire as a vehicle for making moral points.

Spurred on by the success of the *Sketches of Young Ladies*,[112] Caswall next embarked upon a companion set of *Sketches of Young Gentlemen*.[113] 'On calm deliberation', however, he put it aside, having decided to seek ordination rather than pursue a full-time career as a writer.[114] Still, Caswall's gift for humour had attracted the attention of another aspiring author: Charles Dickens wished to meet him, and Dickens ultimately continued with the *Young Gentlemen* as well as *Sketches of Young Couples*, and eventually all three works, having first been published individually, were brought out in one volume anonymously.[115]

The moralist

Geoffrey Rowell, in *Hell and the Victorians*,[116] writes of the 'didactic use of death-beds'[117] in vogue in Victorian literature – that is, Victorian authors were fond of using death-bed scenes to inculcate a moral lesson. 'Not only was death used didactically in this way, the tradition of graveyard musings, most notably represented by James Hervey, continued in articles with such titles as "Contemplations in P-N Churchyard" and "The Village Churchyard" by Aliquis, which

110 The *Sketches* can safely be regarded as evidence that Caswall would not have personally subscribed to the Tractarian valuation of celibacy.

111 Nearly ten years later Caswall wrote in his journal, 'On looking back to those sketches now I really do not think that they contain anything to be ashamed of. I remember that in writing them I really wished to do good' (1, no. 229).

112 This was the work the phenomenal success of which caused him 'at the time to think of turning my attention to writing as a profession' (Bellasis, 'Biographical Preface', p. 7).

113 London: Chapman & Hall, 1838.

114 Bellasis, 'Biographical Preface', p. 7.

115 Ibid., pp. 7–8.

116 Oxford: Clarendon Press, 1974.

117 Ibid., p. 8.

were characteristic of Evangelical journals in the earlier part of the century.'[118]

Edward Caswall's next published work, *Morals from the Churchyard*,[119] is an allegorical narrative in the vein of Victorian 'graveyard' moralizing. It presents a debate among the graves in a particular churchyard as to which of the graves is 'the most worthy' (p. 1). An old, wise grave proposes that they each tell their story, and at the end all the brother graves would decide among the various claims. Throughout the fable the old grave's voice acts as a unifying force to further the story and to point up the moral, which is about the fleetingness and vanity of all earthly things and the importance of seeking the things of heaven; for in the end, as the wise grave says, each person 'must come to us in the end!' (p. 18).

This venerable old grave speaks first, in order to oblige the others who wish to hear his story. He is more than four centuries old and thus predates the Reformation, an event to which he alludes in his reference to 'a new people ... who used no incense in their prayers' (p. 6) and who followed the great-grandchildren of his own generation. Although he had made no claim to be worthiest, the other graves judge him to be very worthy indeed.

A rich man's grave, a gaudy grave with 'a square tomb of hewn stone', richly decorated and surrounded by protective iron railings, proudly recalls the fancy funeral with purple coach and boasts of his own ornateness and the silver coffin within. To be sure, 'we saw [the rich man] not here on Sundays' (p. 10). The other graves are not impressed, however. The old grave recalls that the rich man was loved by no one; he never spoke a kind word and spent his wealth only on himself, never giving to beggars.

Then comes the turn of a little child's grave. This is the grave of innocence; it holds the remains of a little child who had scarcely had a chance to live. The other graves, while considering him worthy, counter that 'innocence which hath never been tempted, equalleth not the innocence which hath survived temptation'. Worthier would be the grave of someone who 'after much tribulation had reached heaven' (p. 16).[120]

Days and seasons pass while each grave takes its turn, since they can only speak at night. This affords the author the opportunity to create interludes describing the surrounding nature and introducing

[118] Ibid., p. 9.

[119] ... *in a Series of Cheerful Fables, with illustrations by H.K. Browne* (London: Chapman & Hall, 1838).

[120] This is an unusual perspective in an era that tended to sentimentalize childhood.

guardian angels who have specific responsibilities. Almost everything contributes to furthering the moralizing function of the story. After a spell of hot, dry days, for example, the graves beseech the angels to bring rain, which they do. A happy butterfly then flits among the graves. The old grave remembers how the beautiful butterfly was once a lowly chrysalis with no beauty, hanging down from a tree bough by a delicate thread, pelted by rain and swung about by wind. 'It was despised. But behold! one morning it left its place, clad in burnished wings, and soared into the air ... It is admired by all the insects. Its hues shame the pride of kings. Let man learn of the butterfly. For such as it was, so are the despised of this world' (p. 39).

Christmas Eve comes, and the Archangel visits the graveyard. The old grave requests his help in the graves' dispute, and the Archangel tells him to 'Behold where the first snow-drop shall spring up in the new year; that is the most worthy grave' (p. 43). When a thaw comes all the graves at last see a snowdrop on a lowly, neglected, and despised grave with no tombstone and no tree by its side. How did it deserve its honour? This is the grave of an aged beggar. The beggar once had a happy home and children. But he was deserted by his friends and wandered far and wide with no companion except a dog who loved him and whom he looked after. Eventually people killed his dog, and he sat down here and died. Despite all the sorrow he experienced he never complained, 'but bowed in all things to the will of his God' (p. 57). His grave deserves the title of worthiest because the beggar's 'faith held fast in adversity' (p. 116).

Several things are noteworthy about this little book. First, it is the earliest work written by Caswall 'for the amusement and instruction of the young' (p. v), a concern that would occupy him on and off for much of the rest of his life. Second, it is 'written in a kind of prose poetry'[121] – a style that crops up in several works that he sketched (and, in some cases, completed) but never published.[122] Third, Caswall observed of *Morals from the Churchyard*, 'I can detect traces of a leaning toward the old Catholic theology, but I do not think I was aware of this at the time'.[123] His characterization of Protestants as 'people who used no incense in their prayers', and the reminiscence of the angel who tends a little spring in the churchyard – 'Time was when they reverenced my waters as a cure for disease. This honour they give me no more' (p. 58) – suggest a nostalgia for

[121] Bellasis, 'Biographical Preface', p. 6.
[122] Material from one of these manuscripts, 'Benedicite', eventually found its way into his published poetry, and a comparison of the 'Benedicite' with Caswall's published Odes (see chapter 6) will afford insight into his creative processes.
[123] Quoted in Bellasis, 'Biographical Preface', p. 8.

pre-Reformation piety; the song of the angels as they attend the sabbath service – 'Glory to the church of Christ, the old church, the church of ages. Saints for ever are its martyrs; saints before the throne of God' (p. 24) – anticipates his later decision about the Roman Church having antiquity on its side.

Finally, Bellasis remarks that *Morals* 'marks [Caswall's] change to serious thought'.[124] This is accurate in the sense that it does not employ any overt humour or satire; however, as we have already seen, even Caswall's satirical works tend to have an underlying serious purpose. That he made a conscious decision in this work to highlight its moralizing purpose is obvious from the change of the title from its original manuscript title, *The Fable of the Graves*.[125] The final, published title reflects his awareness that the moral to be imparted took precedence over the fable *per se*, although he discloses in the Preface that he has chosen fable as his vehicle because he is satisfied that fables are more pleasing to the young than any other mode of instruction.[126]

Besides these early published works, Caswall left several unpublished manuscripts from the 1840s, some of which bear investigation because they encompass concerns that would occupy him throughout his life.[127] One of these works, *The Elements of the World*,[128] was sketched in detail and dated at the end 'April 18th, 1840'; thus he was working on it during the period immediately following his ordination to the Anglican priesthood. His intention with this treatise was to consider in detail the 'elements of the world and their correlatives ... in themselves and as aids towards ascertaining the true Church'.[129] His achievement was to set down a systematic cosmology that inspires and informs his later work, and especially his poetry. Following are its main points:

1. The existence of two worlds: visible and invisible

This, states Caswall, is revealed in Scripture, and just as these two worlds are connected rather than separate, so is the human soul 'mysteriously connected' with both of these worlds. The invisible

[124] Ibid.

[125] Ibid., Note †.

[126] Caswall, *Morals*, p. vi.

[127] Ibid., p. 8, Note ‡, lists several manuscript works, among which 'History of a late Term at the University' after the plan of Niebuhr and a sketch of 'The Life and Adventures of Paul Pickering' appear to have been lost; at any rate, they are not among the holdings of the Birmingham Oratory archives.

[128] This work is variously titled 'The Elements of the World considered in themselves and as aids towards ascertaining the true Church' and 'An Essay on The Empire of the World in the Soul of Man'.

[129] From the ms. title page.

world consists of the Heaven of Heavens, the triune God, the Angels and Saints, Paradise, and Hell with its powers of darkness. The visible world has three components: Nature (the material Universe), Art (artificial objects made by human labour, e.g., cities), and Human Life. This division and subdivision will recur in Caswall's later (published and unpublished) works that treat of Creation. The visible world is subservient to the invisible world but tries to supplant it in the human soul through the agency of Satan, who gradually and imperceptibly changes human hearts.

2. The sacramentality of the visible world

While Caswall does not actually use the word *sacramentality*, it does appropriately sum up his view of the natural world:

> That the sights and sounds of the natural world ... are of a character to lead towards the invisible and eternal such as are willing so to be led, there can ... be little doubt and indeed the truth of it is not only to be acknowledged but to be maintained. St Paul himself says that the invisible things of God even his eternal power and Godhead may clearly be seen from the things that are made.

Remarkably, he attributes a significant role to *conscience* in bringing this sacramentality into effect. Conscience, he says, seems to be 'an immediate faculty of the soul by which it corresponds with the invisible system and becomes a recipient of it'. Such things as the ideas of Responsibility, a Divine Being, heaven and hell, and so forth, constitute 'the admission of the invisible world into the soul through the openings of conscience'. Conscience, then, is that faculty through which the invisible world affects the human soul, and nature depends on conscience in order to 'infuse religious sentiments towards its creator ... the degree of religious impression which Nature makes on the soul depends entirely upon the previous state of the conscience and is to be referred to it. ... the impressions [made by nature] are in themselves indifferent but depend for good or evil on the state of the conscience.'

In the absence of a properly formed conscience, the impressions made by nature on the soul can lead to idolatry or Pantheism:

> Thus as to those who love God it is their happy privilege that they may also love nature with safety because their love does not rest in it but passes through it to God, ... so it is the condemnation of the evil that to them even the pure mirror of nature is tainted and smeared as it were by their own breath ...

He specifically takes to task nature-worshipping Romantic poets, singling out Byron's *Childe Harold* as an example of nature being loved for itself rather than for God. Thus nature must be feared, for the impressions it makes 'tend to the deification of Nature in the Soul and to a certain adoration of it'. It is in this way, through our sensory faculties, that Satan works, 'gluing us down to the earth lest we should attempt to struggle upwards'.

3. The ambiguity of the artificial world in affecting the individual's relation to God

Having divided the visible world into Nature, Art, and Humanity, Caswall does not view these components as entirely separate but allows that nature and art, in particular, can combine in various degrees in the artificial world to produce what he calls 'mixed works of Art' in which art 'seems to guide or modify Nature'. Thus the works of the artificial world fall under different degrees or 'stages', depending on the extent to which the human is intermingled with nature:

'Lowest': (1) Cornfields, gardens, vineyards, orchards, hedges
↓ (2) Cottages, barns
(3) Streets, shops, merchandise, public buildings
(4) *a* Works of fine art (sculpture, painting, etc.)
'Highest': *b* Railways, gas lights, steam vessels, etc.

Like nature, these works of the artificial world can have a deleterious effect on the soul, possessing the potential to distract one from the things above. Here Caswall is thinking particularly of people who live in 'civilized countries'. Among the factors influencing one's likelihood of being so distracted are the possession of wealth and an 'innate curiosity for and predisposition towards the artificial world in preference to the natural'. It is interesting that he does not single out living in industrial towns as intrinsically more likely to produce distraction than living in rural areas;[130] presumably the possession of riches and an innate tendency to prefer the artificial world over the natural are quite independent of where one lives.

4. The vanities of the present world

In the preface Caswall recalls his mother's custom of having all her children recite their catechism on Sunday evenings; he emphasizes the impression made on him by the words 'the pomps and vanities of this wicked world and all the sinful lusts of the flesh'.[131] The

[130] One thinks of the Tractarian preference for rural over urban areas, which later was taken up by Gerard Manley Hopkins in his concern that living conditions among the urban poor would diminish their feel for the transcendent.

[131] The catechism to which he refers is that contained in the *Book of Common Prayer*, to be learned by each person before his or her confirmation. The answer to the third question says that the first of the three vows made in our name by our godparents at baptism was to 'renounce the devil and all his works, the pomps and vanity of this wicked world, and all the sinful lusts of the flesh' (*Book of Common Prayer* [London: R. and A. Suttaby, *c.* 1868], n.p.).

concept of 'vanity' recurs throughout Caswall's writings (for example, in his 1843 letter to Henry Formby he twice uses the word in connection with his profanation of Scripture in the earlier editions of *The Art of Pluck*). Tracing his emerging understanding of 'the world', he arrives at his present (1840) understanding of it as 'a great reality surrounding us on all sides'. Thus for Caswall the world is not in itself an evil thing, nor are the 'vanities' of the world coextensive with the world itself. Rather, vanity for Caswall can be defined as positing oneself as an absolute value; acting or thinking without any reference to God or any consideration of transcendent meaning.

The vanity of the present world became the theme of an allegorical fable variously titled 'Modern Sinbad, or, The Castle Builder, Travels to Castles in the Air', and 'A Visit to Cloudland'. Subtitled 'Fata Morgana', it shows Caswall at his most intensely moralizing. Bellasis lists it among 'other humorous works sketched out',[132] but what actually emerges is a horrifying tale of the human alienation that results from materialism, selfish ambition, and the conviction that the present is all that matters. A young traveller to Cloudland – the story is written in the first person – experiences a variety of adventures, sometimes frightening, sometimes amusing, that eventually (for he is stubborn and determined) teach him the paradoxical lesson that the eternal, unseen, and intangible are more real than the temporal and what can be experienced through the senses: 'nothing was certain and sure but religion and virtue'.

'The Castle Builder' has elements of Gothic horror that recall Horace Walpole's *The Castle of Otranto*, while its moralizing intent, its use of castles to represent vice, and its occasional deliberately archaic language suggest James Thomson's poem *Castle of Indolence*. Perhaps most striking, in terms of relationships to other works, are the three supernatural figures who turn up at various points and attempt to dissuade the young adventurer from pursuing his delusions further. The first, an angel who appears to him in a seemingly endless graveyard and warns him against seeking the 'vain castle', points to various tombstones and bids him read their inscriptions. Two of them contain Scripture texts exhorting one to value eternal rather than temporal things, while on the third he beholds his 'own name at full length, to all appearances just carved on the stone'. The similarity to Dickens's *Christmas Carol*, published in 1843, is compelling. Exasperatingly, Caswall's manuscript is not dated, but

132 Bellasis, 'Biographical Preface', Note ‡, p. 8.

evidence suggests that it probably was written in the late 1830s or very early 1840s.[133] The manuscript was written out in great detail – what looks to be a final version – until Chapter 10, apparently quite close to the end of the story, but then it suddenly stops. Whether the rest has been lost or whether Caswall never completed it is uncertain.

Sympathy with pre-Reformation piety, faith-formation of children, the existence of and relationship between the visible and the invisible worlds, the vanities of the temporal world – these themes, already conspicuous in Caswall's work as a very young man, continue like red threads throughout his life and writings. The next chapter considers his service as an Anglican clergyman and surveys his publications during those years.

[133] The handwriting is young, and Bellasis (ibid.) mentions it with other published and unpublished works that date from the late 1830s.

Chapter Two

The Anglican Clergyman

The year 1838 saw Edward Caswall wrestling with a career decision. Encouraged by the phenomenal success of *The Art of Pluck* and *Sketches of Young Ladies*, should he choose writing as a full-time occupation, or should he enter the Anglican ministry? As we saw in the last chapter, he was in the midst of preparing a sequel to *Young Ladies*, *Sketches of Young Gentlemen*, when 'on calm deliberation' he resolved to set it aside and 'give [him]self up to the ministry'.[1] Accordingly, he was ordained deacon in 1838 at Wells, in the diocese of Bath and Wells, and the following year was ordained priest at Bath.

There followed in quick succession a series of brief assignments as curate: first at Norton Fitzwarren and then at St Michael's in Milverton, Somerset, where he served 'under the Reverend John Trevelyan, brother of Sir Charles Trevelyan'.[2] It may well have been in the course of one of these assignments that he met Louisa Stuart Walker, whom he married on 21 December 1841. Louisa was the only child of Major-General Charles Augustus Walker of Whetleigh House in nearby Taunton.[3]

[1] Edward Bellasis, 'Biographical Preface', in Edward Caswall, *Hymns and Poems Original and Translated* (London: Burns & Oates, 1908), p. 7. There are no sources extant to indicate whether Caswall had embarked upon his university studies with the explicit intention of preparing for the ministry, or whether he had still been open-minded about his career choice in 1832.

[2] Ibid., p. 8.

[3] Described by her sisters-in-law as a 'pretty butterfly style of a girl', Louisa was said to have been 'dark and very handsome, and most particular about proper manners in children' (*Memoirs of the Caswall Family*, p. 17).

Caswall's next move was to St Dunstan's in Fleet Street, London, a post he eventually left because 'the churchwarden represented me to the Rector as having too weak a voice',[4] as he explained to his father some years later when the elder Caswall, on his deathbed, was trying to persuade Edward to take over his incumbency at West Lavington. Edward protested that he was not 'strong enough for so large a church', qualifying it to apply to his voice when his father objected. Against this his father maintained that the churchwarden's real problem with Edward was that the latter was not an Evangelical. While no other account exists as to Edward's physical delivery as a preacher, it is true that he had a speech defect, probably a cleft palate,[5] that caused John Henry Newman's sister Harriett Mozley erroneously to describe him as possessing 'a speech and manner so mincing that at first it seems a silly piece of charity not to allow it most abominably affected'.[6] Wherever the truth lies, this exchange between father and son does confirm that already as a newly-ordained clergyman Edward's religious leanings were toward the 'high' end of the spectrum rather than toward Evangelicalism. After a final brief appointment at St Martin's in Shenley, Herts., Caswall 'settled down at length ... as perpetual curate of Stratford-sub-Castle, near Salisbury'.[7]

Perpetual Curate at Stratford-sub-Castle

The parish of Stratford lies within walking distance (for the reasonably fit) of Salisbury and incorporates the town of Old Sarum, the castle of which gave the parish its designation 'under the Castle'. As the historian R. B. Pugh describes it, 'The lofty hill on which the ruined castle stands, clothed with yews and beeches, is the most striking feature. On the east the [River] Avon flows roughly southwards.'[8] Stratford is nestled in a peaceful pastoral setting, and even today sheep- and cow-dotted green hills rise up from the area surrounding

[4] Edward Caswall, 'Journal 1846–47,' p. 406.

[5] An obituary of Caswall noted that '[a]s a preacher, Mr. Caswall laboured under some disadvantage owing to a natural impediment in his speech' (obituary, no publication details available, filed in Birmingham Oratory archives under Oratory Letters right after Newman's letter of 2 January 1878 to Caswall's sister).

[6] Harriett to her sister Jemima, 9 May 1841, in Dorothea Mozley, ed., *Newman Family Letters* (London: SPCK, 1962), p. 104.

[7] Bellasis, 'Biographical Preface', p. 8.

[8] R. B. Pugh, 'Stratford-sub-Castle', in Elizabeth Crittall, ed., *A History of Wiltshire*, vol. 6 (London: Published for the Institute of Historical Research by Oxford University Press, 1962), p. 193.

the church. In the nineteenth century the population of the parish hovered between three and four hundred[9] and in 1841, the year after Edward Caswall was inducted as Perpetual Curate, it stood at 374.[10]

The exact age of St Lawrence Church is not known. A 'consecration' took place in 1326, but since there had been a chapel on the spot since 1228, it is not known whether the 1326 event implied an entirely new building, for example, or a desecration followed by a reconsecration.[11] Stratford itself became a separate parish by the late fourteenth century, and the church was regarded as a parish church from 1394 at the latest.[12] It underwent various repairs up to the early eighteenth century, when a major renovation was funded by Thomas Pitt in 1711. The pulpit dates from Jacobean times and thus is the very one from which Caswall preached. Ironically for someone in whose life sacred music was to play so significant a role, the church had no organ during Caswall's incumbency; not until 1855 was a barrel organ installed.[13]

The record of Caswall's induction into the Perpetual Curacy of Stratford is preserved at the Wiltshire County Record Office at Trowbridge and indicates that on 7 November 1840, 'Edward Caswell [*sic*], Clerk, M.A.' was licensed to the Perpetual Curacy of 'Stratford under the Castle in the County of Wilt. and Diocese of Sarum' by the Dean of Salisbury, 'the said Edward Caswell [*sic*] having first taken the Oaths and made and subscribed the Subscription and Declaration in such case by Law required'.[14]

The living of Stratford-sub-Castle was under the patronage of the Dean and Chapter of Salisbury and its value was £80 per year.[15] Caswall records an average attendance of 100 parishioners, of which around fourteen were children, at his eleven o'clock Sunday morning services, while the three o'clock afternoon services were attended by 35 to 50 people, including children. During his incumbency he performed 29 baptisms, 41 funerals, and 10 weddings.[16]

[9] Pugh gives the population successively as 352 (in 1801), 385 (1821), and 307 (1871) (ibid.).

[10] Personal communication from Mr Gerard Tracey, Birmingham Oratory archives.

[11] Pugh, 'Stratford-sub-Castle', pp. 210–11.

[12] Ibid., p. 210.

[13] An inscription to this effect stands on the rear inside wall of the church. The present instrument is a respectably adequate pipe organ.

[14] 'Stratford under the Castle, P.C. Licence', in *1837. Register. [Archbishop] Denison*, W.R.O. D1/2/33, Folio 96. In effect a perpetual curate, which is rather uncommon these days, was essentially the same as a vicar, and possibly was appointed in place of an absentee rector.

[15] Personal communication from Mr Gerard Tracey, Birmingham Oratory archives.

[16] W.R.O. Fiche 7/2474/1. Two of the five weddings at which Caswall did not personally officiate were performed by his friend and fellow Brasenose graduate

As Perpetual Curate Caswall occupied an imposing residence called Mawarden Court, a fifteenth-century property described by Newman's brother-in-law Tom Mozley as 'an old mansion full of historical associations'.[17] Mozley was Rector of nearby Cholderton from 1836 to 1847 and thus appears to have seen rather a good deal of Caswall. He also had a connection with him through the Burgess side of the family: one of Mozley's friends from childhood, a fellow pupil at Charterhouse (the school) and later a fellow student at Oriel College, was a nephew of Bishop Burgess.[18]

Mozley and his wife, Newman's sister Harriett, have both left accounts of Caswall from that period. Mozley describes the twenty-seven-year-old clergyman as 'one of the quaintest of men, but ... quaint after the manner of men ... [with] a vein of humour all his own'.[19] In a letter to her sister Jemima, Harriett recorded an encounter with their 'new sharp and witty neighbour Mr. Caswall'[20] at a decanal meeting at Netheravon in May 1841. This was her first meeting with him; she describes his bubbly and irrepressible nature and his fascination with and insatiable curiosity about her famous brother, and admits to having been quite taken with him:

> He lost no time in making up to me without any introduction and bounced at me into the thick of every thing, talking of his brother[21] and mine – and relating innumerable anecdotes, interspersed with reflections sentimental and moral, without end – he is a most entertaining and enthusiastic creature ... He again got next me at dinner, and hardly ate any thing for talking – at least he despatched each plate at the end while the things were clearing. He was resolved to get all he could out of me concerning J.H.N. – his birth, education and character ... He wanted to know if I knew what was *in* J.H.N. all his life, seeming to have a natural wonderment as to how he came to be what he is ... You see I had an amusing companion.[22]

Henry Formby, both on 'St Peter's Day' (29 June) 1841 (ibid.). Formby preceded Caswall into the Church of Rome.

17 Tom Mozley, *Reminiscences, Chiefly of Oriel College and the Oxford Movement*, 2 vols. (London: Longmans, Green, 1882), vol. 1, p. 12. The property may have been named for Richard Mawarden, a knight of the shire who held lands in Stratford in 1403 (Pugh, 'Stratford-sub-Castle', p. 205).

18 Mozley, *Reminiscences* vol. 1, pp. 419–20. Mozley refers to the nephew only as 'poor little Burgess' and describes him as the only son of 'the well-known manufacturer of sauces and pickles in the Strand' (p. 419).

19 Mozley, *Reminiscences* vol. 1, p. 12.

20 Mozley, ed., *Newman Family Letters*, p. 103.

21 Henry, who knew Newman before Edward did.

22 Mozley, ed., *Newman Family Letters*, pp. 103–4.

From this naturally arises the question of the extent to which Caswall was influenced by Newman and the Oxford Movement at this stage of his life. Unlike his exact contemporary, fellow Oxford student, poet, and hymn writer Frederick William Faber, Caswall never explicitly identified himself as a Tractarian or actively proselytized on behalf of Tractarian ideology, although this is not to assume lack of interest in or agreement with the principles of the Movement on his part. For one thing, it is highly unlikely that he would not have gone to hear Newman preach. As Mozley records, in the early 1830s 'Newman was now one of the preachers of the day ... By the year 1831 undergraduates from [all over England, as well as Ireland and Scotland] were all coming up and securing the next Sunday afternoon a good place at St Mary's.'[23] Caswall's published writings, as we have seen, reveal that he enjoyed being *au courant* with all University events; moreover, Brasenose College lies in Radcliffe Square at a right angle to St Mary's, with about one minute's walking distance between the College gate and one of the church entrances. Surely both natural curiosity and geographical convenience would have put him among the crowds of students converging on St Mary the Virgin for Newman's sermons, and surely his intense interest in Newman as recorded by Harriett Mozley must have initially been sparked by hearing Newman preach. Further, as Perpetual Curate of Stratford-sub-Castle Caswall was exposed to a significant amount of Tractarian thought. The youthful bishop of Salisbury,[24] Edward Denison, had been a fellow of Merton College, Oxford, and Vicar of St Peter's-in-the-East there. He came from Oxford to his new diocese 'when the tractarian movement was at the height of its power and prosperity'[25] and could be considered a Tractarian sympathizer, if a somewhat qualified one. In his Charge to his clergy in 1842 he

> set out the achievements of the tractarians, who had revived 'the study of sound theology', 'raised the standard of the ministerial character', ... 'successfully vindicated the important truth of the nature and constitution of the Church', 'given the sacraments their due place in the scheme of our holy religion', and 'warned men not to rest contented in the mere beginnings of Christian life, but to endeavour still to go on to perfection'.[26]

[23] Mozley, *Reminiscences* vol. 1, pp. 238–9.
[24] He was thirty-six at the time of his consecration in 1837 (Crittall, ed., *History of Wiltshire* vol. 6, p. 58) and the immediate successor to Caswall's great-uncle Thomas Burgess.
[25] Ibid.
[26] Ibid., p. 59.

At the same time, however, Denison supported the condemnation of Tract 90. In 1845, in the crisis following Newman's secession from the Established Church, he was noncommittal about the ritualistic questions now coming to the fore: '[He] told his clergy, "I could not lay down any rule which I could either require or advise you to adopt universally", and, "I do not look to any legislative enactments for a remedy to our present distractions".'[27]

Further, Mozley himself at Cholderton was busy proselytizing for the Tractarians: 'The *Tracts for the Times* were still appearing, and Mozley was among those who received parcels of the leaflets to distribute. He has described how he took bundles of them on pony-back from parsonage to parsonage on Salisbury Plain. Coming from Oxford, the *Tracts* were welcomed by many country clergy...'[28] One can assume with reasonable certainty that the young Perpetual Curate of Stratford, described by Newman's sister as 'quite an Oxford man',[29] was among those who welcomed the Tracts; he mentions having begun to read the *Tracts for the Times* in the early 1840s,[30] and it was probably the very copies passed on to him by the pony-riding Mozley that provided his reading matter for the bleak evenings on Salisbury Plain.[31]

Probably the most compelling argument in favour of Caswall's espousal of Tractarian principles is provided by the evidence of his ministry: he held two services a day and celebrated Communion monthly[32] in a parish in which four or five Communion services per year had been common for over 250 years.[33]

Mozley was well aware of the difficulties faced by any clergy who attempted to put Tractarian principles into practice by introducing 'daily services, fasting, confession, and new doctrines among parishioners who were "all day at work," who "fasted already in the poverty and scantiness of their daily fare," and who preferred "a good understanding between all opinions and sects" to a stricter

[27] Denison, *Charge of 1845*, pp. 7–9, quoted in ibid.
[28] Crittall, ed., *History of Wiltshire* vol. 6, p. 58.
[29] Mozley, ed., *Newman Family Letters*, p. 104.
[30] Bellasis, 'Biographical Preface', p. 9.
[31] Mozley has described the lonely and secluded lives experienced by many of the Wiltshire clergy. 'There were but scanty means of enlivening their rural solitude with newspapers and periodicals' (*Reminiscences* vol. 1, p. 324, quoted in Crittall, ed., *History of Wiltshire* vol. 6, p. 59).
[32] Caswall, 'Journal' vol. 1, p. 40.
[33] Communion was celebrated 'regularly' (four times a year, although five times was 'almost as common') from 1578 (Pugh, 'Stratford-sub-Castle', p. 213). Henry Caswall, while Vicar of the Church of St Michael and All Angels in nearby Figheldean in the early 1850s, celebrated the sacrament on four Sundays per year, plus Christmas, Easter, Ascension, and Whitsun (D. A. Crowley, ed., *History of Wiltshire* vol. 15, p. 117).

churchmanship'.[34] The clergyman who persisted 'had the church day after day, year after year, to himself alone, and perhaps two or three school children'.[35] Stratford-sub-Castle was no exception, as Mozley discovered during a visit to Caswall's home: 'As Caswall had to leave early the next morning, I was asked to take the early service for him. The congregation consisted of the clerk, some school children, and a bright-looking old fellow, with a full rubicund face and a profusion of white hair ...'[36]

It speaks for Caswall's zeal and determination that he continued this ministry in the face of the indifference of his flock. Despite his diligence in attempting to promote devotion, his efforts did not excite 'the least religious sympathy whatever' in his parishioners.[37] In fact, one reason he eventually gave to Bishop Denison for resigning was that the daily services were 'a source of annoyance and suspicion to the people' (virtually no one attended them except his servants).[38] Thus Caswall's experience of what he regarded as the lifelessness of the Church of England proved to be a significant factor influencing him to reconsider the relative positions of the Established and the Roman Churches and ultimately helping to convince him of the validity of the latter's claims. He initially had the hope that Tractarianism would be the effective antidote to this lifelessness rather than regarding it as an ideology to be espoused for its own sake. And if some Tractarians have been accused (often erroneously, to be sure) of putting ecclesiastical principles ahead of social concerns, this cannot be said of Caswall. He seems to have made it a practice to invite the children who had attended the morning service into the parsonage and feed them breakfast,[39] and on the anniversary of their baptism he gave them 'some help towards buying clothes which is very serviceable for the wages here are only 8s. a week'.[40]

34 Crittall, ed., History of Wiltshire vol. 6, p. 58.
35 Mozley, *Reminiscences* vol. 1, p. 410; quoted in ibid., p. 59.
36 Mozley, *Reminiscences* vol. 1, pp. 12–13.
37 Caswall, 'Journal' vol. 1, p. 9.
38 Ibid. vol. 1, p. 37.
39 Mozley recalls that after the early morning service that he took for Caswall 'the children went to the parsonage for the breakfast they had well earned' (*Reminiscences* vol. 1, p. 13).
40 Caswall, 'Journal' vol. 1, p. 41.

Publications

The Child's Manual

On a board in the Stratford parish schoolroom there hung a calendar on which the children's baptism days were marked – concrete acknowledgment of the significance of this day for the individual child as well as for the clergyman and the entire community. Caswall used the baptism days as an opportunity not only to extend material assistance in the form of 'some help towards buying clothes' but also for faith formation: 'On their baptism days', he wrote in his journal, 'they come to me, and I hear them say their private prayers, and speak to them seriously.'[41]

Like his great-uncle Bishop Burgess, Caswall took the Christian formation of children very seriously. Out of his experience with the children of his parish was born one of the two books he published during his incumbency at Stratford, *The Child's Manual: Forty Days' Meditations on the Chief Truths of Religion, as Contained in the Church Catechism*.[42] Written with the aim of instilling into young people the habit of meditation upon the truths of the Christian faith, the *Manual* offers forty brief chapters or meditations, to be used regularly, one chapter per day over six weeks. The topics include God, the Trinity, God the Father Almighty, God the Son, God the Holy Ghost, the Creation, the Incarnation, My Baptism, Heaven, Hell, the Life of Christ, the Holy Scriptures, the Christian Sacrifice, My Duty towards God, My Duty towards My Neighbour, and so forth. Instructions for the use of the *Manual* explain step-by-step how the child should proceed:

1. Open the book; read the subject or title for the day's meditation.
2. Spend two minutes placing yourself in the presence of God.
3. Say a prayer for grace:

    Sign of the Cross

    'My God, I believe Thee to be present within me, and I worship Thee from my inmost soul.

    'Holy Father, grant me grace, that I may gather fruit from this Meditation.'
4. Read the meditation slowly, with pauses, taking at least ten minutes for this.

[41] Ibid. vol. 1, pp. 40–41.

[42] London: James Burns, 1846. In the preface he states that the meditations have been 'written for the use of young persons known to the author, whose ages vary from ten to fifteen' (p. viii).

5. Say the prayer at the end of the meditation, then make a good resolution for the day
   and say:
   'O blessed Jesu, give me the gift of Thy holy love, pardon of all my sins, and
   grace to fulfil this good resolution, and to persevere unto the end. Amen.'
6. Say your morning prayers if you have not already said them. Remain still for two minutes before going away.[43]

The idea is to inculcate a certain ritual into the child so that the child will learn to do the meditations with reverence and care. Each day for the first seven days some aspect of the instructions is repeated: for example, Day 1 gives a brief précis of the instructions and after the meditation the child is reminded to kneel and say a prayer and make a resolution (given in the text); then the closing prayer is repeated and the child reminded to say his or her morning prayers. On Day 2 the child is reminded to consider the subject for the day, to say the prayer for grace, to make a resolution 'such as ...', and to say the prayer for blessing 'as before'. By Day 5 it is suggested that the child ought to be able to formulate his or her own resolution (although the author continues to give one), and by Day 7 the author places confidence in the child to be able to continue without needing reminders – by then the child should have mastered the ability to 'attend exactly to the rules' as given in the preface.

Noteworthy about the *Manual* is Caswall's distinction between the intellectual appropriation of Christian truths and the nurturing of a personal relationship with God. For living the true Christian life the former is insufficient on its own: cleverness in Scripture, he cautions, does not necessarily indicate a well-formed conscience,[44] and a quarter-hour silent meditation each morning is, he claims, more fruitful that 'a whole hour's noisy inculcation of Christian truth upon the mere intellect – a custom in many schools which cannot be too greatly deplored' (p. v). Nevertheless, the meditations in the *Manual* respect and engage the child's thought processes: many of them either begin with several questions or have questions interspersed throughout, because '[t]his was the only mode that presented itself to the author as really likely to lead children to

[43] Caswall, *Child's Manual*, pp. 1–2.

[44] It is interesting to compare Caswall's definition of conscience in the *Manual* – 'the voice of God within the soul of man' (p. 75) – with that in his sketch for *The Elements of the World* – 'an immediate faculty of the soul by which it corresponds with the invisible system and becomes a recipient of it'.

exert their thinking powers' (p. vii). Consistent with the author's purpose, however, the questions do not quiz the child on his or her knowledge of the Catechism but, rather, challenge the child to meditate on Christian faith truths in the context of his or her relationship with God. Thus, for example:

> Day 1. Concerning God: Do I often think about God? (p. 3)
> Day 3: Concerning God the Father Almighty: Am I happy when I think that He is also my Father through the same Jesus Christ, since in my baptism I was made a member of Christ, and so the child of God? (p. 5)
> Day 8: Concerning the Incarnation: Do I . . . often think about Jesus Christ? do I love Him for His great goodness towards me? (p. 14)

Further, throughout the *Manual* there is an emphasis on '*my* Baptism' and its implications (e.g., Do I keep the three parts of my baptismal vow?) and on *my* status as God's child and a member of the holy Catholic Church. Appropriately, the author directs that the book should be used by each child individually rather than as a class; and while the book was written to aid those 'who have the spiritual direction of the young' (p. v), he recommends that ideally it should be the parents who guide their children in using the *Manual*.

Some of the meditations, because of their pronounced moral slant, come close to resembling a typical examination of conscience;[45] not unexpectedly, references to the vanity of this world occur in two of these (Day 19: Concerning My Three Enemies and Day 21: Concerning the World). The *Manual* also employs quotes from Scripture whenever suitable, thereby both presenting opportunities for the child to learn biblical passages and teaching the child to use Scripture-based prayer. In Day 1, for example, the question 'Do I recollect that God heareth all that I say, and knoweth every thought of my heart?' is followed by an excerpt from Psalm 139; and Day 7, Concerning the Creation, ends not with the same type of prayer as before but with verses from Psalm 148 ending with the Doxology. The Creation meditation also reveals the influence of the *Benedicite* canticle, which would be so important in his later work; characteristically, Caswall divides Creation into the visible creation and the invisible creation.

Caswall completed the *Manual* in October 1845.[46] In it, he wrote in his Journal, 'I stated my entire belief that the English Church

[45] A brief form of self-examination is added at the end of the book since this was increasingly being recognized as essential for the formation of Christian character.
[46] The preface is dated October 1845; cf. also his Journal vol. 1, p. 4.

was the Catholic Church in this country.'[47] It was to be not the last book he would write, but the last book he would publish, as the incumbent of Stratford-sub-Castle.

Sermons on the Seen and Unseen

Tom Mozley remembered Edward Caswall as someone who 'loved to hover free between the seen and the unseen world'.[48] This penetrating and picturesque insight succinctly sums up Caswall's earthly journey: his literary corpus shows him equally comfortable on the one hand critiquing and satirizing the real world as he experienced and observed it and, on the other, conjuring up fantasy worlds inhabited by talking graves and mysterious supernatural messengers; while his life in general reveals a man who could function creatively in the intellectual and artistic realm as well as efficiently in the nitty-gritty of everyday pastoral and administrative tasks. But more than that, the division of the world into seen and unseen and the relation between the two realms represented Caswall's *Weltanschauung* that informed all that he wrote and did.

Caswall's acknowledgment of the existence of visible and invisible worlds has already been noted in the 'Creation' meditation of *The Child's Manual* and in *The Elements of the World* sketch, which attributes importance to the role of conscience in maintaining the proper relation between the two worlds. A passage from the Second Letter to the Corinthians was to provide him with the means of placing this concept within a theological framework and thereby enabling it to inform his preaching; the results appeared in the last book he was to publish as an Anglican, *Sermons on the Seen and Unseen*.[49] The passage is 2 Corinthians 4:18, and it is worth quoting in its context for its full import:

> For which cause we faint not; but though our outward man perish, yet the inward man is renewed day by day. For our light affliction, which is but for a moment, worketh for us a far more exceeding and eternal weight of glory; while we look not at the things which are seen, but at the things which are not seen: for the things which are seen are temporal; but the things which are not seen are eternal. (2 Cor. 4:16–18 AV)

The core message of this passage, as well as of Caswall's collection

47 Ibid.
48 Mozley, *Reminiscences* vol. 1, p. 12.
49 London: James Burns, 1846.

of sermons, is the equation of the seen with what is transitory and ephemeral, and of the unseen with what is eternal and lasts forever, and the tension that often exists between the two. The reference '2 Corinthians 4:18' appears on the title page as the motto of the book, and the 'Advertisement' sums up the theme of the sermons as 'the influence of The Unseen upon the Christian'. Christianity is 'that religion which teaches man his true position in the Universe both Visible and Invisible', and as Christians our duty is to discern that position and to act always mindful of 'our condition as beings of another system besides this which we see'. In the course of the twenty-six sermons (which he actually preached before his congregation) he draws out a variety of implications of the Christian challenge to be aware of the 'depth of mystery surrounding us on all sides' and to act accordingly.

The motto text of the collection, 2 Cor. 4:18, is also the text of a sermon entitled 'Looking at the Invisible'. According to Caswall's exegesis, St Paul 'believed fully ... that there are ... two worlds ... each equally real': the things seen and the things unseen, and among the latter are not only created things but also the Creator, 'the principal and chief amid unseen realities',[50] as well as Christ, who was sent by the Father to teach us the existence of this invisible world and is presently invisible (p. 135).[51] Paul gave priority to[52] the unseen, because these things 'are eternal, the other temporal' (p. 135). The true Christian is called to walk by faith and not by sight, and by so doing is prepared to enter the invisible world and enabled to bear tranquilly 'any manner of tribulations' (p. 141). The emphasis on faith is echoed in a funeral sermon on 'Christ's Secret Providence' that speaks of 'the necessity of submitting in faith to all the dispensations of Christ's providence, whatever they may be ... we are all of us at different times called upon to yield ourselves up in faith to what seems inexplicable' (p. 146). We will eventually know God's reasons, not in time but in eternity.[53]

[50] Caswall, too, includes God among invisible realities in *The Elements of the World*, but not in *The Child's Manual*, because in the latter the relevant meditation treats only of Creation.

[51] Despite Caswall's frequent references in these sermons to the present invisibility of Christ and, in this sermon, to Christ's mission role as revealer of the invisible world, nowhere in *Sermons on the Seen and Unseen* does he draw out the sacramental implications of Christ's role as mediator between the visible and invisible worlds, although, as we have seen, he does allude to the sacramentality of the visible world in *The Elements of the World*.

[52] Caswall points out that the Greek for 'look at' can also mean 'aim at'.

[53] I find here an uncanny echo of John Henry Newman's meditation: 'I have my mission – I never may know it in this life, but I shall be told it in the next ... [God] knows what He is about.' (Quoted in *Meditations and Devotions of the late Cardinal Newman* [London: Longmans, Green & Co., 1893.])

The opposition between faith and sight is the theme of a sermon 'Faith and Sight' that really forms the cornerstone of the book. Taking as its text John 20:29 ('Jesus said to [Thomas], "Have you believed because you have seen me? Blessed are those who have not seen and yet have come to believe."'), and using St Thomas's refusal to believe without seeing as a paradigm of the worldly system, the sermon contrasts worldly grounds of belief, embraced by those who do not believe 'except on actual sight' (p. 118), with Christian grounds of belief, embraced by those who 'believe without seeing' (p. 119). The former is the *law of sight* – 'Seeing is believing' – and the latter, contrary to the rules of the world, is the *law of faith*. While acknowledging the prudence of acting by the law of sight in a normal mundane context, Caswall warns that it becomes a 'snare' if people apply it to Christianity and thus 'learn to give very little belief to what in Christianity is unseen', for in Christianity 'the greater matters' are invisible and thus beheld only by the eye of faith (pp. 119–20). In a passage that echoes *The Elements of the World* he admonishes the hearer to keep created things, however good in themselves, in their proper perspective so that they do not lead one astray:

> The woods, the fields, the mountains, the valleys, the clouds, the ocean, all the wonderful, and beautiful, and amazing works with which God has enriched this lower order of things, – all these celestial and terrestrial wonders, great as they are in themselves, greater in their Creator, yet have nevertheless the tendency, if we do not watch ourselves, of withdrawing our minds from spiritual realities, from Eternity, from Christ, from Heaven, from Hell, from the Resurrection of the dead, from the Judgment to come. And thus it is that many, who could appreciate and describe very well the amazing scenes which are exhibited in the natural world, have nevertheless shewn themselves to be without a sense of things unseen, which certainly contain by far the greatest wonders of creation ... (p. 121)

Yet in seeming contrast to *The Elements*, in which he describes inhabitants of 'civilised countries' as being vulnerable to material distractions, and yet makes no explicit mention of cities, here he singles out those who live in large cities, where 'a constant succession of artificial objects is presented to their eyes' (p. 122) so that they are ever surrounded by 'a multitudinous abyss of things temporal' (p. 123) that prevent them from focusing on the transcendent things of Christianity.

As often occurs in Caswall's thought, there is a pronounced apocalyptic tinge to his concept of the transitory nature of life. He is ever aware of the presence and possibility of death, and consequently a sense of urgency marks his exhortation to focus on unseen, eternal things:

> Faster than on eagle's wings we are all of us being borne along into the realms of the invisible. They only are eternal; they only are imperishable; – imperishable bliss, eternal torment ... we are all moving onward ... to drop down silently into the depths of an unseen existence. Our course is inevitable; no power can make it pause. (pp. 129–30)

His favourite 'vanity of vanities' theme is strongly implied in this picture of the fleetingness of the world. The sermon 'The World Perishable, the Christian Imperishable', with its imagery of 'the perishable and perishing things of this world, which cannot last for any length of time, but must always be shifting and changing and falling to pieces' (p. 305), recalls the various landscapes in Cloudland, beautiful and seductive yet suddenly crumbling, and, in one Ciceronian paragraph, distils the entire message of *The Elements of the World*:

> Only recollect, for instance, what those who have been even slightly educated amongst us know from what they have read of history. How empires have succeeded upon empires in the procession of past ages; each thought sure to last by the historians and mighty men of its own time; each, however, obliterated either suddenly or by degrees, and giving place to some new kingdom, new races of men, new forms, new polities, which in their turn again have become old and perished. This, in particular, we have learnt as respects the four great Empires mentioned in prophecy, Assyria, Persia, Græcia, and Rome; how they have been swept away, leaving few vestiges, those vestiges no better than ruins of ruins, scattered over the world in perpetual desolations, continual mementos of that fate which in due time awaits all the pride and pomp and glory of present monarchies and empires. (pp. 306–7)

A sermon for the First Sunday in Advent refers to the Mystery of the Incarnation as 'that great Union of the Seen and Unseen' (p. 1): that 'the Word was made flesh' means that the Invisible became visible. Such eternal mysteries are virtually beyond human capacity to comprehend; as sinners our minds are darkened – 'Doubtless the holy angels do understand it far beyond what we do' (p. 3). That God became human, 'how difficult it is to realize it in our minds; what earnestness, and faith, and deep meditation it requires to represent to ourselves this most wonderful truth! ... To apprehend this doctrine with the intellect is but a small part of Christian knowledge. It is necessary also to receive it in the heart' (pp. 7–8).

Already in *The Child's Manual*, in the context of the religious formation of children, Caswall had distinguished between the intellectual appropriation of Christian truths and the cultivation of faith. Now he applies it to the adult response to the great Christian mysteries, adding the complementary opposites 'heart/intellect' to 'faith/sight' and 'unseen/seen'. What is understood by means of the intellect is, in a sense, seen: frequently we say 'I see' when we mean 'I understand'. What is appropriated by faith, on the other hand, belongs to the realm of the unseen; it is an inward reality, a matter of the heart.

But heart is, for Caswall, not only an opposite of intellect but also the seat of the inner life as opposed to outward actions. The Wise Men who came to adore the infant Jesus not only gave him precious material gifts but also, more valuable, was the 'unseen offering' of a simple faith and humble mind, and a holy heart that 'resigns the wisdom of this world as foolishness with God' ('The Wise Men', p. 88). A Lenten sermon on 'Contrition: How to Be Attained' points up the inward/outward tension in the context of the right heart needed to obtain God's forgiveness. The text is from Psalm 51, the great penitential psalm that refers to truth in the innermost being, prayer for a right spirit, and God's desire for a contrite heart as the acceptable sacrifice. '[O]ur eternal condition depends upon the state of our inward hearts [not on ouroutward life] ... To what purpose is it that a person should outwardly live a respectable life, if inwardly his heart is gone astray from God? Of what use are outward observances to him who within has a heart hardened against his Maker ... ?' (p. 224).

Caswall recommends confession as one of four means (along with meditation, self-examination, and prayer) to assist in developing a contrite heart. This is consistent with his pastoral practice: his private talks with each parish child on his or her baptism day were intended as 'a sort of groundwork for confession'.[54]

If this is taken together with some of the other sermons, Caswall seems here to anticipate the notion of the fundamental option in contemporary Roman Catholic moral theology, which holds that one's fundamental moral orientation in life is paramount over the collection of discrete actions one performs. The idea of *choice* of life-orientation is essential to the fundamental option; so, too, Caswall says of the worldly, '[T]hey made their choice to go along with the perishing world, and live by it and for it' (p. 315). The one impor-

[54] Caswall, 'Journal', vol. 1, p. 41.

tant distinction between the fundamental option concept and Caswall's thought is the chronological relation between choice/orientation and actions: the fundamental option posits that our actions ultimately determine our basic orientation toward good or evil, whereas Caswall holds that our orientation determines (by enabling) our course of actions. Without the right heart, he claims, 'it is impossible for us to do any good action at all' (p. 225). But the important shared element is the emphasis on the paramountcy of inward orientation or 'right heart' over outward actions, for it is on the former that we shall be judged.

A notable aspect of the nineteenth-century Romantic movement's turn inward was its concept of the relationship between inner and outer vision. Such thinkers as the poet William Wordsworth[55] and the German theologian Friedrich Schleiermacher[56] warned against making the inner eye of the mind a slave to the physical vision of the outer eye and living lives determined solely by one's external situation. Caswall theologized the Romantic concept of the tyranny of the outer eye in a sermon on 'Discerning the Time', in which he preached about the importance of seeing with the inner eye instead of being distracted by the external and ephemeral. 'The great errors which persons make in religion arise commonly from their not seeing, and not being willing to see, the crises or turning-points of their lives,' he states (p. 71). For example, someone may have had his or her mind 'softened by affliction and been offered the consolation of the Holy Spirit'. But instead of acknowledging and accepting this consolation, the person let the affliction pass over, quenching 'the holy fire of the Spirit in a flood of unbelief. He did not discern the present time' (p. 72). Or the person may have had a God-given opportunity to make 'one or two truly religious friends' who could have been of great benefit, '[b]ut he did not discern that time which was then present. He did not see its privileges' (p. 72). And if it is so difficult to 'discern the present time in life's ordinary events, how

[55] Wordsworth wrote of freedom breaking through at those times of

> ... deepest feeling that the mind
> Is lord and master, and that outward sense
> Is but the obedient servant of her will. (*The Prelude* XI: 258–77)

[56] 'Whoever sees and recognizes only the outward spectacle of life instead of the spiritual activity that secretly stirs his inmost being, who merely constructs a picture of life and its vicissitudes from impressions gathered far and near instead of facing his essential self, will always remain a slave of Time and Necessity ... [I]n the image which he constructs of himself, this very self becomes something external, ... and everything in such an image is determined by external circumstances.' (*Soliloquies*, trans. Horace Leland Friess [Chicago: Open Court, 1957], p. 15.)

much more difficult is it with respect to using the great seasons of the Church year as occasions for grace and for religious growth'.

Caswall completed *Sermons on the Seen and Unseen* while in the throes of preparing to leave Stratford. There was a definite sense of urgency in his intention to have the book published as quickly as possible: 'My idea is to show to my relations and friends by these sermons that, whatever hereafter may become of me I at least am acquainted with the Christian religion. It will be a sort of legacy before going abroad.'[57] By the time the book appeared in print, Caswall was no longer Perpetual Curate at Stratford: his 'Advertisement' is dated 14 May 1846, from Mudeford, a coastal village near Bournemouth where the Caswalls had gone for Louisa's health, and his resignation of the Stratford incumbency had taken effect on March 28.[58] His journal in June 1846 contains a poignant mention of his having sent twelve copies of the *Sermons* back to twelve of his former parishioners. In August he quotes a letter from Canon W. K. Hamilton of Salisbury who writes glowingly that 'I have never read sermons (with the exception of Newman's) which have so thoroughly pleased me as yours'.[59] Caswall notes that a review in the *English Churchman* also compared his sermons to those of Newman – a comparison that, as Caswall hesitantly anticipated,[60] would prove to be prophetic.

[57] Caswall, 'Journal', vol 1, p. 48.
[58] W.R.O. D1/2/34, Folio 180–1.
[59] Caswall, 'Journal', vol. 2, pp. 397–98.
[60] Ibid.

Chapter Three

Journey to Rome

In his study of conversions to Roman Catholicism during the era of the Oxford Movement[1] Peter Nockles concludes that 'the Oxford Movement played a crucial role in fostering conversions to Rome . . . Of the one hundred Anglican clerical converts of the period 1845–55, most were the product of Tractarian influence.'[2] The 'peak periods of Tractarian conversion', he points out, were in 1845–6 and 1850–1.[3]

In listing a variety of factors operative among the Tractarians who eventually submitted to Rome, Nockles draws upon an extensive body of literature left by converts as accounts of their experiences. Among the authors of such accounts are Newman,[4] the poet and hymn writer Frederick William Faber, and the former clergyman Thomas W. Allies, who became an important figure in Catholic education after his conversion. Caswall's journey to Rome, then, was not a solitary one. He shared a number of the concerns of several other Tractarian converts, and like many of them he, too, wrote an account of his conversion journey, in the form of a journal. Unlike Allies[5] and others, however, Caswall never

[1] Peter Nockles, 'Sources of English Conversions to Roman Catholicism in the Era of the Oxford Movement', in V. A. McClelland, ed., *By Whose Authority? Newman, Manning and the Magisterium* (Bath: Downside Abbey, 1996), pp. 1–40.

[2] Ibid., pp. 25–6.

[3] Ibid., p. 7.

[4] Acknowledging Newman's 'initial reluctance to give reasons' for converting (p. 2), Nockles considers *Loss and Gain*, *Lectures on Anglican Difficulties*, and *Apologia pro Vita Sua* as examples of this genre.

[5] Allies compiled his journal, which he titled *A Life's Decision*, in 1853, from notes and sketches he had made during the years of his struggle between the Church of England and the Church of Rome (1845–50). He first published it in 1880, at his son's urging.

published his journal, and thus it has remained unknown even to scholars of the period. It is chiefly from this journal that my account of Caswall's conversion to Rome is drawn. Using the study by Nockles as background and Allies' account of his conversion as a touchstone for comparison, I will draw primarily on this unpublished material to relate Caswall's conversion journey from the time when his doubts about the Church of England grew serious enough to impel him to begin recording them, to his reception into the Church of Rome eleven months later. I will trace Caswall's literal, external journey: the trauma of his resignation of the living at Stratford and the ensuing suspicions and interrogations to which his and Louisa's families subjected them; the visit to Ireland to witness Roman Catholic religion and life at first hand; the further family confrontations in the face of the Revd Robert Clarke Caswall's impending demise; and the final, decisive trip to Rome. But at the same time I will also chart Caswall's inner – his spiritual, intellectual, and emotional – journey: his incipient doubts about the church of which he was minister and the motivating factors behind his initial suspicions that the Church of Rome offered the fullness of religious truth; his turmoil over the family's reaction and remorse over the impending pain; his search for God's will and prayer for the grace to carry it out; his meticulous investigation of whatever literature could help to resolve his questions of doctrine and discipline. In thus describing Caswall's journey to Rome I will offer the first detailed account of the conversion experience of someone who then went on to surrender himself totally to sharing the Oratorian vocation with Newman.

Caswall's journal first came into being as a notebook begun on 13 February 1846 and initially titled 'Thoughts on the English Church'. The 'thoughts' are numbered, some of them in the form of a question or questions, and at first most of them are brief. Before long, however, this catalogue of thoughts developed into a 630-page journal that chronicles his inner and external life journey from midwinter 1846, when the conversions of three of his close friends, together with his first reading of Newman's *Essay on Development*, jarred him into doubts about the validity of the Church of England, until approximately one month after his reception into the Church of Rome on 18 January 1847.[6]

[6] The journal is housed among Caswall's files in the archives of the Birmingham Oratory. I have to thank the late Gerard Tracey, Oratory archivist, for bringing it to my attention and making it available to me. The journal is valuable also because into it Caswall copied in their entirety letters he sent to or received from family and friends as well as excerpts from relevant material that he was reading. Unlike several other nineteenth-century Anglican converts to Roman Catholicism (e.g., Frederick William Faber and Thomas W. Allies), Caswall never published the account of his conversion journey, although he later told Bellasis, 'I have

The stated purpose of the journal was to 'discover from it the habitual state of my views and convictions as regards the great controversy between England and Rome'.[7] Besides Caswall's original thoughts it includes material that he copied into it, such as letters and excerpts from books that he had been reading. After three months on the project he admitted that he sometimes found keeping the diary 'a great bore' (p. 233), yet he never doubted the value of the enterprise, which was, at what he termed 'a critical point' in his life (p. 220), 'by means of the thoughts contained in this book to be able to judge fairly what are my real views, and their continued bias, and upon that judgement to act. I shall endeavour to be careful in setting down every day the events of the day before and what I thought and said' (p. 233).

Initially the thoughts Caswall began recording in the journal 'seemed ... to be mere theoretical speculations, but now they appear to bear on practise [*sic*]. I think that what gave them reality was partly reading Development and partly the secession of some of my friends to Rome' (p. 4).[8] Although on the next page he called Newman's *Essay on Development of Christian Doctrine* 'a very noble and sublime view of the Gospel', it was not until a month later that he set down any more detailed thoughts on it. By then he was reading it for the third time:[9]

> It does seem to me a most matchless work and that for which he came into the world ... My idea is that in the course of years it will alter the face of society. How childish seems our[10] argument from Antiquity after reading Newman anew! And his view is evidently not a private judgment, but only a full drawing out of principles maintained in the

---

sometimes thought of publishing [it] in an abridged form' (Bellasis, 'Biographical Preface', p. 9). Toward the end of his life he went so far as to have one of the Oratory's boy pupils start to make a clean copy – several pages in 'Smith's writing' are extant and were done in November and December 1877, according to a handwritten annotation on the first page – and to calculate how many pages would result in a printed version, but death intervened before anything could come of the project.

7 Caswall, 'Journal', p. 588. Hereafter page numbers in the Journal are given in the text.

8 The pages of the journal, which eventually encompassed three notebooks, are numbered consecutively. Page number references are given in this chapter in parentheses in the text.

9 To a letter sent by Newman at Rome on 15 January 1847 to J. D. Dalgairns, Ambrose St John added a postscript: 'Caswall attributes his conversion to Newman. He has read the 'Developments' [*sic*] four times ...' (*The Letters and Diaries of John Henry Newman*, ed. Charles Stephen Dessain, vol. XII [London & New York: Thomas Nelson & Sons Ltd., 1962], p. 18).

10 An indication as to the meaning of 'our' is given on the next page, on which he refers to 'we Puseyites'. Thus Caswall identified himself with the Tractarians.

> council of Trent. How must it affect me in the end. Must it not inevitably lead me to Rome? I feel quite unable to dispossess my mind of that theory. (p. 66)

Sacrifice as inspiration

Among the numerous factors influencing the English converts to Rome in the 1830s and 1840s Nockles mentions the inspiration of 'the examples of self-denying holiness of Italian missions such as the Rosminian Luigi Gentili and the Passionist Dominic Barberi'.[11] In Caswall's case, however, it was the example of his friends who had converted earlier that touched him so deeply and sparked in him a nagging suspicion that the Church of Rome and not the Church of England was the true Catholic Church in England – and the reason was precisely the sacrifices entailed in such a step.[12] In the middle of the nineteenth century and beyond, Roman Catholicism was still held highly suspect in England. Converts from the Established Church risked alienation from family and friends and – if they were university-educated, as many of them were – automatic exclusion from academic careers. Further, those married converts who had been clergymen now cut themselves off from their livings and thus from economic security, for they could not be reordained as Roman Catholic priests.[13] Caswall noted about his three convert friends John Glenie, Henry Formby, and Henry Coope[14] that they 'have ...

[11] Nockles, 'Sources of English Conversions', p. 3.

[12] Like many of the English converts around this time (see ibid., p. 4: 'Contact with individual Roman Catholics on the part of English converts was rare and limited'), Caswall had never met a Roman Catholic priest until he intentionally set out to investigate the claims of the Church of Rome.

[13] Even twenty years after Caswall, converts, whether single or married, faced these problems, as testified by, e.g., several biographers of the poet Gerard Manley Hopkins.

[14] John Melville Glenie (1816–1878) was an MA of St Mary's Hall, ordained deacon at Salisbury on 22 December 1839, and thus was a contemporary of Caswall's at Oxford (W.R.O. D1/1/33: '1837. Register. Denison', folio 60). He became a Roman Catholic in 1845. Henry Formby (1816–1884), a fellow Brasenose man with Caswall, as an Anglican vicar solemnized two marriages in Caswall's stead at Stratford on 29 June 1841 (W.R.O. Fiche 7/2474/1). He was received into the Roman Catholic Church in January 1846. It was Formby to whom Caswall addressed the letter that was added as a foreword to later editions of *The Art of Pluck*. In the mid 1840s Caswall's publisher urged him, unsuccessfully, to remove the foreword because of the association with a seceder from the Established Church. Henry George Coope (b. 1818), an Anglican clergyman who was an MA of Christ Church, Oxford, became a Roman Catholic in 1845. (Except as otherwise noted, biographical details on these three men come from Bertram C. A. Windle, *Who's Who of the Oxford Movement* [New York and London: The Century Company, 1926].)

forsaken their homes and pursuits, relations, position and the like, which shows that the inducement, or conscientious conviction must have been very powerful. Now on the side where there is self-sacrifice and suffering, there is generally the truth' (p. 4).

Caswall's quest for the truth meant that in all honesty he could not continue as Perpetual Curate of Stratford if his doubts about the Church of England persisted. He decided to give himself until March; if he continued to hold these ideas, he would feel it his duty to resign (p. 5). Not only would continuing in the active ministry compromise his integrity, but he was also concerned about the distractions presented by the material trappings of his living that would imperil his search for the truth:

> It seems to me that while a man is enthralled with various domestic comforts, good furniture, servants, a nice garden, society and other secular advantages, he is not in a capacity to see the truth. Those men who seem to have discovered the length, breadth, depth and height of Christianity in Romanism were chiefly men who for some years had been living in small lodgings ...
>
> It is too true that I took this curacy in part because I found it had a comfortable and most respectable house. Let me now then resign it because I have found it comfortable and respectable. (p. 25)

Thus the 'vanity' theme that figured so prominently in some of his writings at this time (he was then engaged in fleshing out his sketches for *Elements of the World*) now challenged him in an intensely personal way. His response to the challenge was an inexorable determination 'to put off that which is of the world, my house, relations, furniture, servants, garden, poney chaise etc. and to throw myself for a time out of the present system, by which means I shall be better able to see the truth' (p. 31).

Thus it was this material concern rather than any doctrinal doubts that caused him to push forward his decision to leave Stratford. The day after he wrote this last entry, on 20 February 1846, he wrote his letter of resignation to the Dean of Salisbury and delivered it personally that very afternoon. As reasons for his course of action he cited Louisa's health and the fact of his daily services being a source of annoyance and suspicion to the parishioners.[15] He proposed to leave at Lady Day and did not intend to take another curacy just yet; instead he thought to move about a

[15] A few pages later he confided that these two factors 'would not have been suffered to influence me unless I had also thought there might be great truths in the Roman Church worth risking all to obtain' (p. 46).

little to be able to 'remove some perplexities which perhaps without cause I was sensible of having felt lately in regard to ecclesiastical affairs' (p. 37).[16]

Accordingly, with no fixed place in which to settle and with the possibility of extensive travel on the horizon, Caswall and Louisa prepared to sell most of their possessions – their furniture and other contents of their house, entrusting the process to Mr Brownjohn, a local auctioneer. Caswall proposed to Louisa that they give £50 from the proceeds of the sale – £5 apiece to ten neighbouring clergymen – 'for the good of the poor', following Christ's injunction to 'sell what you have and give to the poor'. Without this element, thought Caswall, his undertaking would lack consistency (p. 84). It was not long before the stark reality of what he was doing struck him; characteristically, he gave it a theological significance:

> This Evening [April 4] I saw My Goods advertized in the Salisbury Paper for Sale by auction ... It seems a bitter thing to behold all my property thus exposed to an inquisitive and hardhearted public. But I ought to consider that at this very season[17] Christ was exposed naked on the Cross for my sake. O God I rejoice to think that I can thank thee for what is now taking place, and that I can regard this sale of my private treasures as a Sacrifice to thee and a Crucifixion from the world. (p. 90)

Some days later, after a man from Brownjohn's had been to the house to ticket the furniture of the auction, Caswall commented that he might fancy himself dead and become his own executor. 'Oh that I were dead in the best sense and my life hid with Christ in God. I do not regret that all these painful things are being done during Passion week' (p. 104).

His feeling of renunciation was intensified by the fact that he was now alone – Louisa had already left Stratford to spend a fortnight at her aunt's some one hundred miles away, with the intention of joining Edward later in London. Like her husband, Louisa was torn between sadness at leaving a beloved home and the desire for a simpler life. 'She had great pain', he wrote, 'in parting from this place and I really admire her for being so ready to give up for ever such a quantity of worldly property which she has long felt to be a great temptation' (p. 85).

Whatever his parishioners' feelings were about the daily services,

[16] Caswall's resignation was officially accepted on 28 March 1846 (W.R.O. D1/2/34, folio 180).

[17] It was the evening before Passion Sunday.

they must otherwise have held Caswall in high esteem, to judge from their reactions to the news of his impending departure. When he made his farewell visits to them he found them 'very sorry' that he was leaving; many had tears in their eyes. The little children apparently took the news very hard, one woman in particular telling Caswall that her two sons were crying in bed because he was going. Aware that he and Louisa intended to go abroad, the people had got the notion that they planned to travel to Jerusalem and wished them a safe voyage, 'wondering at Louisa's boldness in undertaking it' (p. 108).

On Passion Sunday, 5 April, Caswall preached his farewell sermon. Using Psalm 1 as his text, he described the blessedness of a Christian life, set out various duties, including self-examination, attendance at church services, private prayer, and the reading of Scripture, and went through the chief points of faith as contained in the Creed. He concluded by promising to pray for them and asking their prayers for him: 'Pray ... for me in the time to come that I may have grace to know what things I ought to do, and strength and power faithfully to fulfil the same' (p. 97).

On Good Friday afternoon, 10 April Caswall finished visiting the poor and distributing gifts. That night his friend Geldart, a cousin of Louisa's, slept at Stratford so as to be able to help him with some packing the next day. At noon on Holy Saturday he left two of the servants in charge of the house with instructions to have the carpets taken up in readiness for the auction the following week. Then he walked into Salisbury with Geldart while a servant, Bedford, took his luggage up the hill. Along the way he met several of the poor people, 'who wished me goodbye very heartily' (p. 114). Three hours later Caswall arrived at West Lavington, where his father was vicar. There he found his parents, his sisters Emma and Olivia, and his brother Alfred with his wife and two children. As there was no spare bedroom for him in the vicarage he took a little room over a shop. 'And so here I am without a home in the world! Glory be to thee O Lord' (p. 114). Although he did not know it at the time, he and Louisa were never again to have a fixed abode of their own.

Family concerns

Prospective and actual converts had to run a gamut of painful social trials, not the least being estrangement, sometimes permanent, from family and friends. Thomas Allies mourned over Mr Baron

Alderson, Mr Justice Coleridge, and the Revd E. Coleridge: 'How can one remember such friends without grieving at the loss of them?' William Palmer confided to Allies that as a result of his conversion his relations with non-converts were all either 'snapped or frozen'.[18] Thus in his quest for religious truth Caswall was not alone in being confronted with family pressures as well as challenged to resolve certain doctrinal and devotional issues.

In his study of Catholic converts Patrick Allitt points out that 'becoming a Catholic in Britain or the United States often prompted accusations of disloyalty to the nation, its Protestant heritage, even its sense of common decency'.[19] That one's own family would have been a primary source of such accusations was inevitable. Given the strong family tradition, on both the Caswall and the Burgess sides, of service to the Established Church, Edward's family would have regarded defection to Rome as a traitorous action. The pressure even came from beyond the family on behalf of the family; in reply to the gift of a copy of *Sermons on the Seen and Unseen* an old family friend, Mrs. Beauchamp, wrote to remind Edward of his proud heritage: as 'Grand son and Son of two most simple minded and sincere Christian Pastors and the great nephew of ... an ornament to our venerable establishment', it would be a shame if he were to forsake this faith–heritage 'to follow cunningly devised fables' (p. 462).

As early as February 1846, when he became aware of his difficulty with some of the Thirty-nine Articles, Caswall wrote to his parents and to Captain and Mrs Fischer, the aunt and uncle who had raised Louisa,[20] informing them that he thought he should resign Stratford. The unpleasant reactions apparently were not long in coming: Edward reported in his journal on 5 March that '[s]ome of the letters which we have received lately from relations have seemed harsh and suspicious'. In his very next entry, made the same day, he mentions having just received from his mother a guard chain that she had been working for him: 'Should I ever turn a Roman Catholic what a bitter bitter pang it would give her and to my father also' (p. 51).

[18] Thomas Allies, *A Life's Decision*, p. 251. See also, e.g., Patrick Allitt, *Catholic Converts: British and American Intellectuals Turn to Rome* (Ithaca and London: Cornell University Press, 1997), pp. 5–8.

[19] Allitt, *Catholic Converts*, p. 5.

[20] In her will, dated 5 May 1847, Louisa Stuart Caswall refers to her father as 'the late deceased Major General Charles Augustus Walker' and to General Walker's will dated 26 April 1842, but the date of his death is not given (W.R.O. no. 776/1103, a copy in Edward Caswall's handwriting). Very possibly General Walker had early been widowed (Louisa's mother is nowhere mentioned in any documents or sources) and his military duties compelled him to entrust Louisa, his only child, to the care of her aunt and uncle.

On the one hand, then, Caswall was beset by remorse at how his possible secession from the Church of England would affect the parents he loved and who loved him. On the other hand, however, Jesus' assertion that 'He who loves father or mother more than me is not worthy of me' (Matt. 10:37) haunted him, sometimes making him wonder whether his delay in taking the final step was sinful vacillation. These two opposing forces would continue to vie for dominance in Caswall's attitude toward his family throughout his journey toward Roman Catholicism. As early as his first week in Lavington he was able to perceive and sum up this conflict. Having taken a walk with his mother and explained his doctrinal difficulties to her, he found her to be 'very affectionate ... [she] said she constantly prayed for me that I might be directed aright':

> Sometimes when I look at father's grey hairs, I think to myself that someday I may be the cause of bringing them with sorrow to the grave. Yet has not Jesus said whosoever loveth father or mother more than me is not worthy of me? If thc Roman Catholic Religion should go on to press itself upon my conscience as containing the real length, breadth, depth and height of Christianity I must follow it at all hazards. How nobly my father treats me at this time, with what exquisite delicacy. My tears blind me as I write and think of him ... must I cause pain someday perhaps to so good a father? (pp. 122–3)

Throughout his journey toward Rome, Caswall considered it of the utmost importance that he be seen to act with great deliberation and not with haste. For one thing, he felt that his position as a clergyman demanded that he not take such a step lightly; he wanted to avoid giving scandal to friends as well as family and believed that giving himself a good amount of time 'will give more weight to what I do when I do it' (p. 374).[21] But there was an aspect to the family circumstances that increased his self-imposed pressure to appear deliberate, and this was the fact that his younger brother Tom had also been showing signs of Roman sympathies. Two years before this, Tom had suffered a period of mental illness – Edward refers in his journal to Tom's 'insanity' or 'derangement' – and the family was only too ready to regard Tom's interest in Roman Catholicism as a symptom that mentally he was not entirely out of the woods. In September 1846, when the family were gathered at the bedside of their dying husband and father, Edward's brother Alfred confided

[21] Lest it seem that he regarded others' opinions of him too highly he added that he thought that 'considering the nature of my mind, God will be more pleased at my deliberating for a much longer time' (p. 374).

to Edward his certainty that Tom intended to 'become a Romanist' after their father died. Tom's fellowship at Clare Hall, Alfred pointed out, must be worth £300 a year, and such a step would compel him to forfeit it. 'Alluding to his share in putting Tom with Dr Munro's lunatic asylum three years ago when Tom was deranged, [Alfred] said that ... he had immense power of intimidation over Tom and that he would use it now in case of his attempting to turn papist and would rather put Tom in a madhouse than suffer it' (pp. 413–14).[22]

Edward, therefore, was determined to exercise considerable deliberation in his investigation of the Roman Church since, should he decide to convert, he did not want to appear to be 'acting precipitately': 'I wished the step when it came to be entirely deliberate and also to appear so to others' (p. 400). Even on the verge of his reception into the Church of Rome, in an interview with Newman in which he gave Newman an account of his deliberations since leaving Stratford, he 'particularly mentioned my wish to be deliberate especially because of Tom's having been once insane' (p. 576).[23]

Both Edward and Louisa felt the pressure from Louisa's family as well. On Easter Thursday Edward went to Devizes to meet Louisa, who had just arrived at the home of his sister and brother-in-law Maria and Benjamin Dowding. She had had

> a very painful fortnight at Castle. On the day before she came away her uncle asked her solemnly whether I intended becoming a Papist stating that he had seen the report in the paper. She told [him] that I did not intend. He then asked whether she thought I ever should. She replied she could not answer how it might be in four or five years. He then asked what she should do if I do. She replied that she would change with me. He greatly wondered at my excessive weakness in giving up Stratford. Mrs. Fischer also was greatly pained. It is a great grief to me that I should cause these two dear friends such misery, especially since they have reposed such entire confidence in me. May God eternally bless them, but I foresee I can never hope that in this life they will think well of me again. (p. 135)

Two months later he was still admitting that the 'deepest pain' he felt in resigning his curacy was the effect of his actions on Captain and Mrs Fischer: they

[22] Edward commented in his journal, '[W]hat can be better than, in a question of religion, for conscience' sake to give up £300 a year and to run the risk of infinite family evils?' (p. 422).

[23] Tom had by then (January 1847) become a Roman Catholic.

> entrusted [Louisa] to me in our marriage after entirely bringing her up . . ., and I can most fully see and understand how acutely painful it must have been at the change of ideas which she exhibits in her letters from Protestant to Catholic and our giving up our happy and respectable home and at the loss of character which must more or less have fallen on me. A military man must especially feel himself degraded in having a connection with one who has deserted his post. (p. 284)

In June 1846 Edward, his brother Tom, and Louisa travelled to Ireland to observe the practice of Roman Catholicism there. On 31 July they were summoned home with the news that their father the Revd Robert Caswall was ill and not expected to survive. This further intensified family pressure on Edward to remain in the Church of England. After they had returned to Lavington, Edward's mother informed him that his father, now seventy-eight years old, had lately been 'a good deal troubled by several things. One of the principal things has been my leaving Stratford and my unsettled state in regard to religion . . . If father had died it might have been said that I had contributed to his death' (p. 372).

At this point Edward was keenly aware of the deeply painful effects his 'determination . . . to enquire into the truth' was having on his parents. Yet he realized that it would never occur to him to give up his quest. After some soul-searching he decided that this mindset of his most definitely was not mere obstinacy on his part: he could never cause such pain to his parents 'for the mere sake of obstinacy'. He now felt the determination more strongly than ever, suspected it to be of divine origin, and resolved to continue with his enquiries, including eventually a trip to Italy to observe Roman Catholicism there (pp. 372–3). When his father had improved somewhat he asked Edward to stay for three weeks and to take his Wednesday and Friday morning services. Edward complied.

> I think mother fancies that by getting me to do this a step has been obtained toward bringing me back to regular duty. But she is mistaken. I could not at the present time take a parish conscientiously, and I do not think I shall ever be able again. I consider there was no harm in my taking the Wednesday and Friday services since it was a case of mercy rather than sacrifice, and besides I always have the regular daily service in private by myself or with Louisa. (p. 379)

By the end of August hope had been lost for the Revd Robert Caswall's recovery. About this time the elder Caswall asked Edward to be his curate, saying that he would arrange it with the bishop. 'He seemed to have an idea that were I thus to assist him officially I might have a chance at coming in for the living.' Caswall replied 'that as a son I was really happy to assist him in the duty so long as I stayed here, but that I did not wish to undertake it officially' (pp. 405–6). Analysing his feelings about his father's impending death, Edward thought that one reason why he did not 'sufficiently sympathize with and for' his father was that it might be a mercy for him not to live to see two of his sons turn Roman Catholic, especially given that older generation of Anglican clergymen's prejudice against Rome, which would cause him to regard his sons as 'idolaters' (p. 405).

The Revd Robert Caswall died on 4 September 1846, without ever knowing of the reception into the Roman Catholic Church of his son Tom, which had taken place shortly before. Edward was glad that this matter had at last been resolved for Tom, whose own health had given his brothers cause for concern that he would not outlive his father.[24] Edward alone, of course, had shared Tom's anxious dilemma over the timing of his entry into the Church of Rome: should he turn Roman Catholic as soon as possible and thus risk hastening his father's demise, or should he wait until after his father died and thereby endanger (as he and Edward believed) his own salvation if he himself should die without having followed his conscience?

Tom, then, was now at peace, at least for the time being. Edward, on the other hand, was feeling the pressure on account of Tom's secession as well as his own 'questionable' status in the Church of England. Captain Fischer wrote him:

> I heard with much regret that your brother Tom had become a Roman Catholic, for I fear his example may shake the faith of many others in the soundness of Protestantism ... [I]t does appear to me strange that proselytes can ever be made to a religion which enjoins the worship of images and other such mummeries, particularly when they have been brought up in the principles of the Church of England which adheres so rigidly to the sense and spirit of the 2nd Commandment. (p. 460)

There it was again: the accusation of idolatry, of image-worship, that Edward would be compelled to disprove in the course of his Romeward journey. If he knew it in his heart to be false, he would need to marshal actual intellectual or experiential evidence to satisfy his relatives.

[24] Tom lived another sixteen years and died just short of his forty-sixth birthday in New York, where he is buried in the Evergreen Cemetery in Brooklyn. See chapter 7, p. 200.

As late as mid-November 1846 the doubts as to whether his lengthy deliberation was justified returned to haunt Caswall. Was he deceiving himself in regarding it as necessary? Could he be overdoing it? The fragility of life could not be ignored in this matter; in a moment of striking insight he wrote: 'Might I not die suddenly? ... It must be considered that the Church is a means not an end. To join Rome is not to come to a conclusion but to make a beginning, and all the hard work will come afterwards. Now is life sufficient for long delays in questions of this sort?' (p. 515).

Again, he questioned the validity of his position that 'my friends and relations demand deliberation of me ... [I]s not this a seeking the praise of men?' Asking himself whether he would be thinking differently if he had no friends or family to consider, he was forced to admit that in all likelihood he would have joined Rome by now. Was he not, then, ignoring Christ's command to leave all and follow him, especially since he was convinced that his impulses toward Rome were from God and not from Satan? 'These are grave questions.' He had given up Stratford in order to be free from entanglements, yet he appeared to have taken on new entanglements through his exaggerated concern over his family and friends. 'Neither', he reminded himself, 'have I anything to suffer in the way of income' (pp. 515–16).

It was finally during his and Louisa's sojourn in Rome in December of that year that Caswall resolved once for all 'to regard my mother brothers sisters Capt & Mrs Fischer and all other relations and friends as dead or rather as never having existed, and to put them utterly absolutely and altogether aside as having nothing whatever to do with my decision in the present question. This is what our Saviour commands ...' (p. 587). On literally the very eve of his reception into the Church of Rome he wrote that if the step he was about to take should cause his family and friends great pain, 'it must be firmly borne in mind that Christ can make them a thousandfold compensation for that pain' (p. 612).[25] This was his mindset as he entered the Roman Catholic Church, and once the deed had been done, he looked back with gratitude on his various relationships, deciding that they could have behaved more objectionably; at least they never actually stood in the way of his deliberations in the eleven months since he had resigned Stratford (pp. 612–13).

[25] Cf. Allies' rejoinder to Palmer on being told of the loss of his friendships with non-converts: 'But He who created friendship itself will repay the loss of it.' Allies, *A Life's Decision*, p. 251.

Methods of investigation

Consistently with his view of the equality of heart and intellect, Caswall's methods of investigating the truth of Roman Catholic claims over against the Church of England took two basic forms: *intellectual*, that is, the reading of pertinent source materials and discussions with helpful persons, and *experiential*, or the observation of Roman Catholicism in its actual practice. The publications he read ranged from historical treatises that helped him contextualize his questions about the validity of Anglican orders and jurisdiction to contemporary works that aided his evaluation of Tractarian claims, while his observations of Roman Catholicism took place in two chief phases: a trip to Ireland, accompanied by his wife, Louisa, and brother Tom, in the summer of 1846 and a trip to Rome on which he set out with Louisa in the autumn of the same year and which ended in their reception into the Church of Rome in January 1847.

The intellectual quest

Early in April 1846 Caswall recorded that he had begun reading *The End of Religious Controversy* by the English Catholic apologist John Milner[26] after finding a copy of the book that his friend Coope had left at Geldart's home. Milner's book was very influential in helping Caswall clarify his position on doctrinal concerns.

Another of the earliest books that Caswall read in hopes that it would shed light on his dilemma was *The Unity of the Church* by Henry Edward (then Archdeacon, later Cardinal) Manning. This book, published in 1842, was Manning's 'first significant theological treatise'.[27] Manning's concern with 'the scandal of schism'[28] must

[26] John Milner, *The End of Religious Controversy in a Friendly Correspondence between a Religious Society of Protestants and a Roman Catholic Divine*. Addressed to the Rt. Rev. Dr. Burgess, Lord Bishop of St. David's, in answer to His Lordship's PROTESTANT'S CATECHISM (New York: D. & J. Sadlier, 1844). The book consists of a long series of letters written in late 1801 and early 1802 and mostly addressed to a James Brown, Esq., president of the Friendly Society of New Cottage or the 'Salopian Society'. The later decision to publish the letters – the opening address to Burgess was written in 1818 – because of the increasing attacks to which Catholics were subject, and especially because of Burgess's own recent *Protestant's Catechism*, which 'teaches [Protestants] to *hate* and *persecute* their elder brethren, the authors of their Christianity and civilization' (p. xiii), an attitude unseemly in a Christian bishop.

[27] David Newsome, *The Convert Cardinals: Newman and Manning* (London: John Murray Ltd., 1993), p. 149. I am indebted to Newsome's book for the précis of *Unity* that follows.

[28] Ibid.

have attracted Caswall, who throughout his journal agonized over the question of whether the church of his birth was a schismatic church. He starts out with a statement, which he bases on the authority of the Fathers, that 'a belief in the Unity of the Church forms an article in every Baptismal creed of every church, both in the East and in the West'.[29] 'Unity in plurality' existed since the time of the apostles, he argued; it was plain 'that the divinely appointed ministry of the church was the bond which knit together the members of Christ in one visible communion'.[30] Unfortunately, observed Manning, reality fell far short of perfection. Schism exists – and who, he asked, is to blame? To a large extent he found Rome guilty 'because of the claim of the successors of St Peter to universal jurisdiction, in defiance of the fact that the commission to Peter was afterwards given to all the Apostles'.[31] Manning attacked Rome 'for the damage that it had inflicted on the organic, or objective, unity of the Church by acts of usurpation, making claims that assemblies such as the Council of Florence and the Council of Trent were general councils when they were not, and – most of all – in claiming jurisdiction over the *Ecclesia Anglicana*, whose credentials for its independence from Rome went far back into the Middle Ages.'[32]

The Unity of the Church may have 'establish[ed Manning] as a theologian of consequence in the eyes of contemporaries such as Gladstone and Robert Wilberforce',[33] but Caswall was not impressed. Manning made the church to be one visible empire episcopally organized. But, argued Caswall, episcopacy must produce 'that Unity for which it subsists', and Manning errs if he believes that the Church of England enjoys the same visible unity as Rome (p. 90). Episcopacy alone is not sufficient, but, rather, an episcopacy united over the face of the earth. Only Rome possesses this. Indeed, Caswall maintained, Manning more than once describes attributes of the church to which only Rome can validly lay claim; for example, states Manning, '[t]he testimony of the Church Catholic compels assent by its universality ... all embracing all absorbing Church of Christ which takes up into itself all nations languages people and tongues ... and blends them into one.'[34]

Further, declared Caswall, Manning contradicts himself. After his

[29] Manning, *Unity of the Church*, p. 19; quoted in Newsome, *Convert Cardinals*, p. 150.
[30] Manning, *Unity of the Church*, pp. 77, 85; quoted in Newsome, *Convert Cardinals*, p. 150.
[31] Newsome, *Convert Cardinals*, p. 150.
[32] Ibid., p. 151.
[33] Ibid.
[34] Manning, *Unity of the Church*, p. 217; quoted in Caswall, 'Journal', p. 91.

descriptions of unity and his statement (indeed, the starting point of his thesis, as we have seen above) that the unity of the Church is an object of faith and thus a fact (which means *what is* and not what ought to be), at the end he claims that there is no unity in the church. Manning closes by expressing the hope that the now 'miserably divided' church may 'be once more united'. Thus, when Manning states in the Creed his belief in 'one holy catholic and apostolic church' he is not saying 'I believe *there is*' but 'I believe *there ought to be*' (p. 92).

Caswall also read a book by William Sewell entitled *Plea of Conscience for Seceding from the Catholic Church to the Romish Schism in England*.[35] He disagreed with Sewell's conception of the nature of conscience[36] and strongly objected to Sewell's belief that conscience unaided by the art of casuistry cannot reach a decision about whether to join the Church of Rome.[37] Further, he took issue with Sewell's criteria for distinguishing whether a voice within is really the voice of conscience: (1) the voice must be prohibitive and not affirmative (Caswall: as if conscience cannot exhort us in a positive way!); (2) it should contradict the bias and inclination of the heart as if 'a good man might not have a good bias and inclination'; (3) it should be supported by some human testimony external to ourselves. Here Caswall's objection was to the implication that the consciences of those who have joined Rome were not 'supported by the human testimony of a vast number of Catholic Fathers and 250 million living Roman Catholics'[38] (p. 100). To Sewell's claim that 'Rome has no external evidence to produce' 'for by the claim of supremacy she absorbs all witnesses in her own person'[39] Caswall replied that 'Milner and others draw many arguments in support of the Roman doctrines from the fact that the Heterodox Eastern bodies which split off from Rome in the early centuries hold the same doctrines ...' (p. 100).

[35] The *Plea of Conscience* was a sermon that Sewell preached before the University of Oxford on 5 November 1845 (the anniversary of the Gunpowder Plot). It was published the same year, along with other sermons, by J. H. Parker of Oxford. Sewell also wrote a novel entitled *Hawkstone*, which Caswall, who mentions having met the author, read with disapproval and described as anti-Jesuitical. The most memorable aspect of Caswall's disparaging remarks about the novel, and about novels in general as means of edification, must surely be his exclamation, 'What should we all think if Newman were to write a novel?'

[36] It will be recalled from chapter 3 that Caswall defined conscience as 'the voice of God within the soul of man' (*Manual*, p. 75) and 'an immediate faculty of the soul by which it corresponds with the invisible system and becomes a recipient of it' (sketch for *The Elements of the World*).

[37] Sewell, *Plea of Conscience*, p. xiii.

[38] Ibid., p. 11.

[39] Ibid., p. 42.

Caswall challenged Sewell's assertion that every development of revelation 'must be attested by the more sure word of prophecy' (and thus Roman Catholicism cannot prove any right of such development).[40] Defining the nature of a development as 'a deduction from other deductions, an evolution from previous truths conducted on fixed principles', he cited as an example the doctrine of the Trinity, which has developed from certain truths but did not need 'the more sure word of prophecy' to arrive at it (p. 101).

Caswall's reaction to Sewell's work was not entirely negative, however. He quoted with approval a passage that spoke positively of converts to the Church of Rome:

> [S]ay of those who have abandoned their church that they were earnest, say they were zealous, say they were yearning after visions of things better than the poor realities around them. Slight not their acts of self-sacrifice. Let us compare ourselves with those who are gone – men of zeal, men of piety, men of prayer and watchings and fastings and almsgiving and purity of life. They have despised their Church as believing that it is despised of God. They left us for a rule more stern. They offered to Almighty God a sacrifice of many a comfort, many a pleasure, more than He required. They impaired their bodies perhaps their judgment by excess of mortification. (p. 49)

At the same time, he remarked on the slight dig implied in the last sentence: recalling a rumour that had circulated to the effect that 'Newman through his mortifications had ... nearly lost the use of his intellect', he points up 'the falsity of this notion' by citing the *Essay on Development*, 'the profoundest book that ever yet appeared' (p. 102).

One passage from Sewell struck at the very heart of Caswall's current enterprise; he quoted it with assent and resolved to 'strive to carry it out' (p. 103). Sewell admonishes someone with doubts about the Church of England to 'turn to the acknowledged standard of the will of God, to some divinely authorized plan of ecclesiastical polity' for clear proof that the charge is 'fatal to its character as a true member of the body of Christ'. If the doubter cannot find this clear proof yet still remains in serious doubt, he must (1) guard 'against the danger of propagating a system of possible error' by 'retiring ... from the ministry of the Church if he serve at its altar' and from any other work that 'contributes to its extension'; (2) 'guard ... against the possibility of belying traducing and despising one who may be notwithstanding his doubts his spiritual mother'[41] (p. 103).

[40] Ibid., p. 44.

[41] Caswall does not give the page number of this passage.

Caswall challenged, however, Sewell's assumption that those who go over to Rome are filled with bitter remorse over having thus far spent their lives, albeit ignorantly, 'in the service of Satan': 'Now I have had five friends go over and I know for certain that none of them think thus. None of them think that while they were earnestly discharging their duties in the English Church they were serving Satan. They know well that they were serving God, and believe that God has rewarded them' (p. 103). In this connection Caswall believed Sewell to be unaware of the Roman Catholic belief that those who truly desire to be Catholics and reckon themselves as such, even though ignorantly in schism, are really Catholics 'to a considerable extent' (p. 103). He summed up his judgment on Sewell's *Plea of Conscience* by saying that it seemed 'forced out for the occasion, and not to have the appearance of reality' (p. 104).

From volume 6 of Jeremy Collier's *Ecclesiastical History of Great Britain*, which he was reading in Barham's edition, Caswall quoted a number of passages on the English Reformation, mainly dealing with authority and jurisdiction, although one – concerning the Queen's order that the English Common Prayer be translated into Latin probably for the sake of 'foreign princes'[42] – he interpreted in the context of a connection between the use of a universal language (Latin) and the universality of the church, stating that 'they' showed that 'an English service would only do for an insular and insulated Church' (p. 147). But what touched him most personally was Collier's reference to 'the Supremacy bill for restoring to the crown the ancient jurisdiction over the state ecclesiastical and abolishing all foreign power repugnant to the same – Nothing can be more comprehensive than the terms of this clause. The whole compass of Church discipline seems transferred upon the crown.'[43] Caswall commented:

> It is evident from this that when afterwards the Queen deposed all the existing Bishops of the English Church and imprisoned them she did it by Authority of Parliament and of the Church so that to all intents and purposes those fourteen Bishops still continued Bishops in the eye of God and the new ones were state intruders. Now it so happens that my own ordination comes from those new ones, and the question is whether time can make it valid what at its commencement was invalid. Surely I am bound to look back to the rock from whence I was hewn ... [W]e are bound to look to the invalidity of Parker. (p. 146)

[42] Collier, *Ecclesiastical History*, p. 308.
[43] Ibid., p. 224.

Another source that Caswall consulted was the seventeenth-century divine William Chillingworth, a fellow Oxford man and the godson of Archbishop Laud. Caswall had been 'reading a good deal' of Chillingworth from a single-volume collection of all his works, of which the principal work is one that he does not name but describes as the author's 'answer to a Roman Catholic work called "Charity maintained by Catholics". The entire Roman Catholic work is published Chapter by Chapter and after each Chapter there comes a Chapter by Chillingworth in answer' (p. 533). The work in question was *The Religion of Protestants a Safe Way to Salvation* (Oxford 1638), which 'caused a stir' upon its original publication.[44] Although Caswall did not judge Chillingworth to be adequate to the task he set himself, he did acknowledge that the latter saw that 'the only ground on which he could consistently oppose Rome was a purely Protestant ground and not a via media ground' (p. 534). Chillingworth regarded the Church of England as 'absolutely one with the Calvinist and Lutheran bodies'. Caswall quotes the passage with Chillingworth's famous dictum 'The Bible I say, the Bible only is the religion of Protestants' as that wherein all Protestant bodies agree and 'which they all subscribe with a greater harmony as a perfect rule of their faith and actions'[45] – here he includes the Church of England – in distinction to the Roman Catholic Church, which takes the doctrines of Trent as that on which all of that body agree.

'Now', commented Caswall, 'the real question is whether a man of plain sense like Chillingworth in thus regarding the Church of England as integral portion of Protestantism does not regard it in the right way in which it should be regarded.' If Chillingworth is correct, then 'the view which Pusey Manning Keble and others now take of the Church of England is manifestly unreal ... For they evidently do not regard our Church as a part of the Protestant body' (pp. 534–5).

The experiential quest

John Milner in *The End of Religious Controversy* lamented that 'there is hardly a lisping infant, who has not been taught that *the Romanists*

[44] Patrick Collinson, *The Religion of Protestants: The Church in English Society 1559–1625* (Oxford: Clarendon, 1982), p. vii. The work that Chillingworth was answering was *Mercy and Truth, or Charity Maintained by Catholicks* (1638) by Edward Knott (1582–1656).

[45] Interestingly, Newman writes about Chillingworth in the Introduction to his *Essay on Development*, implicitly referring to the latter's dictum about the Bible.

pray to images'.[46] The memoirs of individual converts bear this out. The architect Augustus Welby Pugin (1812–52) recalled having been brought up 'thoroughly imbued with all the popular [anti-Catholic] notions of rocks and faggots, and fires, idolatry, sin-purchase, etc., with all the usual tissue of falsehoods so industriously propagated throughout the land'.[47] Caswall, too, records having been inculcated with stories about the alleged Roman Catholic worship of images as well as their idolatrous attitude toward Mary and the saints,[48] and the influence of such beliefs upon his relationship with his family has been noted. Impressed by the conversion of his clearly intelligent and educated friends, he began to question whether these things could be true.

A second question that dogged Caswall about Roman Catholic practice was rooted in his radically pastoral orientation: How could the Latin liturgy have any true meaning for the average Catholic, and especially the poor and uneducated, who did not understand the language? Caswall's resolution of this question is dealt with later in this chapter.

Deciding that the only way to resolve these issues would be a first-hand observation of Roman Catholicism in operation, Caswall set out for a tour of Ireland in late June 1846 with Louisa and his brother Tom. Because in Ireland the Roman Catholic Church existed side by side with the Church of Ireland, the tour would also afford him an immediate comparison between the two religions, something not available had he chosen to visit one of the predominantly Catholic countries on the Continent. During the trip he faithfully and meticulously recorded his observations and impressions: the services he attended and popular devotions he observed, the schools he visited, his conversations with Religious and lay people. Consequently, Caswall's journal is a valuable source of eyewitness information about Roman Catholicism as practised in Ireland in the middle of the nineteenth century.

Caswall's main methods of experiential investigation were, first, visits to the churches to observe and sometimes participate in liturgical or paraliturgical services or private devotions, and often simply 'counting heads' at the various churches in the mornings; and secondly, visits to religious institutions, which were usually

[46] Milner, *The End of Religious Controversy*, Letter xxxiv, 'Religious Memorials', p. 233.

[47] Pugin, quoted in Michael Trappes-Lomax, *Pugin: A Medieval Victorian* (London: Sheed & Ward, 1933), p. 57; quoted in Allitt, *Catholic Converts*, p. 46.

[48] For example, in an aside he describes the English, himself included, as 'bred up as we all have been to consider Popery tantamount to idolatry' ('Journal', p. 86).

involved in educational work, to converse with those in charge and to observe them at work.

Visits to churches

Caswall regularly made early-morning pre-breakfast visits to the numerous Roman Catholic churches and chapels, often just to look in and count the number of persons present, note whether a Mass was in progress or about to begin or had just ended, and then go on to the next church. Usually finding large numbers of persons attending Mass,[49] he was also impressed by the numbers of visitors to the churches when no service was in progress. Cork was the Caswalls' first port of call. Immediately after they arrived and had secured lodgings, Edward headed for the Roman Catholic cathedral. It was a Sunday morning and the church was 'cram full of people'. Very soon after this congregation left, 'another crowd had entirely filled the building' for the next Mass (p. 304).

High Mass was celebrated only on the 'grand festivals', and since the next day was St. Peter's Day Caswall planned to attend this Mass as well as afternoon Benediction. Again he found the cathedral very full for both services. The devoutness of the worshippers impressed him: there was 'no chatting or smiling whatever on the part of any person either on taking their seats or on leaving or during the service' (p. 305). He also thought 'that I never saw so much actual kneeling in my life as I have seen during the last two days' (p. 307).

Commenting on the very basic, functional appearance of most of the chapels – in Dublin he saw twelve and noted that with one exception they were 'without architectural beauty and ... devoid of ornament' – Caswall observed that the worshippers were nonetheless 'evidently very fervent. This shows that the Roman Catholic religion really does not depend in the least on an outward gorgeous show. It is evident that it depends on some strong spiritual ideas, and on the freedom which the worshippers find in praying according to their individual bent' (p. 353).[50]

In contrast to the vast numbers of worshippers in the Roman Catholic churches, Caswall counted fewer than 150 in the congregation at the Sunday service in St Fin Barr's Protestant cathedral in

49 E.g., one weekday morning in Dublin he saw ca. 300 persons at St Andrew's at the 7.30 Mass, 30 persons at prayer in another church where no Mass was going on, and between 300 and 400 at the 8.30 Mass at St Francis Xavier. Sunday Mass congregations would reach between 800 and 1,200.

50 This comment was made in the context of his observation that the Latin liturgy, by not binding the congregation to a strict following of the text, allowed each worshipper the freedom to pray as he or she saw fit, everyone being bound by the 'idea' of Christ's Real Presence in the Eucharist.

Cork, while on a visit to St Patrick's Protestant cathedral in Dublin he was outraged by the neglected state of the building: a 'sickening wretched disheartening miserable sight' with 'not the least appearance as if [it] had been used as a religious building for centuries' (p. 349). Noting the renovation work going on there, he wondered,

> where are they to get the living stones, the poor, to fill the building? My firm belief is that the population of this country will never again return to St. Patrick's till it is Roman Catholic, and considering its present desolate state, and the unattended condition of the Church of Ireland Churches all over the country I must say I almost wish that time was come. (p. 350)

Whatever he has seen of the Roman Catholic Church in Ireland 'corresponds entirely with what I have seen of it in Switzerland, Italy, Germany, France & Belgium' (p. 359). The Established Church, on the other hand, 'is not equal to being the Church of all nations, not even equal, as we see in Ireland, to be the Church of one nation' (p. 360).

Caswall's landlord in Dublin took him to witness a young Carmelite novice taking the black veil.[51] It was an entirely private ceremony, attended by about thirty ladies and children, with Caswall, his landlord, and the nun's father and brother the only men present. 'It was a touching service.' At the breakfast reception afterwards he noted that the young nun 'had a very cheerful appearance'. 'I came away filled with admiration and a greater sense of the loveliness of Christianity than I ever before experienced. She had had several offers [of marriage] before entering the convent' (p. 357).

Visits to religious institutions

Given his keen interest in the formation of the young during his curacy in Stratford, it was natural that Caswall should have considered an investigation of its educational operations to be of paramount importance in assessing the viability of the Roman Catholic religion. Accordingly, he took every opportunity to visit the Catholic schools, speaking with those in charge, observing lessons in progress, and frequently asking questions of the pupils themselves. In a school run by the Presentation Brothers in Cork he observed a class of ten-year-old boys going through their paces in

[51] The young woman had previously been apprenticed to the landlord's wife, a dressmaker.

geography, Shakespeare, arithmetic, and English history. The brothers regarded preparation for the sacraments as their chief responsibility; thus regular attendance at Mass and Communion and at least monthly confession were *de rigueur*.

At two Christian Brothers schools Caswall watched the boys as their teacher, a 'particularly intelligent man' (p. 321), took them through reading, singing, geometry, and arithmetic. He was extremely impressed, commenting that all three schools compared very favourably with the English national schools. His experience in the Cork schools led him to declare that Roman Catholicism was 'a thorough practical hardworking Religion' and that there was 'a real spiritual work going on here' (p. 322). The Presentation Brothers and Christian Brothers together had over 2,000 boys in their care, 'and the effect upon the city of Cork has been wonderful'. If it is true that 'by their fruits you shall know them', then 'the Church of Rome is more a true Church than ours' (p. 330).

Visiting the seminary at Maynooth, where young men studied for the priesthood, Caswall was struck by the apparent poverty of the students as evinced by their threadbare clothing. He came away with the impression that their theological education[52] was 'infinitely superior ... to that at Oxford' (p. 370).

On 31 July Caswall received news from his brother Henry about their father's serious illness. The three thus returned home, having spent a little over a month in Ireland. Toward the end of November Edward and Louisa left for the Continent to see the church in operation in Rome. On the eve of their departure Edward was troubled by the possibility that his motives for this journey were not entirely pure, that in addition to or instead of religious considerations the trip 'may be the offspring of an idle curiosity and love of excitement' (p. 539). A jumble of conflicting motives danced through his head, making it difficult for him to discern the 'correct' or at least the most important one. By the time he reached Genoa he concluded, 'The sole object for which I go to Rome is that by the help of English Roman Catholics whom I hope to meet I may have an opportunity of knowing what the Roman Catholic religion really is in Rome itself' (p. 556).

In the course of the actual journey through France and Italy Caswall recorded his observations of religious practices both in and out of the churches, and was clearly quite affected by the paraliturgical and private devotions he witnessed as well as by the formal

[52] He noted that for the last four of their six or sometimes eight years they 'study only divinity' (p. 370).

liturgies. In Rome itself, true to the resolve expressed in Genoa, he tended more to record his conversations, such as those with Newman (whom he asked about devotion to Mary and the saints) and with a Dr English, with whom he discussed the position of the Church of England.

While their methods of investigation differ – the architect pursuing scholarly research and the pastoral clergyman conducting field observation – the experience of Pugin and Caswall strikingly parallel each other: both concluded that the stories of Roman Catholic 'idolatry' with which they had been raised were totally unfounded.[53] Writing to Louisa's aunt, Mrs Fischer, four days before his reception into the Church of Rome, he declared, 'I have been unable to find here those superstitions of which I had heard so much. It is absolutely certain that in regard to images including that of the cross Roman Catholics pay them no divine worship whatever'; and the idea of their worshipping Mary and the saints is also 'entirely chimerical' (p. 598). Indeed, all the charges that 'it is the custom' to level against Roman Catholics in England are 'founded upon most extraordinary misrepresentations' (p. 599). Thus, by meticulous observation Caswall divested himself of the misconceptions about Roman Catholicism implanted in him as a 'lisping infant'.

Doctrinal and devotional concerns

The validity of Anglican orders

Apostolic succession

At the heart of a constellation of issues revolving around the question of the validity of Anglican orders was the debate about apostolic succession in the Church of England.

In April 1846 Caswall confided to his friend Glenie, a recent convert, and to Mrs Trevelyan, widow of the Revd John Trevelyan whose curate he had been at Milverton, that the chief point that demanded his serious investigation was the validity of Matthew Parker's consecration (p.165) and thus the validity of his own ordination as derived from Parker (p. 141). The Anglican clergy's claim 'to the entire powers of the Priesthood' with respect to offering a Sacrifice of the Altar and absolving in confession is one 'from which as a body we have entirely shrunk during the last three centuries'

[53] For Pugin cf. Allitt, *Catholic Converts*, p. 46.

(p. 165), and now that it was being revived by the Tractarians, there emerged the necessity of establishing beyond any doubt the validity of Anglican ordinations.

It is no coincidence that Caswall had just been reading Milner's *The End of Religious Controversy*, for Milner's arguments treating the question of validity find a strong echo in Caswall's own, and from the beginning Caswall had obviously been troubled by the Catholic apologist's conclusion that Anglican orders 'are, to say the least, exceedingly doubtful'.[54] Caswall is quite clearly convinced that the validity of priestly orders depends on whether they can be traced back in unbroken continuity to the apostles. As proof that the church needs to demonstrate this unbroken continuity he adduces Jesus' saying 'Ye shall be my witnesses because ye have been with me from the beginning' (p. 185). But, asks Caswall, can the Church of England truly claim this apostolic succession? That the validity of Roman Catholic orders was a certainty, while the validity of Anglican orders was still contested, tormented Caswall throughout the period of his investigation. Roman orders derive from 'a vast number of chains of Bishops. Ours through one chain and through one individual' – Matthew Parker. 'If we fail in Parker we fail altogether' (p. 94), and 'the more the circumstances of his ordination are investigated the more difficulties are found to surround it' (p. 165).

For Caswall the arguments against the validity of Parker's consecration, and thus against the Church of England's claim to have the apostolic succession, could be reduced to two chief points: (1) there was a formal defect in Parker's consecration; (2) apostolic succession is a matter of *fact* and not of *faith*, and the weight of authority was against the Church of England's having it.

Caswall pointed out that the stress on apostolic succession requires 'that there be no invalidity or informality [i.e., defect of form] in the transmission of it'. But all Anglican orders can be traced to Parker, and was there not 'a great informality in [Parker's] consecration?' (p. 115). Caswall recorded numerous discussions on this subject, with himself and with friends and relatives. He maintained that Parker's consecration was certainly deficient in form, so much so 'as to have invalidated any legal process' (p. 95). Following Milner's argument about the inadequacy of Edward VI's ordinal with respect to ordinations, Caswall states that Parker was consecrated not according to the form that existed in the 1840s but

[54] Milner, *The End of Religious Controversy*, Letter xxix: 'Apostolic Succession', p. 202.

according to the form of Edward VI which, declared Caswall, 'would have done better for a confirmation' (p. 95).[55]

'Present' Form	*King Edward VI's Form*
Receive the Holy Ghost for the office and work of a bishop in the Church of God committed unto thee by imposition of our hands in the name of the Father and of the Son and of the Holy Ghost and and remember that thou stir up the grace of God who is given thee by this Imposition of our hands for God hath not given us the spirit of fear but of power and love and soberness.	Take thou the Holy Ghost and remember that thou stir up the grace of God which is in thee by the imposition of hands for God hath not given us the spirit of fear but of power love and soberness.

By replacing Edward VI's form with the other form one hundred and three years later, Caswall contends, the Church of England 'has virtually condemned [Edward VI's form] and thrown a slur upon it. I should think a lawyer would find great difficulty in Parker's form knowing how necessary it is to be exactly accurate in forms' (p. 95). Caswall takes issue with those who would minimize the difficulty in the form of Parker's consecration by denying that 'a change or omission in a mere form could affect the transmission of hierarchical authority'. After all, 'it is certain that the exact observance of forms is necessary at Coronations, and this Queen Elizabeth herself felt who was crowned according to the exact Roman Ritual' (pp. 119–20).

Finally, Caswall adopts Milner's arguments against the Church of England's continuity with the apostolic church, and in so doing he not only contends on an intellectual level but also battles with a family ghost. Milner's book, as its subtitle indicates, is '[a]ddressed to the Rt. Rev. Dr. Burgess, Lord Bishop of St. David's, in answer to His Lordship's PROTESTANT'S CATECHISM' – that is, to Caswall's great-uncle. In various pamphlets Burgess argued against the supremacy of Peter and therefore of the Church of Rome, by citing various scriptural passages that contradict Peter's supremacy and attempting to prove that the British church was founded not by St. Peter but by St. Paul; thus the true church in the British Isles descends from this original Pauline apostolic church and not from Augustine of Canterbury, who was sent by the Roman Pope. Milner

[55] The wording of the forms as given here follows that given in Caswall's journal, p. 95. Cf. Milner: 'according to [Edward VI's] ordinal, bishops were consecrated ... by a *form* which might be used to a child, when confirmed or baptized' (*The End of Religious Controversy*, Letter xxix: 'Apostolic Succession', p. 203).

counters by citing New Testament passages in support of St Peter being 'any way superior to the other apostles'[56] – some being the same passages Burgess uses *against* it – and by quoting Bede's account of Pope Gregory I's directive to Augustine of Canterbury regarding the mission to the British Isles: 'When Augustine asked [Gregory] how to treat other bishops, Gregory said, '... we commit all the bishops of Britain to your care, that the ignorant among them may be instructed, the weak strengthened, and the perverse corrected by your authority.'[57]

Caswall does not mention Burgess by name – perhaps he was taking no chances that his journal would not be read by a family member – but in echoing Milner on this point he clearly disagrees in no uncertain terms with his great-uncle:

> I must say I think it is childish and absurd to argue for the Independence of our Church from the fact of their having been a British Church here before Augustin [*sic*] came. Anyhow our present orders if derived in succession at all come from Augustine and not from the Old British Church. We are Saxons and have not connexions with the older inhabitants of this country. Or at least if there is a connexion it is so slight as to amount to nothing. To go back to the British Church is a mere theory and amounts to real dissimulation and false argument. (p. 204)[58]

In his journal Caswall expresses his position that the apostolic succession of any church is not a matter of pure faith but, rather, a fact that admits of proof and demands the evidence of the reason. The weight of authority is against the apostolic succession of the Church of England, he claims, because of the widespread denial of its presence. The apostolic succession in the Church of Rome is 'a standing fact acknowledged by the whole world. In the Church of England it is a theory denied by the world and by many of our own bishops' (p. 203). There are too many groups who deny the continuity of the Church of England with the pre-Reformation Church and instead hold that the Church of England as it now exists began at the Reformation; these groups include Dissenters, Roman Catholics, all Evangelicals, indeed 'the world in general' (p. 185), all of whom

56 Milner, *The End of Religious Controversy*, Letter xlvi: 'Papal Supremacy'.

57 Ibid., p. 305. In question here were 'the British prelates in Wales, and the Pictish and Scotch in the northern parts'.

58 How ironic that Milner's statement in his opening address to Burgess, written in May 1818 – 'the most fruitful source of conversions in the Catholic Church, are the detected calumnies and misrepresentations of her bitterest enemies' (p. xxvii) – should eventually come to apply to Burgess's own great-nephew!

claim that Queen Elizabeth was the source of the Church of England's existence and organization. Caswall's own father denied apostolic succession and held that the Church of England's power and jurisdiction are from the state, and even Parliament 'claims all Church property on the principle of a denial of genuine continuity' of the Established Church with the Church of the Apostles.[59]

In maintaining his position Caswall opposed the Tractarians in whose camp he had hitherto regarded himself, disagreeing with the very basis of their claim for the Church of England as an apostolic church rather than a creation of the state. Dr Pusey, Isaac Williams, John Keble, and Charles Marriott still hold to the continuity between the Established Church and the pre-Reformation Church, while Newman, W. G. Ward, Frederick Oakeley, and Frederick William Faber 'have ceased to believe it' (p. 203). In one of his conversations with Dr Pusey, Caswall reiterated his position on this issue, contrasting the apostolic succession as historical fact with 'the truths of Christianity, [which] were to be received by faith', and came away with the abiding impression that Dr. Pusey, 'absorbed in the old Fathers, ... has not really studied the history of the English Reformation but has taken our Orders in faith' and thus firmly believes 'that we are exactly as much a Church as is Rome' (pp. 256–57). Early on, Caswall made a remark that foreshadowed his ultimate conclusion: 'I see now why when the Tracts began to make much of the Apostolical succession all persons said it would lead to Rome' (p. 61). Considering the vast numbers who reject the apostolic succession of the Church of England, and finding Parker's consecration to have been 'informal', Caswall observed that there were two choices, either 'to give up the belief in Apostolical succession at all, or else to join Rome, for in Rome the Apostolical succession is absolutely certain beyond any doubt' (p. 203).

The Eucharist: Sacrifice and Real Presence

Early in his investigations Caswall affirmed his 'strong' belief that Christ's sacrifice on the cross was the first of a series of sacrifices

59 In November 1846 Caswall read in the current issue of the *Oxford and Cambridge Review* that Sir Robert Peel and the conservative party regarded the Church of England 'only as an establishment, ... as a human invention, the creature of the state'. This could be seen from reading Peel's speeches, which 'never acknowledge any higher origin to the Church than Parliament, or any more ancient than the Reformation. He doggedly and determinedly confines the term Catholic to the Romanists'. Caswall comments that Sir Robert Peel is a double-first Oxford man and 'more than any other man of his time is in the habit of regarding things as they actually are' and thus may 'be quite right'. In this Sir Robert also agrees with Newman. He 'is well aware of the nature of High Church views and of all the questions raised by the Tracts' (pp. 532–3).

and 'the Holy Eucharist is the continuation of it' (p. 109). He questioned, however, whether this was a valid belief in the Church of England, for (1) the power to offer sacrifice is not conferred at ordination; (2) the ecclesiastical courts recognize no altar; (3) the entire body of the clergy deny that the Eucharist is a sacrifice in the sense of a continuation of Christ's sacrifice, and nearly all in any sense whatsoever; (4) the laity 'altogether abhor such a notion and therefore cannot be said to assist the priest in the Sacrifice, but without the assistance of the laity can it be a valid sacrifice'; (5) the Thirty-first Article, with its *wherefore*,[60] confirms the notion of one sacrifice.

At the time he wrote his meditation on the Christian sacrifice for *The Child's Manual*, 'I saw no difficulty in appropriating the doctrine to our Church. But now [spring 1846] I do see it' (p. 111). Accordingly, in June 1846 he broached the topic during one of his conversations with Dr Pusey, who also held a view of the Eucharist as sacrifice. To Pusey he expressed his belief that the priest offered the sacrifice on the part of the people; but if the people did not assent to the notion of the sacrifice, how could the priest offer it? Pusey maintained that the assent and assistance of the people were not necessary – after all, Roman Catholic priests offered Mass in private – while Caswall replied that in the Roman Catholic Church the entire parish assisted, even if they were not present, 'by being united in the idea of a sacrifice', but in the Church of England even the notion of the sacrifice did not exist. To Pusey's question on what authority he claimed that the people's prayers must be added to the priest's for a perfect sacrifice, Caswall answered that it seemed natural, 'and at any rate unnatural to go on year after year offering a sacrifice which the people did not offer with me' (p. 284). Later, Caswall reflected that his appeal to nature in this discussion was 'really sound. Certainly at all the ancient heathen and Jewish sacrifices the people were not opposed to the notion of a sacrifice. But amongst us they are opposed to the very notion' (p. 300).

In a lengthy discussion with Tom Mozley and William Palmer in Oxford in June 1846 Caswall expounded on his view of the Eucharist as a commemorative (as opposed to a figurative) sacrifice, emphasizing the meaning of *commemorative* as it applies to an eternal event:

[60] 'Wherefore the sacrifices of Masses, in the which it was commonly said, that the Priest did offer Christ for the quick and the dead, to have remission of pain or guilt, were blasphemous fables, and dangerous deceits.' *The Book of Common Prayer* (New York: The Church Hymnal Corporation and The Seabury Press, 1977), p. 874.

> The Sacrifice of Christ on the cross had two aspects from the fact of Christ being God and Man in one Eternal Person. So far as he was man it was a temporal event ... So far as he was God it was an eternal event ... The Sacrifice then on the Cross was a temporal event and is also an eternal event at the same time and the commemoration of it as performed by Himself through his Priest in his Church partakes of the same nature ... When therefore we speak of a commemorative sacrifice in the Eucharist ... we must mean not a mere commemoration as of any temporal event such as of the Queen's birthday but also the commemoration of an eternal event. But an eternal event admits of no past or future. A commemoration then of an eternal event ... must be one with the event. Hence ... the Sacrifice of the Eucharist is mystically ... the same as the Sacrifice of Christ on the Cross. (p. 263)

The words *real* and *unreal* are significant terms in Caswall's evaluations of things.[61] It was no wonder, then, that he held the Real Presence of Christ in the elements of bread and wine to be such an important part of Eucharistic doctrine. Initially he perceived no conflict between belief in the Real Presence and Church of England doctrine. An incident that occurred around Christmas 1845 led him to reflect on this:

> I was administering the Communion to a dying man who holding up the bread between his thumb and finger said to me, earnestly repeating the question 'Is this the flesh of Christ?' To which I answered Yes. And upon that he eat [*sic*] it. But on mentioning my answer afterwards to other clergymen they considered that I had given an answer contrary to the doctrine of the English Church. This led me to consider what that doctrine was, and I still think that the answer which I gave, though contrary to the tendency of the Reformation, is not contrary to the actual words of the English ritual. (pp. 11–12)

Further reflection and investigation, however, threw up doubts as to whether the beliefs he held concerning the Real Presence really did conform to Anglican doctrine and eventually led him to conclude that they did not.[62] By Easter 1846, when he received Communion from his father, he was writing:

[61] The discipline of Oxford was 'insufferably lax and unreal' (p. 231), as was Pusey's view of the Church of England (p. 534); the more Caswall attempted to verbalize his difficulties over the Church of England, the more 'real' they seemed to become (p. 247). In writings such as *The Castle Builder* he graphically equates the vanities of this world with what is unreal.

[62] This was a common pattern in Caswall's conversion journey.

I know perfectly well that Father abhors the notion of the bread becoming the body of Christ, and I observed that he laid a particular stress upon the word remembrance. 'Take and eat this in *remembrance* that Christ died for thee and feed on him in thy heart by faith'. Surely those words ... virtually reject and pass by the doctrine of a real presence ... (pp. 115–16)

By late summer of that year Caswall seems to have conceded that a real, objective presence of Christ in the Sacrament belonged strictly to Roman Catholic doctrine, as against the receptionist belief of his Anglican confreres. Attending to his dying father he commented, 'I can fancy it a great comfort to a dying Roman Catholic to know that the reality of Christ's body in the Sacrament is an external fact independent of his own weak faith' (p. 412). Shortly thereafter, in a discussion with his brother-in-law and fellow clergyman Benjamin Dowding, he concluded that in the Church of England the elements were not changed but remained vehicles by which each person according to his or her faith received (if at all) the body and blood of Christ, and he speculated that power to effect transubstantiation was lacking due to the invalidity of Anglican orders. He gave a simple and characteristic interpretation of the Roman doctrine of transubstantiation: 'there are two laws, the laws of The Seen and the Laws of the unseen ... according to the laws of the Seen the substance is bread, according to the laws of the Unseen is Christ, and this I believe' (p. 458).

At Michaelmas 1846 Caswall acknowledged that his views were 'decidedly Roman Catholic' (p. 448). The previous Sunday he had attended the Communion service with his mother and two sisters Emma and Olivia, and he could not avoid considering that the Church of England regarded the consecrated elements not as Christ's body and blood 'but only [as] a vehicle instrumental towards the reception of his body and blood, that reception dependent on the receiver'.

Nor could Caswall now refrain from acknowledging that the validity of the consecration depended on the validity of the consecrator's orders. This commemoration and the power to offer it were, for him, inextricably linked with the apostolic succession and valid priestly orders. At the Last Supper, he observed, Jesus offered a sacrifice of himself 'under the figures of bread and wine', identical with and inseparable from that offered on the cross. Jesus then commanded the apostles and, by extension, their successors to do what he had done. Thus the 'true successors of the Apostles ... offer in the Eucharist a sacrifice identical with that on the Cross' (p. 381)

– that is, a commemoration of the God-Man's eternal sacrifice that is one with that eternal sacrificial event.

Already at the outset of his enquiries, in February 1846, Caswall recorded, 'I ... sometimes dread to administer the sacraments, as one who possibly may not be authorized' (p. 61). Whatever roads he travelled during his investigations, a core concern for him always remained the quest for certainty that his own orders were valid. Six months later, asking himself why he did not feel constrained to become a Roman Catholic immediately in light of his positive feelings about Roman Catholic devotion to the Eucharist, he acknowledged that, although he felt that his orders were doubtful, he was not certain that they were invalid. Consequently he wrestled with the question of whether he was not 'bound to reject a Church with doubtful orders, and join a Church with undoubted orders' (p. 374) and whether it was lawful for him to be willing to live in such doubt. If someone doubts that the consecrated bread and wine become the body and blood of Christ in the Church of England, should he receive the sacrament if he can receive it in the Roman Catholic Church without doubt? Caswall held that the presence of the body and blood of Christ in the sacrament depended on the validity of the consecration, which in turn depended on the validity of the orders, and because of his practical doubt about the validity of Anglican orders he questioned whether he was justified in continuing to receive the Eucharist in the Church of England.

Caswall harboured such strong doubts about the validity of Anglican orders 'in the full sense of validity' that he hesitated to use his own orders lest he be doing something wrong (p. 450). Clergy 'must have an absolute certainty in the external validity of their own orders', he maintained; but he had no such certainty about his own – in fact, he thought it 'very doubtful whether the late Bishop of Bath and Wells who ordained me was to all intents and purposes a real Bishop, and if he was a real Bishop then I still greatly doubt what jurisdiction he had, that is ... what right to ordain?' (pp. 457–8). Caswall's doubts about jurisdiction complicated the matter of validity of orders. 'Even if our orders are valid, there still remains the question of jurisdiction, that is to say, by what right we exercise them, and who gave us that right. Certainly no king could give it' (p. 121). In his eyes the improper usurpation of power by Queen Elizabeth struck at the very foundations of the English Church. Elizabeth's reorganization of the Church on the monarchical principle instead of the papal principle that had previously subsisted in England and still did so in the rest of the world gave rise to the invalidity of orders. Her acting without any reference to the Church as a whole – 'a mere local act in a small portion of the body' – amounted to a destruction of the Church of England (p. 459).

Thus Caswall's enquiries into the validity of Anglican orders were not mere theoretical speculations; rather, they generated searching and sometimes painful reflections on how that validity affected his own ministry to the souls in his charge. The spectre of the dying parishioner who held up the sacrament and begged to know, 'Is this the flesh of Christ?' haunted the young clergyman throughout the course of his journey toward Rome.

The Church of England's relationship to the One Holy Catholic Church

Could the Church of England, a national church, be a part of the universal church, or was this necessarily a contradiction? Caswall asked whether the idea of a simply national church is not absurd in itself. Frequently he stated that a *Catholic* church must necessarily be *universal*. How does the Church of England show that it is universal? Is the Church of England a Catholic church? The very nature of this set of issues seemed to require resolution chiefly by logical deduction, and this Caswall attempted to do. Characteristically, his reasoning was almost invariably reinforced by his observations.

(1) Does the Church of England belong to the Holy Catholic Church?
If there is one Holy Catholic Church, Caswall reasoned, then to pass from one portion of that church into another cannot entail a real change of religion.

> But to pass from the English to the Roman Church is a real change of religion. Therefore either there is not one Holy Catholic Church and the Creed is false, or else the Roman and English Churches are not two portions of the Holy Catholic Church. But if they are not two portions of it, then one of them does not belong to it. Is it then the Roman or the English that does not belong to it. Not the Roman for at best the English comes from the Roman. Therefore the English Church is not a portion of the Holy Catholic Church. (p. 186)

What Caswall observed of the Roman Catholic Church in Ireland during his visit there in the summer of 1846 corresponded with what he had seen of it in several countries on the Continent: the Roman Catholic Church is 'the same Church' in all the places in which it exists. The Church of England, on the other hand, 'is not equal to being the Church of all nations', let alone of one nation (pp. 359–60), as he witnessed in Ireland. His experience in Ireland was, for him, dramatic testimony that the Church of Rome and the Church of the Establishment certainly are not one with each other.

(2) Is the Church of England a Catholic church?
'Catholic', wrote Caswall, means existing everywhere. 'One' means one. Thus, to believe in one Catholic church is to believe in a church that is everywhere one. But, he reasoned, the Church of England is not everywhere one but only in England, the colonies, Ireland, Scotland, and the United States. The Roman Catholic Church, on the other hand, really is everywhere one. It exists throughout the globe and everywhere is 'one body teaching one doctrine on fundamentals'. The Anglican Church, in contrast, is 'simply a national church, not a Catholic one'.

Roman Catholic doctrines involving the Communion of Saints

The roots of Caswall's affinity with the Communion of Saints can be found in Tom Mozley's description of him as one who 'loved to hover free between the seen and the unseen world'.[63] Caswall possessed a strong sense of the presence of the invisible world. For him the *Communion* of Saints implied *communication* between the visible and the invisible worlds, especially between the Church Militant and the Church Triumphant. Already at the outset of his deliberations about Roman Catholicism he noted that he found himself continually walking along representing himself as 'having the invisible world round about me, and having my conversation in heaven' (p. 51).

In the letter to his sister Maria, Caswall 'observed that the question [of which church had the correct belief about the dynamics of intercessory prayer] depends upon ... whether there are real means of communication between the Church on Earth and in Heaven' (p. 480); thus he argued that the visible and the invisible worlds enjoy a closeness that facilitates communication between them. Reflecting on the custom of reckoning distance in terms of time (e.g., a certain place is an eight-hour journey away), and considering that it takes us but a moment to pass from the visible to the invisible world at the time of our death, he concluded that

[63] Tom Mozley, *Reminiscences* vol. 1, p. 12.

> [t]he invisible world then being but a moment off is in reality through our whole lives as near to us as it is found to be at our death. Thus the Saints may well have a communion with us, especially as being one with us in Christ. And thus the asking them to pray for us may not after all be more absurd, than asking a living person to do so. (p. 89)

Indeed, he contends, the distance between the two worlds consists precisely in their contrasting properties of visibility and invisibility and not in any element of space. A proof of this 'wonderful spiritual nearness between heaven & earth, and also between the saints in heaven and men on earth', is Jesus' injunction, 'Take heed that ye despise not one of these little ones; for I say unto you, That in heaven their angels do always behold the face of my Father which is in heaven' (Matt. 18:10), which shows that the angels who guard the little ones on earth are at the same time always in heaven (p. 142). Further proof of the closeness between the two worlds is provided by Jesus' ability to pass between (or perhaps even his simultaneous coexistence in) the two worlds during the forty days after his resurrection (p. 223), and by the fact that St Stephen could see the heavens open and Jesus standing at God's right hand (p. 181). '... I suppose if any of us were vouchsafed to see the heavens opened now we should see another sight, not Christ alone but Christ surrounded by his saints, the Virgin Mary, the apostles, Martyrs and others' (p. 47). The vehicle by which this would happen is faith. 'Faith is the evidence of things not seen. It makes present that which is invisible,' he wrote while in the midst of preparing the *Sermons on the Seen and Unseen* for publication. 'By faith then the Virgin Mary and all the saints are made present' (p. 139).

Caswall maintained that the dead are fully aware of what happens on earth (and thus can hear our prayers). He deduced this from a passage in the Book of Isaiah (14:9–17) that commemorates the death of the king of Babylon:[64]

> Hell from beneath is moved for thee to meet thee at thy coming: It stirreth up the dead for thee, even all the chief ones of the earth ... All they shall speak and say unto thee, 'Art thou also become weak as we ... How art thou cut down to the ground, which didst weaken the nations!'

According to Caswall, 'Evidently the Holy Spirit speaking by Isaiah

[64] Caswall identifies this king, not named in the Book of Isaiah, as Nebuchadnezzar. Recent scholarship, however, postulates that the passage (Isa. 14:3–23) refers either to Sargon II or to Sennacherib. See *The HarperCollins Study Bible* (New York: HarperCollins, 1993), p. 1033.

here declares to us that the dead have a knowledge of what the living do. And if this is the case with the dead in general, much more with those who fall asleep in Christ and being absent from the body are present in the Lord' (p. 89).

The Invocation of Saints

By February 1846 Caswall acknowledged that he could no longer in good conscience subscribe totally to the Thirty-nine Articles, and he singled out Article XXII as one with which he had particular difficulty: 'The Romish Doctrine concerning Purgatory, Pardons, Worshipping and Adoration, as well of Images as of Relics, and also Invocation of Saints, is a fond thing, vainly invented, and grounded upon no warranty of Scripture, but rather repugnant to the Word of God.'

Both the Church of Rome and the Church of England believe in intercessory prayer and hold that if the saints in heaven can hear supplicants on earth it would be right to ask their prayers. But the Church of Rome claims that the saints can hear us, while the Church of England denies that they have the means to hear; they intercede without being asked. Either way, said Caswall, it is an assumption on both parts, but he appealed to antiquity and to a sort of *sensus fidelium* – a principle of universality – in support of the likelihood that the Roman Catholic assumption is the correct one: in a letter of October 1846 to his sister Maria Dowding defending his 'sinful errors' concerning the invocation of saints, he pointed out that

> the Roman Catholic assumption is fifteen hundred years old, the English three hundred, the Roman Catholic assumption is that of the whole Christian world, the English that of a little island. It lay with us to establish our negative assumption on some kind of proof before we gave up the Roman Catholic positive assumption, but this we have never done, nor can possibly do to any real purpose, assumptions not admitting of proof. (pp. 480–1)

Earlier, too, he had commented, 'We are so unacquainted with the nature of Spirits and of our connection with the Spiritual world that I really think it is impossible to pronounce with certainty against the practice of so many millions of religious persons living and dead, that the Saints cannot hear the ora pro nobis' (p. 206).

Initially Caswall distinguished between the 'ora pro nobis' – asking the saints to pray for us – and 'direct invocation' or addressing the saints in any other way. The former he considered acceptable from the outset, and in fact admitted that it came quite naturally to him. In the journal passage referring to his 'having [his] conversation in heaven' he disclosed: 'And often without any effort I catch myself saying to myself Sancta Dei genetrix ora pro nobis peccatoribus nunc et in hora mortis nostrae. Sancte Petre ora pro nobis. Sancte Paule ora pro nobis. Omnes sancti apostoli orate pro nobis' (p. 51).

On Holy Saturday 1846, he decided absolutely that the Roman Catholic practice of the ora pro nobis was not idolatrous. Idolatry bypasses God. But prayers are made possible only by God: 'All prayers for us avail only through God. It is only through God giving us breath that we are able to ask the living to pray for us. God may give an analogous invisible breath by which we may ask the Saints to pray for us ... I must say that our litany appears to me even deficient without addresses to the saints' (p. 115). The Roman Catholic litany, he points out, puts the saints in their proper context, always subject to God. In the litany the addresses to the saints 'never come barely by themselves but always in due subjection to the glory of the Eternal Trinity and divine Word incarnate, and they imply in the Saints no power of their own except that of Prayer' (p. 208). That same faith which makes the Virgin Mary and the saints present to us renders the address to them legitimate: 'If [the Virgin and the saints] are present by faith, they are actually present to all spiritual purposes. Therefore the Ora pro nobis is lawful to faith, although unlawful to sense' (p. 139).

The direct invocation to saints was, however, more problematical. During their trip to Ireland in August 1846 Caswall and Louisa were reading together some Roman Catholic devotional books Louisa had bought, and they 'both unanimously set aside' a prayer to the Guardian Angel. He would permit only the ora pro nobis in the context of the litany in which the Trinity is addressed first. 'But in saying any prayer with Louisa I have never addressed the Saints or angels, and feel a repugnance to do so' (p. 371). Yet at the same time he admitted, 'It is conceivable that this very invocation of saints which, when practically carried out, causes me trouble, yet may one day be to me the chief attraction to the Church of Rome. Only grant it to be altogether true, and I can conceive nothing more excellent' (p. 377).

Contrary to Article XXII's assertion that the Roman doctrines concerning the Communion of Saints are 'grounded upon no warranty of Scripture', Caswall 'consider[ed] that these doctrines may possibly flow necessarily from certain relationships established in Scripture' (p. 5), and throughout his journal he reflected on and drew out the implications of this early speculation. Like Milner, he even reached back to the Hebrew Scriptures for texts to substantiate his claim, including a number that appeared to legitimize the invocation of saints. Such a practice was not, he contended, unknown among the people of the Old Covenant: Saul's invocation of the recently dead Samuel via the medium at Endor (1 Sam. 28) is 'a kind of case of Invocation of Saints' (p. 399). Caswall also cites the remark of the bystanders at Jesus' crucifixion – 'Listen, he is calling for Elijah ... let us see whether Elijah will come to take him down' (Mark 15:35, 36) – as demonstrating that 'the idea of invocation addressed to an ancient Jewish Saint did not seem strange to the Jews' (p. 2). The Psalms, Caswall pointed out, often invoke angels, as does the Benedicite canticle: 'O ye angels ... O ye spirits and souls ...' etc. It is absurd, he declared, to hold that these are merely figurative expressions (p. 242). Jesus' description of the rich man in the parable of Dives and Lazarus as invoking Abraham ('the great Saint of the old covenant' [p. 124]) 'with a direct prayer' 'I think ... establishes the principle of direct Invocation of Saints' (p. 361); here he develops Milner's contention[65] that the notion of the poor Lazarus resting in Abraham's bosom (Luke 16:22) demonstrates the existence of a 'middle state' between earth and heaven, or purgatory.

What legitimates the practice of the invocation of saints and especially the ora pro nobis is the jurisdiction promised and accorded the saints by Jesus. Interpreting John 16:23[66] as a promise by Jesus that in the next life the apostles will have influence with the Father through Christ, Caswall concludes that the Virgin Mary and all the other saints must enjoy the same influence, and 'it is worthwhile to obtain the benefit for ourselves of that influence'. Thus the ora pro nobis, which is the means of obtaining that benefit, 'does not seem unreasonable. Hence I feel that I can legitimately say Sancte Petre ora pro nobis ...' (pp. 208–9). In the parable of Lazarus, too, Jesus 'certainly ... encourages the notion of Saints in Heaven having Power. For if under the Old covenant it was so how much more under the new' (p. 124). Eventually Caswall connected the Roman concept of patronage of the saints with this jurisdiction and influence:

> Our Saviour speaks of His servants after death being appointed over many things, being entrusted with the true riches. Now I suppose this is what Roman Catholics mean when they speak of the Saints

[65] Milner, *The End of Religious Controversy*, Letter xliii: 'Purgatory and Prayers for the Dead', p. 282.

[66] 'On that day you will ask nothing of me. Very truly, I tell you, if you ask anything of the Father in my name, he will give it to you'.

> having Patronage. They mean that those who whilst on earth have been faithful in their own sphere do, on being admitted into Christ's presence, enter upon a wider sphere still in connection with the Church. (p. 290)

Later, and more importantly, he interpreted the saints' jurisdiction and patronage as a share granted them by God in the distribution of divine providence:

> If the Saints and the Virgin Mary ... reign with Christ with whom all power is given in heaven and earth, then they have a share with him in his government as having been entrusted the true riches. But his government lies in the secret course of his Providence towards individuals and bodies. The Virgin Mary then and the saints have some sort of authority and power in the dispensations of divine Providence. (p. 365)

He was careful to emphasize, however, that the saints did not act autonomously; rather, their will 'is in every respect the will of God, ... they being one with Christ as heirs with God' (p. 366).

Marian devotion

Like many other mid-nineteenth-century English converts to Rome, Caswall was 'impressed by the sheer spiritual power of the Catholic Church on the Continent, as evidenced by the practical impact of the dogma of the Real Presence and doctrines of the Intercession of Saints and of the Blessed Virgin in inspiring popular devotion'.[67] But Caswall's deepest and most lasting impressions of the practical devotional side of Roman Catholicism came during his trip to Ireland in the summer of 1846.

On 30 June 1846, Caswall described an experience he had had that day in a Roman Catholic chapel in Ireland:

> This evening ... I heard a bell ringing near me and found myself near the South Chapel. The side door was open, in which I went, and found about twelve poor persons praying. There was one little light on the altar and two tallow candles on a form just in front of the altar rails. At this form ... five poor men were kneeling and some other men and women behind them. The middle one of the five was an old man and had a book. I do not think he could have been a priest, since he was dressed in a brown coat and yellow neckerchief. He was reading a litany in English and the others answered him. It was said in a very low voice and so very rapid I could catch but very few of the

[67] Nockles, 'Sources of English Conversions', p. 21; see n. 109.

> words, but all present seemed to enter heart and soul into what they were doing. Presently one of the five said the Lord's Prayer as far as 'as it is in heaven', on which all the others began at 'give us this day our daily bread' and completed the prayer. Then the man in the middle said another prayer, and then all of them together said, 'Holy Mary, mother of God, pray for us sinners now and at the hour of death' [*sic*]. Then another of the five began the Lord's Prayer and was taken up by the others as before, upon which the middle man said another prayer, and all again said 'Holy Mary' as before. This went on through all the five and then some change came, but still the Lord's Prayer went on as before ... At times they crossed themselves simultaneously and at certain intervals all together said 'Glory be to the Father'. Bowing their heads, they knelt all the time. This is the first time I ever heard any devotion to the Virgin. A thrill passed through me at the first moment, but I presently saw that it could not possibly be idolatrous. There was too much appearance of love, humility and real religion in the poor men for idolatry to be possible. I knelt down with them all till all was over. Every word was in English, and I must say, if ever I saw true praying it was then. (pp. 309–10)

This passage is worth quoting at length because, although he apparently was unaware of it at the time, it records Caswall's first encounter with the rosary; it also marked a turning point in his attitude toward Roman Catholic devotion and especially a rejection, on his part, of commonly held anti-Roman misconceptions. 'I was perpetually suspecting that in the Invocation of the blessed Virgin there must be some latent spirit of idolatry,' he confided to a friend following his conversion.[68] After this experience, however, he concluded that '[i]t is evident ... that in the Roman Catholic religion an immense scope is afforded to poor persons beyond what we have any idea of in our Church. It is evident, too, that their religion does not lie in incense or show, but is a spiritual, internal system' (p. 310).

The subject of Marian devotion had come up in Caswall's conversations with Dr Pusey. When he confided to Pusey that he thought that, contrary to Article XXII, the ora pro nobis was 'very likely to be part of the fullness of Christian truth', Pusey replied that the problem was not with the ora pro nobis as such but with 'a vast system of direct worship of the Virgin, in which she was addressed

[68] Letter to 'George', 15 March 1847; repr. in *The Oratory Parish Magazine*, n.d., pp. 6–7. The magazine entry claims that Caswall wrote the letter to his brother. He had no brother named George, however; the letter was most likely written to his good friend George Copeland.

in the same terms as the Blessed Trinity'. Pusey had seen a Roman Catholic prayer that addressed the Virgin as if she were divine. To Caswall's objection that he had spoken with some poor Roman Catholics who denied this mariolatrous view, Pusey countered that it might not apply in England but friends who had travelled on the Continent had assured him that there Mary had 'quite supplanted her Son in the minds of the people', and the Church of England could never unite with Rome until this system of worship was put down by authority (pp. 248–9).

To some extent this exchange reflected the occasional tension or even conflict between popular practice and formal doctrine. Caswall was correct in his view of the litanies, as described above, as he was in his statement that the Council of Trent did not go beyond the ora pro nobis, but the existence of a vast body of devotional literature and popular practice that goes beyond what is officially acceptable cannot be denied. Pusey continued to maintain that a large number of Roman Catholics 'in point of fact did substitute the Virgin Mary in the place of her Son', and he based this on some devotional books of exaggerated Mariolatry (he cites Liguori in particular); thus he held that the ora pro nobis, while admissible in itself, was 'only the outskirts' of a vast system of Virgin worship, whereas Caswall believed it to be the foundation of and 'always implied' in Marian devotion (p. 250).

Nonetheless, Caswall did have enough respect for Dr Pusey to continue to mull over the question of Marian devotion throughout his investigation into Roman Catholicism. In Ireland, reflecting on his talks with Dr Pusey, he saw that one of the 'two points to which [his] attention must be particularly directed was to ascertain whether the mass of the Roman Catholic people invocate [*sic*] the Blessed Virgin in such a way as to obscure her Eternal Son' (p. 301). It was shortly after this that he had his first experience of the rosary. Still somewhat concerned about 'that prayer, "Holy Mary, mother of God, pray for us sinners now and in the hour of death" [*sic*]', and determined to be absolutely thorough, he decided he would examine some of the children upon this point in the Catholic schools he was visiting (p. 321). Accordingly, while on a visit shortly thereafter to a school run by the Christian Brothers, '[a]t my request [one of the Brothers] asked [the boys] about the Virgin Mary, whom they pronounced a creature, stating that to give her divine worship would be idolatry' (p. 328).

Having frequently stated in his journal that only actual experience would ultimately enable him fully to understand certain aspects of Roman Catholicism, by the autumn of 1846 he had begun practising the rosary: '... I think nothing can equal [it] in leading Christians to realize the Incarnation' (p. 477).

> That the immaterial Deity should become matter and as such ally himself to the entire material Universe was the greatest event next to the Creation of the Universe, perhaps even a greater one, when we contemplate its future results through all Eternity. Now the Virgin Mary was that choice material substance obviously prepared from before the foundation of the world, out of which the Deity drew a material body for himself, and this not without her own freewill which might have opposed the act. From this we can see that the Virgin Mary is the turning point of the Universe. (pp. 481–2)

By November of 1846 Marian devotion had become the major issue that he had to resolve. Writing to Mrs Trevelyan of his great doubts concerning 'the reality of my own priesthood', he added that if in Rome he were to find 'Mariolatry' to be not really idolatrous 'it would become a question with me how far I should be justified in continuing in a system which denounced Roman practices as such' (p. 522).

In January 1847, less than one week before his reception into the Church of Rome, he visited Newman and asked him whether Roman Catholics were bound to believe anything of the Virgin Mary beyond what is contained in the profession of faith. Newman assured him that they were not – that 'whatever was believed of the Virgin Mary's influence upon the course of Providence was based entirely upon the ora pro nobis, and that the means of communication between us and her and the other saints was to be considered as nothing inherent of itself but simply the Holy Ghost.' Caswall found Newman's views on the subject of divine providence and the saints to be 'the same as that which I have set down from time to time in this book', and thus he 'was entirely satisfied with what he said upon the subject' (pp. 596–7).

Ultimately, then, both Caswall's own experience and his questioning of a variety of Roman Catholics satisfied him on the major stumbling block of Marian devotion: he came to realize Mary's significance within the context of the doctrine of the Incarnation and to accept that it was in this context that the Church of Rome addressed her in prayer.

Purgatory and prayers for the dead

As has already been noted, Caswall possessed a strong sense of the presence of the invisible world. For him this meant that the recently-discovered knowledge of geology and the other developing sciences did not diminish or negate the principles of faith but rather could be used analogically to reinforce them. He applied this to the Roman Catholic doctrine of purgatory, which holds the afterlife to be a transitional rather than a static state. Referring to the Book of Common Prayer doctrine that the good rest with Christ, he observed:

> Still its view of the intermediate state as one continuous sameness of condition does not appear to me so philosophical as the notion that the intermediate state is a transition state. We find that all Nature is in a transition state and created on a transition principle. Geology shows us through what vast transitions this globe has gone through great lengths of time. It is not likely then upon principles of analogy that God would leave so vast a field as the intermediate state in inaction. There is therefore some growth or passing on of the soul in it, not to such sense as to alter its ultimate state, but as to work out its bias on which it died. (p. 126)

Every state, argued Caswall, implies a locality: heaven for a state of happiness, hell for misery. Thus for a state of transition there must be a corresponding intermediate world or locality, 'one for the good and another perhaps for the evil, in which an advance is made by each class of souls towards their ultimate destiny. This locality in the case of good seems to be all that is meant by Purgatory' (p. 127).

Caswall recorded often having noticed a strong intuition of purgatory among the sick he visited as curate in Stratford. A parishioner named Mary Bedford, suffering excessive pain and difficulty in swallowing due to throat cancer, told him during one of his calls that 'she trusted she had had all her sufferings here', thereby implying belief in an intermediate state in which she would otherwise be expected to suffer before entering Paradise (p. 127).

Caswall commented early on that the Church of England's 'not having prayers for the dead is a most terrible witness against us, and I feel it more and more' (p. 150). He was to feel it in a particularly personal and painful way at the time of his father's death in early September 1846. One week after the Revd Robert Caswall died, his son wrote:

> My father has now been dead seven days, and I have been thinking what has his soul been doing during that period? Did it go at once to be with Christ in his glory, or has it had to wait till further purified? Certainly it has not been quiescent and inert during the last week. But since all created things are continually in progress, and since my father's soul is a created thing, it must have been in progress during

> these last seven nights and days, and in progress towards a certain end, unless it has already attained that end. (pp. 436–7)

Periodically thereafter Caswall noted that 'all this time' the Church of England has been offering no prayers for his father's soul, 'yet all this time that soul has been progressing in one direction and no doubt would have been benefited by prayers of the faithful' (p. 457). Here not only the potential convert but also the son and, especially, the pastor of souls was speaking.

At the very beginning of his journal Caswall observed that '[m]any clergymen believe in and practise prayers for the dead ... There may then be certain doctrines of no small influence which may be privately carried out in the Church of England ...' (p. 5). Thus the practice of prayers for the dead along with the notion of purgatory was not a doctrine or practice of whose validity he needed to convince himself; rather, it was something that he intuitively accepted all along, but he wished to belong to a Church that officially admitted it.

Caswall considered the Roman doctrine of Communion of Saints in its various aspects to be a most effective safeguard against pantheism:

> Pantheism holds that souls when they die lose their individuality and merge in the universal soul of the Deity. Now in the Roman Catholic Church there is a strong safeguard against the entrance of this idea, in the Invocation of Saints ... The practice of invocation of Saints and prayers for the dead uphold strongly the individuality of the soul after death ... Hence the system which will effectually oppose Pantheism will most likely be the Roman Catholic. (pp. 365, 412)

Indeed, the great advantages he saw to the Communion of Saints moved him to express concern for the consequences of neglecting it. 'It seems to me', he commented, 'that by leaving out the saints in our devotions we neglect bringing to bear a very powerful engine for the conversion of the world' (p. 124). Later he admitted that he sometimes thought of this doctrine as 'a vast element of spiritual improvement maintained to be so by some of the first saints that ever lived, which I am wasting, ... on account of it having been condemned by this little English Church' (p. 481).

The exclusive use of Latin in the Roman Catholic liturgy

Caswall was simultaneously fascinated and irritated by the exclusive use of Latin in Roman Catholic worship. At first he often found the Latin to be 'an invincible obstacle against Rome': how could uneducated folk possibly understand what was going on (p. 46)? He frequently voiced his irritation as well as his concern. Upon attending a Requiem Mass in Cork for the recently deceased Pope Gregory XVI, he expressed his frustration at his inability completely to 'understand what was doing' (p. 332). If this were true for an Oxford graduate in Classics, how much more must it apply to those with little or no education? Reading a book that contained the entire order of the Roman Catholic Holy Week liturgies, Caswall reckoned that the services must be beautiful but he could not imagine how the congregation, especially the many who could not read, managed to 'follow and appreciate the Latin words' (p. 117). Only through experiential knowledge, he decided, could one fathom how this difficulty was overcome: perhaps he would then see that his problem was merely theoretical, 'arising from my ignorance of the practise [*sic*]' (p. 152).[69] Caswall's down-to-earth approach shows his independence of Milner on this point. Except for a brief allusion to the universality of the church being reflected in the universality of the language, most of Milner's arguments in favour of Latin worship are rather far-fetched.[70] Caswall, on the other hand, only ended up approving of the Latin liturgy (and even then not without great difficulty) after his own careful observations, basing his reasons on practical concerns and on explanations he requested and received from priests active in parochial ministry.

After witnessing Benediction and a procession of the Blessed Sacrament in an Irish cathedral,[71] Caswall observed that, despite the Latin services, most of the people obviously 'thoroughly enter into them and comprehend what is going on sufficiently for themselves ... with all my knowledge of the dead languages the poorest person in those congregations knows more than I do as to what he is about' (p. 325). 'Indeed', he felt compelled to acknowledge, 'it is a

69 Compare Peter Le Page Renouf's observation that 'hardly one person in a thousand becomes a Catholic by controversy, they all become so immediately when they hear what the Catholic faith really is' (Peter Le Page Renouf, letter to his parents, 24 March 1842; quoted in Nockles, 'Sources of English Conversions', p. 38). In his journal Caswall records that his convert friends assured him of the paramountcy of experiential over intellectual reasons for converting.

70 Cf. Milner, *The End of Religious Controversy*, Letter xlvii: 'Latin Language'.

71 He thought that he had 'never seen anything even abroad more lovely', and Louisa agreed (p. 325).

most certain fact that the Roman Catholic Church is every where the Church of the Poor' (p. 46) and that 'the poor find more pleasure in Roman Catholic services than in ours' (117).[72] He speculated that the use of Latin cultivated a sense of mystery (p. 46) and he gradually became convinced that the people were possessed of some great idea that transcended the need for a thoroughly comprehensible language, and he decided that this idea must be 'the notion of a Sacrifice at which they are assisting' (p. 130). 'Allow a sacrifice and the language becomes less necessary. Had [the Church of England] a notion of a sacrifice we should not so much insist on words' (p. 177). Deeply impressed by the influence of Roman Catholicism in Ireland, and wondering what the cause could be (one could not credit church architecture, he observed), he thought that it must be 'something in the system itself', perhaps actually connected with the Latin. Because the people cannot follow and do not understand every single word, they instead take up 'certain general ideas' which each person according to his or her ability 'dresses up ... in a particular phrazeology [*sic*]'. This affords 'scope for extempore prayer' (p. 335), something Caswall repeatedly praised as a major advantage of the Roman Catholic liturgy and the lack of which he perceived as a major deficiency of Anglican worship. Twice he commented that the provision of silent intervals for private extempore prayer would have been 'a great preservative' against people turning Dissenters ('Wesleyans and Ranters') out of frustration over their inability to keep pace with the text of the Anglican service (pp. 46, 335). He frequently remarked on the benefits of permitting time for extempore prayer during the service, particularly in its promotion of fervour, but at one point he wrote down an especially perceptive analysis of the subject which deserves to be quoted at length:

> [The Anglican view of common prayer] is that the clergyman is to go through a certain order of prayers aloud and that every person present must simultaneously go through the same mentally completing the prayer with an Amen. Thus all intellects are expected in attending our Church service to go through the same process, and the same mental transitions and course of ideas. No room is left for extempore prayer, nor for adaptation on the part of the individual,

[72] Describing a service he attended in the Church of Ireland cathedral in Cork, Caswall recalled, 'There were present about two hundred and fifty persons of whom only one was a poor person ... [O]ne came away from the service with the feeling as if the religion which had given birth to it was dying out from sheer inanition. Can that be the true religion which attracts no poor, but only a few fashionables?' (p. 324).

> and if his thoughts wander for a moment he cannot recover since the prayers have been going on with the regularity of a railroad, or of some engine. This often causes persons ... to feel disheartened ... Now I have observed that the Roman Catholic view of Common Prayer is quite different. They lay down certain broad demarcations for public service distinguished by ringing of little bells and the actions of the Priest, and then it is left to every one according to his capacity and earnestness and according as he chooses to supply himself with little books, or to learn a few prayers of his own, to join in what is going on. Hence ... the use of Latin really does in many respects tend to give the great majority of the congregation comfort, freedom, ease and spontaneousness in public prayer. And it is most certain that a Roman Catholic congregation does enter into the public service with a more complete identification than an English one does, certain I mean to say so far as I can possibly judge from what I see. Wonderful to say, we with an English service are listless and disheartened. They with a Latin service show every token of understanding what each is doing so far as he goes, and betray no listlessness. (pp. 361–2)

The use of English, Caswall ruefully admitted, by no means ensured adequate comprehension on the part of the average person in the pew, as 'the ignorance of the people in regard to the plainest of things' (p. 117) testified: 'Is it not certain', he asked, 'that in spite of our prayers and reading of Scripture being in English the common people do not really after twenty years attendance at Church understand any one doctrine, and wonderfully misinterpret the facts of scripture, and the meaning of the prayers?' (p. 46). Further, when hymns were sung 'very few of the poor have books, or have any idea of the words sung' (p. 177).

Then there were acoustical considerations. In large cathedrals, Caswall observed, it did not really matter which language was used – neither could be heard. 'The chanting of our psalms cannot be followed even now without a book, and to the poor who cannot read they must be as good as Latin.' Roman Catholics at least had printed translations that they could follow (p. 130). Moreover, English presented problems to clergy as well as to laity. Church builders before the Reformation did not need to take into account a priest's need to project his voice to be understood through an entire service. Thus many clergymen 'were being brought to the verge of decline'[73] because of the Reformers' miscalculation of the

[73] It will be recalled that Caswall resigned his curacy at St Dunstan's because the warden had 'represented me to the vicar as having too weak a voice' (p. 406). Moreover, as someone with a speech defect he would have been particularly sensitive to this issue.

physical power of human lungs (p. 45). The Latin service and the 'silent Masses' were not so trying on the lungs, for the priest did not have to strive constantly to make himself heard. Also, although the Anglicans criticized 'that action which we see in the Mass, ... is it not certain that such action being substituted for speaking saves the lungs?' (p. 245).

Here Caswall hit upon an important characteristic of the Roman liturgy: its rich visual symbolism, which along with 'the notion of a Sacrifice assists wonderfully in dispensing with the vernacular language' (p. 47). Anglicans who criticized the Latin of the Roman liturgy lost sight of this wealth of 'outward signs to make up for words' (p. 177). An effective liturgy, he contended, must appeal to and communicate on other levels of the human person besides merely the verbal. Even in Rome on the verge of his reception into the Roman Church he again questioned what real *ideas* the people manage to grasp with an English liturgy. '[H]earing nothing but English words the people think they have gained more than they have in fact, and ... their religion is in great measure verbal and of the letter not of the spirit, and what is this but formality? ... A good liturgy is a liturgy adapted to the entire nature of man genus homo' (p. 589).

Repeatedly Caswall observed that, despite the Latin, the Roman Catholic religion is a living religion to a great mass of people while the Anglican religion is dead to most people, and he was convinced that this was because (1) the Anglican liturgy made no provision for nor did it encourage spontaneous prayer; (2) unlike Roman Catholicism, the Church of England had not got hold of the great idea of sacrifice, altar, priesthood. So, he asked, 'Which is best, a dead religion with a living language, or a living religion with a dead language?' Operative in the Roman liturgy was a 'language of action' that all understood (p. 311).

These latter comments of Caswall's lead directly into the last of the major doctrinal or devotional concerns entailed in his conversion.

The vitality of the Church of Rome in contrast to the coldness of the Established Church

In his account of factors that motivated English conversions to Rome during this period Nockles refers to 'numerous examples of the positive impact of foreign travel on English men and women on a Continent ... which witnessed abundant evidence of a Catholic revival especially in France'.[74] Writing of the Tractarians specifi-

[74] Nockles, 'Sources of English Conversions', p. 3.

cally, V. Alan McClelland observes that 'nothing interested [them] more than to discover all they could about the religious habits, observances and inner life of the inhabitants of towns visited when journeying abroad. Their diaries indicate that although they were far from devoid of the normal interests of the tourist ..., it was essentially the ecclesiastical polity and quality of religious observance that really captivated their interest'.[75]

Indeed, whatever their original motives for their travels, all eventual converts who had visited the Continent came away deeply awed by the vitality of the Roman Catholic Church there. Frederick William Faber embarked on a tour of the Continent in 1841. On returning home he worked his copious journals into a book, *Sights and Thoughts in Foreign Churches and among Foreign Peoples,*[76] into which he introduces numerous discussions on religious matters which usually take the form of conversations with 'the Stranger', an imaginary representative of the Middle Ages who embodies Faber's own sympathy with the Catholic ethos. At last the author takes the Stranger on a tour of the many parishes throughout England. The book ends with the Stranger's dramatic challenge: 'You have led me through a land of closed churches and hushed bells, of unlighted altars and unstoled priests: Is England beneath an Interdict?'[77]

Thomas W. Allies made several journeys to the Continent in the years preceding his conversion. In August 1843 he visited France with his wife and two other people: 'Never did I spend fifteen days more influential on the course of my thoughts and religious views,' he wrote in the published account of his conversion, *A Life's Decision*.[78] Like Caswall, who began praying the rosary after first encountering it in Ireland, Allies came to realize Mary's role in the Incarnation, which led him to share Caswall's scepticism toward the accusation that Roman Catholics worship Mary.[79] He was struck as well by the people's sense of the church as a house of prayer and by the sight of people kneeling, and he commented on the wider implications for religious vitality: 'Without churches open all day, and the habit of praying in them, I do not see how it is possible for the great mass of Christians to realise the Communion of Saints; and that the good and serious do realise it abroad to an extent we

[75] V. Alan McClelland, '"The Most Turbulent Priest of the Oxford Diocese": Thomas William Allies and the Quest for Authority 1837–1850', in *By Whose Authority? Newman, Manning and the Magisterium*, ed. V. Alan McClelland (Bath: Downside Abbey, 1996), p. 279.

[76] London: J.G.F. & J. Rivington, 1842.

[77] Faber, *Sights and Thoughts*, p. 645.

[78] 2nd edn (London: Burns & Oates Ltd., 1894), p. 20. Orig. publ. 1880.

[79] Ibid., p. 28.

have no conception of here, I feel convinced.'[80]

Caswall was unique in having travelled to Ireland to observe Roman Catholicism, but his interest had originally been sparked by early trips to the Continent. 'In 1835', Bellasis records, Caswall 'had gone abroad so far as Milan, and in 1846 to Switzerland, and was pleased with the Catholic services'.[81] During these trips Caswall observed 'that there was a great deal of fervor arising from extempore prayer in the Roman Catholic Churches' (p. 46).

Contrast his comments on an afternoon service that he attended at Salisbury Cathedral on Monday of Holy Week 1846: 'The service including the responses was simply read ... and had a very bad effect ... There was not even an anthem ... I observed about fourteen ladies and five or six gentlemen some of whom were strangers come to see the Cathedral ... None of the servants belonging to the close were present ... Everything was so desperately formal and lifeless' (p. 99).

Caswall's trip to Ireland later that year afforded extensive direct comparison between the Roman Catholic and the Established Churches. Having gone one Sunday morning in June to the Roman Catholic cathedral in Cork and found it 'cram full of people', he then proceeded to the Protestant Cathedral of St Fin Barr. 'The effect after coming from the other Cathedral was chilling in the extreme, and the appearance of the service was really pitiable' (p. 303). His description of it as 'effete and soon about to vanish' strikingly recalls the language he used in *The Castle Builder*. Further, he reacted with 'vehement rage' to the sight of St Patrick's Protestant Cathedral in Dublin, neglected and looking as if it had not 'been used as a religious building for centuries' (pp. 349–50). On calling at Christchurch he was 'tremendously disgusted' to find it locked and to learn that there had not been a weekly service for six weeks and would not be one for two more since 'the gentleman had a vacation' (p. 354).

On Sunday the Roman Catholic churches held continuous services between 6 a.m. and noon, when the Church of Ireland service was only just beginning. Thus, observed Caswall, the Roman Catholics have 'immense crowds of worshippers while the Protestants are in bed'. Aside from the likelihood that the Roman Catholics had numbers on their side, the other possible causes of this great different numbers on which he speculated were (1) the fact that the

[80] Ibid., p. 30.

[81] Bellasis, 'Biographical Preface', p. 9. From the context and from the fact that no mention of this is made in his journal, it can safely be assumed that Caswall visited Switzerland at the very beginning of 1846.

Church of Ireland service did not leave room for personal prayer and did not admit 'of being twice in the same Church on the same day', and (2) a greater spirit of prayer among Roman Catholics (p. 304). All his experiences proved to him 'that the Roman Catholic Church in Ireland is a Church which encourages prayer infinitely more than the Irish Church does. But prayer is the life of the Church. The Roman Catholic Church then lives the life of a true Church, more than the Church of Ireland does' (p. 354). He later summed up his impressions of the churches in Ireland as follows:

> The Sunday services in the Churches of the Irish Church appear as nothing. My recollections of that body are as of a feeble inanimate system, my recollection of the Roman Catholic body are as of a living active religious self-denying system ... I seem continually to see before me men women and boys without shoes and stockings kneeling down upon the stones in front of an altar and some of them prostrate on their faces in complete adoration of Christ as really present in the Eucharist. (pp. 373–4)

Caswall came to regard Roman Catholicism as possessing a 'great idea' that inspired and nourished its adherents at all levels and thus transcended such difficulties as the inability to understand all the finer details of doctrine or even all the nuances of the liturgical service. Wondering what kept the faithful coming to the Masses in the Irish churches in such great numbers even though they could not understand Latin, he concluded that the people must be 'in possession of some great idea which I have not altogether got hold of ... and this idea lies in the doctrine of the real presence' (p. 364). Shortly afterwards Fr J. Curtis of St Francis Xavier's Church in Dublin confirmed this for him. To Caswall's question 'upon what principle the poor came to Church since they could not know what was going on in detail', Fr Curtis replied, 'much as I had imagined, that they were possessed with one powerful idea of the real presence at the Mass and that this without entering into the details of the service was sufficient for them' (p. 367).

What did Caswall perceive to be the root of the supposed lifelessness of the Established Church? It was something that he hit upon early in his deliberations and that later appeared to him to be borne out in the course of his observations. Reflecting on his own lack of success at 'exciting religious sympathy' in his Stratford parishioners despite his diligence in holding daily services, he speculated:

> May it not be that unmitigated Church of England doctrines and services appear hard and dry to the people. Saints Days in themselves

> unless you can add the Belief in the Intercession of the Saints must be dull things. Regeneration in Baptism as a doctrine must be uninfluential without priestly absolution for sins after baptism. What is a sheer Episcopal authority without Unity? What the Lord's Supper without the Real Presence? What the real Presence without the Adoration of the Host? (p. 9)[82]

Recall Caswall's comment that the Anglican liturgy appealed to the reason, Roman liturgy to the entire nature of the human person. In the above reflection he points up the importance of *relationality* – the church is a community of people and with God, a community that transcends time and space – and of religion as involving the entire person. He appears to have perceived in the Established Religion of his day the absence of a tangible, intensely personal element that comprised a living connection between the individual on the one hand and God or the Christian community on the other.

Caswall's emphasis on the church as community and on the importance of religion's appeal to the entire person show his agreement with Tractarian concerns. It will be recalled that in his *Sermons on the Seen and Unseen*[83] he highlighted the role of the heart in its function of cultivating faith – as opposed to the intellect's appropriation of doctrine – and as the seat of the interior life. In the *Sermons* Caswall opposed the inner life to outward actions, declaring the latter to be meaningless if they have no foundation in the former. His thinking in the journal is entirely consistent with this, but here he contends that even the outward actions, in the sense of ritual and devotion, are absent from the Church of England in so far as such actions are manifestations of an inner life, for the foundation from which these actions necessarily spring – a warmly rich, interior life signifying a living, personal relationship with God – is lacking.

Caswall, then, was one of a number of Anglican clergymen who, inspired by Tractarian principles, set out to revitalize the Church of England and ended up by converting to Rome. On a doctrinal level he began early to doubt the validity of 'Puseyite principles' in the Established Church and to suspect that their legitimate development must necessarily be found in the Church of Rome (p. 114).[84]

[82] This passage strikingly anticipates the comment that another convert priest-poet made some twenty years later: 'Religion without [the Real Presence] is sombre, dangerous, illogical, with that it is ... *loveable*', wrote Gerard Manley Hopkins to a friend.

[83] See esp. the sermon for the First Sunday in Advent and the Epiphany sermon on 'The Wise Men', discussed in chapter three.

[84] Caswall expressed these doubts to his brother Alfred during Holy Week 1846. Among the 'Puseyite principles' he enumerated prayers for the dead, the intercession of saints, confession and absolution, baptismal regeneration, apostolic

Caswall and later Allies had strikingly similar experiences of consulting Dr Pusey about their respective difficulties: Caswall theorized that one factor that kept Pusey in the Church of England was 'a strong faith which has forbidden him to set about investigating its claims',[85] while Allies, remarking that 'Pusey's guidance was a poor substitute for Newman's', commented that Pusey saw the Church of England through 'such an atmosphere of filial love as disguises or sublimates her features'.[86]

For Caswall and other like-minded clergymen, however, Tractarian concerns did not only embrace doctrine, or ideology, or ecclesiological theory; they also had a practical pastoral dimension that strongly affected the clergy in the field. The issue of validity and related concerns called into question Caswall's empowerment to minister to his parishioners. Was his priesthood 'real'? An incident in Faber's ministry eerily paralleled that recalled above in Caswall's.[87] Faber's friend at Elton, Tom Godwin, related what happened on the night of 12 November 1845, after Faber had gone to give communion to a dying woman: 'As we were going home, my master said to me with much solemnity as to impress me greatly, "Tom, I have a strange feeling come over me, and that is that I am not a priest and that what I have been doing has not been a reality."'[88]

Caswall's attempt to achieve what he saw as necessary revitalization at Stratford led to disillusionment. He held a monthly communion service, celebrated 'Baptism Days' for the parish youth as a groundwork for the eventual introduction of confession, and instituted daily prayer services. But the parishioners remained indifferent. He and Allies, who found that his pastoral work at Launton exacerbated his theoretical difficulties, made similar observations concerning their respective parishioners' attitudes toward their clerical role. Allies lamented, 'Reverence for my office they had none; consideration for me as a gentleman and landlord ... they had',[89] while Caswall, noting from parishioners' reactions to

succession, and the Eucharist as mystical sacrifice. Cf. Allies, who recalled that at a time when he still considered himself 'strongly anti-Roman' (ca. 1838–40), he embraced these same doctrines without realizing their incompatibility with the Anglican position. Allies, *A Life's Decision*, p. 10.

85 Journal entry for 27 June 1846.

86 Allies, diary entry for 3 March 1849; quoted in *A Life's Decision*, p. 100.

87 Cf. above, p. 33.

88 Tom Godwin's Narrative in 'Oratory Notes', 1845–1910; quoted in Ronald Chapman, *Father Faber* (Westminster, Md.: The Newman Press, 1961), pp. 113–14.

89 Allies, *A Life's Decision*, p. 18.

his leaving Stratford that he 'really was beloved' there, observed that 'they say goodbye rather to a "kind young gentleman" than to a Priest ... For among those who are most attentive I find some who have never regarded me as a Priest at all, having always attended their chapels in Salisbury instead of going to Church' (p. 109). Writing to his friend Glenie in April 1846, he gave as one of the major reasons for leaving Stratford 'the perception that a further continuation of the daily service would be prejudicial to a parish which after five years trial continued to repudiate it' (pp. 140–1). If the Established Church resisted revitalization, then, concluded Caswall, the truth must be sought in that institution of which vitality was already a hallmark.

Submission to Rome: end of the journey?

The broad lines as well as the details of the conversion journeys of various individuals afford revealing insights into the personalities involved. The outspoken Allies, banished as a young and heretofore promising Anglican clergyman to the bucolic living of Launton, Oxfordshire, for having antagonized Bishop Blomfield of London with his Tractarian views, incurred a storm of episcopal ire (this time from Samuel Wilberforce) by the publication of his *Journal in France* in 1849 and his subsequent refusal to submit the book to further scrutiny by ecclesiastical and academic authorities.[90] Faber's journey toward Roman Catholicism, which can be dated from his tour of the Continent in 1841, was marked by a period of painful uncertainty and vacillation during the years from 1843 to 1845. Sometimes the emotional Faber felt a stronger allegiance than ever to the Church of England, and at other times he often admitted feeling 'more Roman than ever'. His dilemma intensified when he felt increasingly drawn toward Rome yet hesitated to go because of his parish, into which he had succeeded in breathing new life: 'I really cannot without anguish confront the idea of throwing this up, and leaving these souls to – I know not what.'[91] Faber strove constantly to overcome the danger of being ruled by his feelings. A few weeks before he joined the Church of Rome he wrote to

[90] The *Journal in France* contains a detailed account of two fact-finding trips to that country in 1847 and 1848; it was accused of displaying a 'deprecating and even insulting' tone toward the Church of England (Allies, *A Life's Decision*, p. 159).

[91] Faber, letter to J. B. Morris, 3.11.1845; quoted in John Edward Bowden, *Life and Letters of Frederick William Faber, D.D.* (London: Burns & Oates Ltd.; New York: Benziger Bros., 1869), p. 195.

Newman, 'So far as I know of myself, I am in the state of one calmly convinced of the duty to move but wishing to put it to the test of time and prayer, from self distrust arising from a natural tendency to act on impulse.'[92]

Caswall's was a private rather than a public quest, and he remained discreet, methodical, and fair right up to his actual reception into the Roman Catholic Church. On 11 January 1847 he resolved to spend the next few days perusing his journal from beginning to end. 'It will be reasonable to suppose', he wrote, 'that in whatever points [these observations] all agree in those points they indicate the deliberate habitual state of my mind, in other words they will show what my moral convictions really are' (p. 588). In an interview with Newman the following day he asked what he would be expected to profess to believe concerning the Virgin Mary and was satisfied with Newman's answer that belief in the Virgin's 'influence on the course of providence' is entirely based on the ora pro nobis: this coincided with Caswall's own view as 'set down from time to time in this book' (p. 596).

On January 14 Caswall resolved to communicate to Mrs Fischer a general explanation of the results of his investigations without giving a specific decision, feeling that once he had done so he would 'be more at liberty to act exactly according as what I felt disposed [*sic*]' (p. 597). To Mrs. Fischer he acknowledged and regretted the pain he had caused 'and may still cause to others very dear' to him, especially his mother; but after four weeks in Rome he was compelled to admit that he had 'been unable to find here those superstitions of which I had heard so much'. It was quite clear that Roman Catholics paid no divine worship whatever to images or to the saints and the Virgin Mary; indeed, 'in regard to all the charges which in England it is the custom to make against Roman Catholics they are all of them, so far as I have examined, founded upon most extraordinary misrepresentations' (pp. 598, 599). Further, he found himself in an awkward position if, as a clergyman of the Church of England, he was expected to condemn certain things about the Roman Catholic Church that he had discovered not to deserve condemnation (p. 600).

The dates of Edward's and Louisa's receptions into the Church of Rome could not have been more appropriate: Edward on 18 January 1847 (Feast of the Chair of St Peter) and Louisa on 25 January (Feast of the Conversion of St Paul), the one at the beginning, the other at the end of what came to be known as the week of

[92] Faber, letter to Newman, 28 October 1845; quoted in Chapman, *Father Faber*, p. 112.

prayer for church unity. On the day itself Edward noted relief that, far from having any doubts, he felt just as he had done on other occasions on which his decision had proved to be correct: 'If it were wrong there would certainly be a twinge of conscience somewhere,' he observed (p. 612).

Before the actual event he recorded his gratitude to God for various favours: above all for the conduct, over the last year, of Louisa, who, far from presenting obstacles, acceded immediately to his every wish, even to the giving up of Stratford and the traumatic events it entailed. He thanked God also for his father, who 'was of a noble spirit and would have had his children act according to what they thought right, at whatever affliction to himself' (p. 613); and whatever the attitudes of his mother and the Fischers, they could, he felt, have made life much more difficult for him and Louisa had they wanted to.

Edward's journal describes the actual reception ceremony in great detail. After he arrived at the English College at 1.45 p.m. and upon meeting with Dr Thomas Grant (Rector of the College and later Bishop of Southwark), Newman and three young men who accompanied him, and two or three others, they all walked to Cardinal Acton's and were ushered into a room with an altar. Edward was introduced to the Cardinal and directed to kneel down. The Cardinal began by addressing Caswall briefly 'as one who by little and little had been brought to a knowledge of the truth telling me that many difficulties would probably follow upon the present step, but that I must bear them all for Christ's sake' (p. 619).

Caswall was given conditional baptism, read the Abjuration and signed it. 'The Cardinal then offered up some prayers at the altar including the miserere, after which I read the Confession of Faith and at the end of it kissed the Holy Gospel vowing to maintain that faith unviolated' (p. 620). The Te Deum and more prayers in Latin followed, after which everyone present congratulated him. Then the Cardinal engaged him in an informal chat.

Afterwards Edward wrote to his brother Alfred asking him to break the news to their mother, thinking that this would be less painful for her than learning it via a letter. The day after Louisa's reception he wrote apprising Captain and Mrs. Fischer of the events, assuring them that Louisa had 'acted from her own conviction as you will shortly hear from herself' (p. 625), and reiterating his earlier statement that the usual condemnations of Roman Catholicism were based on misrepresentations. After entertaining suspicions on this matter for some time, he said,

> [m]y visit to Rome has forced me to the conclusion that those particular doctrines so far from being false really form a genuine part of the Christian Faith, and I was not long in seeing that if I desired to act honestly I could not possibly undertake again to hold a parish in England and to preach publicly against those doctrines which privately I believed to be sound and orthodox. (p. 623)

Further, it was clear to him that the Church of England was in schism from the whole Catholic Church throughout the world, and this was in opposition to the Lord's command that 'his Church should be one . . .'

> On arriving at this conviction I have felt that there were open to me but two courses, either on the one hand to remain in that Church which has separated from the Catholic Church and by so doing to sin against my conscience or on the other hand setting aside the fear of man to run the risk of displeasing my most beloved friends and relatives, and to join what I believed to be the cause of truth. (pp. 624–5)

Edward begged the Fischers not to believe that he and Louisa had joined a religion that practises idolatry. He also acknowledged 'how strongly it may be felt that by this act I have lowered myself and Louisa also in the scale of society, but what is this in comparison with conscience?' (p. 625). Finally, he assured the Fischers that his and Louisa's love for relatives and friends was undiminished, probably even stronger, '[a]nd as for our love to one another we feel that we shall cling closer together through life in proportion as by this act we become separated (which God forbid) from those whom we most honour and love' (p. 626). Balanced against considerations of family and friends, however, the primacy of conscience remained paramount for Caswall. In a letter to his brother Henry he reiterated that as much as he felt for their mother, 'when it came to a point of conscience I was obliged to obey God rather than man' (p. 628).

Edward Caswall's journey to Rome had reached its climax. But in a very real sense, given the totally unexpected turn his life was shortly to take, his journey was just beginning.

Chapter Four

From Anglican Clergyman to Roman Catholic Priest

Two incidents recorded in Edward Caswall's conversion journal resonate eerily and prophetically with events that were fated to transpire in his life before long. Both occurred during his and Louisa's sojourn in Rome between late 1846 and early 1847.

The first incident took place one evening during dinner at the boarding house where the couple were staying. An old lady asked Edward if he was a clergyman:

> [S]he felt certain I either was one or was going to be one. I replied that I was one, and had been one for many years, upon which she said, Yes, you have been a clergyman, you are one, and you will always be one. It was curious she should have said, will always be one. Such a thing was never said to me before ..., and now it comes just when it is almost no longer true. (p. 595)

The second event involved the general confession that Caswall made to a Fr Glover after his reception into the Church of Rome. Undoubtedly mindful that 'the humiliation of such a confession constituted a considerable penance in itself', the priest gave him a light penance, to recite the seven penitential psalms once. Caswall supposed that 'he thought too that God will provide penances for me as years proceed. Yes and I will endeavour to bear them as from him' (p. 624).

Two and a half years later, in the summer of 1849, England struggled in the grip of a virulent cholera epidemic as a result of the unusually hot weather. Even as summer gave way to autumn the relentless illness had not relaxed its hold. Edward and Louisa had gone to stay at Torquay. On the morning of September 14, Edward went out to Mass. During his brief absence his life would change irrevocably.

Newman continues the story in a letter to his friend Maria Giberne: 'suddenly, without any premonitory symptoms, [the cholera] came down on [Mrs Caswall] and her landlady'.[1] On his return from church Caswall found them both seized. By 11 o'clock that night Louisa Caswall was dead, leaving Edward a widower at the age of thirty-five.

The distraught Caswall immediately contacted Newman, and they arranged that Louisa's Requiem Mass and burial would take place at St Wilfrid's in Cotton, Staffordshire. This was the site of the extensive buildings that Lord Shrewsbury had generously placed in the hands of Frederick William Faber and his convert community, and which eventually became a temporary home for the Oratory when Faber's Wilfridians threw in their lot with Newman's Oratorians. Newman celebrated the Mass and Caswall's friend Henry Formby, a fellow convert who was briefly an Oratorian priest, sang the *Dies Irae*.[2]

Two scraps of paper preserved among Caswall's files at the Birmingham Oratory provide a poignant glimpse into two facets of his character: the depth and durability of his bereavement, and his penchant for keeping methodical accounts, which even at this time of crisis did not forsake him. A tiny newspaper clipping of personal notices includes one of Louisa's death. The request for prayers for the deceased, formulated according to Roman Catholic usage undoubtedly by Edward himself, is striking:

> Of your charity pray for the soul of Louisa Stuart, the beloved wife of Edward Caswall, Esq., and only daughter of the late General Walker of Whetleigh House, Taunton. She died of cholera at Torquay on the 14th inst.

Along with the clipping is a plain piece of paper, dated 14 September 1849, on which Edward had recorded Louisa's last words – a list of some sixteen brief sentences or phrases, ending with the notice that she 'kissed the crucifix. twice'. Underneath the list are Edward's valedictory prayers for and farewell to his wife, and two dated notations, made later,[3] counting the number of days and weeks since she had died.

Louisa Caswall appears to have impressed Newman favourably;

1 Newman, letter to Maria Giberne, 30 October 1849 (*Letters and Diaries* (*LD*) XIII, p. 278).

2 Newman, letter to F. S. Bowles, 19 September 1849 (ibid., p. 259).

3 11 January 1850, and 25 January, the anniversary of her reception into the Church of Rome.

he described her to Maria Giberne as 'a very pleasing, amiable person'[4] and had earlier noted her donation of £20 to the Oratory,[5] a welcome gift to the struggling infant Congregation.

Several letters that Newman wrote around that time[6] invariably refer to 'poor Caswall' and indicate the devastating effect of Louisa's death on him. For the remaining twenty-eight years of his life, Caswall kept not only the newspaper obituary and his intimately personal account of and response to the event but also a pencil portrait of Louisa sketched when she was a very young woman.[7] This is not to say, however, that he went to pieces; a letter he received from his friend Benjamin Wilson, dated 6 February 1850, indicates Caswall's general mood: 'I almost envy your calm resignation and inward peace which evinces itself by your words of devout meekness of spirit ... I have often wondered to see you so quiet and serene.' Perhaps Edward already had an intimation of what God was calling him to do.

Caswall spent the first Christmas after Louisa's death – specifically, from 8 December until Boxing Day[8] – at the Oratory, 'then lately set up by Dr Newman in Alcester Street, Birmingham, "with the intention of joining the community, if it should be judged that I had a vocation for it"'.[9] Obviously he had begun to discern the direction that the remainder of his life would take. Slightly over a month after he had concluded this visit, Caswall contacted Newman with an offer of significant financial assistance to the Oratory.[10] Caswall proposed to transfer £4,000 'out of hand' to the Birmingham Oratory, in the form of stock transferred into their names, plus a gift of £1,000 for Masses to be said for Louisa.[11]

4 Newman, letter to Maria Giberne, 30 October 1849 (*LD*) XIII, p. 278.

5 Newman, letter to Faber (*LD*) XII, p. 116.

6 E.g., to John Edward Bowden, 21 September 1849 (*LD*) XIII, pp. 260–61; to Henry Wilberforce, 19 September 1849 (ibid., p. 260); to Maria Giberne, 30 October 1849 (ibid., p. 278).

7 Newman's show of sympathy when Louisa died, plus the fact that he did not object to Caswall's keeping these mementos, gives the lie to his allegedly anti-marriage attitudes; contrast the fate of the unfortunate convert widower clergyman whom Faber compelled to destroy a portrait of his deceased wife when he joined the London Oratory! Ronald Chapman, *Father Faber* (Westminster, Md.: The Newman Press, 1961), p. 330. The man is not named.

8 Newman, diary entry for Saturday 8 December (*LD*) XIII, p. 333.

9 Edward Bellasis, 'Biographical Preface', in Edward Caswall, *Hymns and Poems Original and Translated*, new edn (London: Burns and Oates, 1908), p. 13. Bellasis, basing his account on information directly supplied by Caswall, gives the date of Caswall's arrival as 7 December.

10 The exact date of Caswall's offer is not known but can be estimated as late January or early February from the date of Newman's acknowledgment, 3 February 1850.

11 The conditions for the latter are spelled out in a letter from Newman to R. A. Coffin dated 11 February 1850; cf. (*LD*) XIII, p. 417. The date of Caswall's 'large donation ... to the Congregation at Birmingham' is recorded in the

One common problem that beset many Roman Catholic converts in mid nineteenth-century England was the loss of livelihood – above all for married clergymen but for other professionals as well, especially academics, since Roman Catholics were not allowed at the universities – and the consequent risk of impoverishment. As Patrick Allitt points out, 'It is difficult to find any example of an intellectual who derived either social or monetary gain from conversion. For many, on the contrary, the material and prestige losses were considerable.'[12] Thomas W. Allies, for example, wrote, 'Had I conceived it *possible* that I should ever be driven to leave the Anglican Church, I should have acted in a far more prudent manner as to money affairs.'[13] Instead he was haunted by 'the most anxious thoughts as to what I shall eat and what I shall drink, wherewithal I shall be clothed, I and mine, and to the drudgery of teaching dunces'.[14]

Caswall was one of the fortunate exceptions to this fate. His landlady in Rome, on learning that he had become Roman Catholic and assuming that this step would bring economic embarrassment upon him, quietly offered to reduce his rent. Though very grateful for her consideration he turned down the offer, because he could well afford to absorb the loss of his clerical living, which was worth £80 per annum. Caswall had the advantage of a private income: indeed in the preface to the first edition of his *Lyra Catholica*, published in 1849, he referred to 'circumstances' that have 'afforded him, during the past year, an unlooked-for amount of leisure'.[15] He had his own investments as well as a small inheritance from Bishop Burgess, and in addition, he had inherited a considerable sum from Louisa. A copy of Louisa's will in Edward's handwriting is preserved in the Wiltshire County Record Office in Trowbridge.[16] Dated 5 May 1847 – three months after Louisa became a Roman Catholic – the will ends with a formula long used by Roman Catholics as a pointed means of identifying their religious faith:

> And as my last act and deed I commend my soul to God in the firm

Decree Book of the Birmingham Oratory as 8 February 1850; cf. Placid Murray, *Newman the Oratorian* (Dublin: Gill & MacMillan, 1969), p. 457.

12 Patrick Allitt, *Catholic Converts: British and American Intellectuals Turn to Rome* (Ithaca and London: Cornell University Press, 1997), p. 6.

13 Thomas W. Allies, *A Life's Decision*, 2nd edn (London: Burns & Oates Ltd., 1894), p. 13.

14 Quoted in David Newsome, *The Parting of Friends: The Wilberforces and Henry Manning* (Grand Rapids, Mich.: William B. Eerdmans, 1966), p. 404.

15 Edward Caswall, *Lyra Catholica: Containing All the Breviary and Missal Hymns with Others from Various Sources* (London: James Burns, 1849) p. vi.

16 W.R.O. no. 776/1103; witnessed as a true copy of the original by Edward's brother Tom and his attorney John Lambert.

> profession of the Catholic Faith and I hereby hope that all Catholic Priests who may hear of and remember me will offer up the Holy Sacrifice of the Mass for the repose of my Soul as often as they can and I earnestly entreat them and all other Catholics to remember me frequently in their prayers.

Louisa bequeathed all her wealth – 'the Sum of £3,333/6/8, 3% consolidated Bank annuities £400 part of a sum of £1,200 secured by a Bond in [a premarital settlement made with Edward] and £4,800 3% reduced Bank annuities and other' – as well as £200 annually 'for and during the term of his natural life' from her deceased father's estate as permitted under the terms of Major-General Walker's will, to her 'dear husband' Edward.[17]

Caswall's offer could not have come at a more fortuitous time for Newman's fledgling Oratory foundation. The English Congregation of the Oratory had been formally set up by Newman on 2 February 1848, and originally housed at Maryvale,[18] a site intended as a launching base for a future establishment in Birmingham. For a variety of complicated reasons, however, Newman was soon compelled to move the Oratory to St Wilfrid's at Cotton Hall, near Cheadle, in Staffordshire, when Faber and his Wilfridian community decided to surrender themselves to him. Its location prevented St Wilfrid's from forming the nucleus of an Oratory, however, since Oratories must be located in urban areas; thus in late January 1849 Newman founded the first Birmingham Oratory in Alcester Street, in 'a gloomy gin distillery of which we have taken a lease, fitting up a large room for a Chapel'.[19] Formally opened on 2 February 1849, the new Oratory flourished,[20] but the largely poor, slum-dwelling congregation was not the '*splendidior, doctior et honestior ordo*' – i.e., the educated upper class that the Papal Brief constituting the English Oratory had specified as the appropriate objects of its ministry. Thus Newman and his Oratorians would have to find a more suitable location for their work, which would, of course, entail considerable financial expenditure. Now, just when it was most urgently needed, Caswall stepped in with his offer of help. On 3 February 1850, Newman wrote to Caswall:

[17] Major-General Charles Augustus Walker's will is dated 26 April 1842, so that he would have died some time between late April 1842 and early May 1847.

[18] This was the old Oscott College 'at that time somewhat outside the main town area of Birmingham'. Murray, *Newman the Oratorian*, p. 96.

[19] (*LD*) XII, p. 382.

[20] See Ian Ker, *John Henry Newman: A Biography* (Oxford and New York: Oxford University Press, 1988), p. 344, for details.

> You have indeed done us the greatest benefit that could be done us at this moment in external matters. At the moment, we do not want any one great thing, but the power to make a great many beginnings ... We want just something to make up the house accounts, something for the music, something for the school, something to start a Church with – and you have answered all these purposes at once.

On 6 February 1850 Newman notified Faber: 'We are in consequence looking out for a site [for a new Oratory] at once,'[21] and on February 11 he wrote to Fr R. A. Coffin:

> We *think* of building an Oratorian House as the *investment* of our £3000 or £4000 ... *This* house, (which we are *in*) will cost us in rent £120 in a few years, £3000 at 4 per cent is £120, £4000 at 3 per cent is £120. So that it will be a good investment, and give us, what no one else will give us, a house – which may proceed in building pari passu with a Church – which the Bishop has allowed us to begin collecting for at once.[22]

Thus the present site of the Birmingham Oratory, on the Hagley Road in Edgbaston, was purchased in May 1850. Two days later the Congregation proposed a resolution to build a house there and to collect money for a church. Construction was started on 13 December of that year, and the Oratorians began moving into the new house in Edgbaston in spring 1852.[23]

Family repercussions

Caswall formally ended his journal with his letter to Henry informing him of his and Louisa's reception into the Church of Rome. There follow the earliest versions of a few of his poems, some of them reworked many times, that were eventually included in his published collection. Two of them, published as 'A Remonstrance' and 'Persecution', express Caswall's only extant verbal response to actual or anticipated reactions to his conversion on the part of family or friends. 'A Remonstrance' addresses in a friendly tone those loved ones who, he allows, mean their best and believe themselves to be serving God by estranging themselves from him. He

[21] (*LD*) XIII, p. 409.
[22] Ibid. XIII: p. 418.
[23] Newman moved in on 16 February 1852, and his fellow Oratorians gradually followed over the next several weeks. See chapter 5 for further details about the choice of Edgbaston as the Oratory site.

prays, out of sincere love and never condescendingly, that they may one day come to perceive the truth. 'Persecution' is more impersonal – it was published under 'Hymns and Meditative Pieces' rather than under 'Poems' – and rejoices that one has been called to suffer for the Lord

> While enemies their arts employ,
> And friends pronounce us fools or mad.[24]

It was not only the converts themselves who suffered the pangs of estrangement: letters to Henry Caswall from one R. M. Chatfield, a mutual friend,[25] and from Henry to Edward enclosing Chatfield's missive, reveal how those left behind experienced the pain of ruptured relations and show a depth of feelings that went quite beyond what those in the other camp might call bigotry. Chatfield had heard a report that Edward contemplated 'returning to the true Faith, in which he was baptised, rejecting the fables, which the traditions of men have introduced into the Romish system'.

> Oh how gladly could I welcome him back to the simple Faith of our apostolic Church ... Earnestly have I prayed for him – We once walked together as Brothers and oh how painful was it to meet one, with whom I once held sweet counsel and walked to the house of God, as a friend, and to feel, that there was now a gulf between us. He a member of a Church, which denounces me, as an accursed Heretic, I a member of Christ, who denounces Rome as Babylon.

Henry forwarded the letter to Edward 'as evincing [Chatfield's] very kind & Christian feelings'.[26] This was obviously not the first time the subject had been broached between the two brothers: Henry refers to an earlier statement of Edward's that his return to the Established Church was 'impossible'. Refusing to accept this, Henry expresses the wish that he had reason to believe the report to be true and the earnest hope that Edward 'may not be still further cut off from us by your receiving Roman Catholic orders'.[27]

It is interesting to speculate on a possible connection between this report of Edward's possible renunciation of Roman Catholicism and Louisa's death three months earlier. Could people have

[24] Edward Caswall, *Poems* (London: Thomas Richardson & Son, 1861), p. 253.
[25] No date, but probably early December 1849.
[26] Henry Caswall, letter to Edward Caswall, 3 December 1849.
[27] The letter closes with Henry's wish that Edward will be with them for the Christmas holidays; thus it is unlikely that Edward had already disclosed an intention of spending the holiday in Birmingham.

assumed that Edward might be suffering from guilt feelings, dogged by the thought that Louisa would still be alive had he remained in his curacy at Stratford and they had not found themselves in Torquay at that fateful time? – or that after the loss of this, the primary relationship in his life, he would have wanted to heal the breaches in his other close relationships? In any case, despite the strength of feelings against the Church of Rome and Edward's submission to it, these letters never exhibit a pervasive sense of personal hostility; they always close affectionately, and Henry ends this particular letter by assuring Edward that the entire family 'feel the most lively interest in your happiness'.

However that may have been, several family members remained reluctant to receive Edward in their homes. In October 1851[28] Caswall wrote to Newman requesting permission to visit his mother, who had invited him 'to see her in her own house from which she has rigidly excluded me since I became a Catholic except on the occasion of my dear wife's death'. Not only was Edward anxious to alleviate his family's concern about his recent illness, but he also believed such a visit would be 'useful in order to show that my mind has not been deranged to that extent which I think they may have supposed and which, from their suspicions about Catholics, they might imagine still to be studiously concealed from them'. Still later, probably in 1854,[29] Edward wrote to his brother Tom from London informing him that he had received a letter from their Aunt Ogle 'refusing to see us as being Catholics'.[30]

Such estrangement could be very long-lasting. After she was widowed in 1870, Edward's sister Maria Dowding wrote to him referring to her having been parted from him 'for many years' due to her sense of responsibility as a mother,[31] and lamenting the fact that 'in all the depth of my sorrows, I could not ask you for that love & Brotherly sympathy wh [*sic*] I had so long refused when in such bliss with my dearest one!' But now her children were mature, two of her daughters were about to be married, and 'I may there-

[28] Edward has dated the letter 16 October 1841, an obvious error; he was recuperating from a serious illness at the time.

[29] The letter is not dated, but its position among other letters in the Oratory archives would allow an assumption of this date.

[30] Jane Ogle was the sister-in-law of their father, the Revd Robert Clarke Caswall, married to Major Robert Ogle of Eglingham Hall (*Memoirs of the Caswall Family*, p. 13).

[31] The letter is not dated, but Benjamin Dowding died in 1870 (cf. his entry in *Alumni Oxonienses: The Members of the University of Oxford, 1715–1886. Being the Matriculation Register of the University,* alphabetically arranged, revised, and annotated by Joseph Foster, vol. I, Later Series [Oxford: James Parker & Co., 1891], and Maria's letter was obviously written not long afterward.)

fore at last ask you to come & see us all & again be my dear dear Brother so long yearned for. – My children all wish it earnestly . . .' She closes by inviting him to one of the forthcoming weddings.

Thus as a recent convert Caswall had reason to anticipate negative repercussions from his family over his sizeable donations to the Oratory. In the four letters Newman wrote to various persons confiding that Caswall was 'doing something handsome for Brummagem'[32] he stressed the need for secrecy, for Caswall feared the consequences should his relations and friends learn what he was doing with his money; indeed Caswall was so anxious 'to keep his gift secret, [that] *he has not even told Mr Lambert his lawyer*'.[33]

Edward's fears were well-founded. His brother Alfred, 'deeply grieved' once he eventually learned what Edward had done, castigated him not so much for having been 'foolish' but for having 'simply done wrong'. To Alfred's mind it would have been more 'acceptable' had Edward instead provided for their brother Tom who had 'sacrificed so much to his scruples', been in a position to help Henry's children were Henry to die, or assisted various other relations (including Louisa's 'poor surviving Relatives') who had much greater claims on him than did 'the Society you have so lately joined'. Instead Edward has neglected his God-given duties in favour of others 'more in accordance with [his] own ideas & fancies'.[34]

It would be grossly unfair to let Alfred's accusation stand unchallenged. Edward's charitable actions, when the occasions for such later presented themselves, proved him to be far from indifferent to the plights of friends and relatives who had fallen on hard times. The Oratory archives preserve a bewilderingly extensive correspondence to Edward from Benjamin Wilson and Mrs Wilson, friends of long standing who were chronically in the throes of misfortune and importuning Edward for assistance, not necessarily of a directly financial nature but in the form of contacts who could help Wilson secure paid employment. Wilson appears to have been a Roman Catholic convert, a teacher by profession, who encountered difficulties in finding and retaining employment after his conversion. Edward dedicated his *Hymns and Poems* to him – addressing him as 'the faithful friend of my school and college life' – and never refused the Wilsons' frequent cries of distress.

[32] Letter of Newman to F. W. Faber, 5 February 1850; *Letters and Diaries* (*LD*) XIII, p. 407.

[33] Letter of Newman to F. W. Faber, 6 February 1850; (*LD*) XIII, p. 409.

[34] Letter of Alfred Caswall to Edward Caswall, 18 May 1852. The fact that Alfred was suffering some financial 'inconveniences' at this time and thus could have benefited from Edward's 'God-given duties' may well have aggravated his acerbic feelings.

Edward's brother Frederick was another noteworthy recipient of his thoughtful consideration. Frederick had emigrated to America and attempted to establish himself first in Carrolton, Kentucky, and then in Akron, Ohio,[35] but, in each case, with singular lack of success. Consequently Edward did at least his fair share of bailing Frederick out of his difficulties. In the autumn of 1852, after Frederick had been involved in some bad speculations, Edward sent him £100, which Alfred advised Edward to regard as a loan rather than as a gift.[36] Frederick was not a good businessman, Alfred observed, and clearly would 'never get on in America'. He had inherited more than either of them from their father and had received more money since then, but he was now worth so little that it was 'a very sickening thought'. In Alfred's opinion the financial rescue efforts should be limited to the education of Frederick's children.

Nearly twenty years later Edward was still helping Frederick – his sole surviving brother. The Revd R. L. Ganter of Akron, Ohio, rector of the church where Frederick was a parishioner, wrote to Edward in February 1871 informing him that Frederick's wife had come to see him about their acute financial difficulties, which had 'rendered [Frederick] helpless': they had two mortgages on their home, one of which was about to be called in. If Edward could see his way to sending £250, this amount would cover both mortgages.[37] Ganter suggested that Edward buy the house and deed it to the children; in any case, Edward should advise Frederick's attorney how he wished the money applied. A further letter in May of that year indicates that Edward's money had been received '& applied as directed', so that Frederick's home was secure.[38] Correspondence from Frederick's attorney Edwin Green[39] shows that Edward had laid out a total of $1,223.46 and apparently taken over the mortgages. Frederick appears to have been an honest man – Green confided to Edward that he had become involved because his own wife had pointed out that Frederick was 'an *honest man* in the true sense of the term and such men are very scarce' – but perhaps was less than responsible. It is noteworthy that in both instances, in the 1850s and the 1870s, emphasis was laid on helping Frederick's children,[40] as if the primary consideration was not so

[35] Frederick Caswall's descendants still live in Ohio.
[36] Letter of Alfred Caswall to Edward Caswall, 30 October 1852.
[37] Letter of the Revd R. L. Ganter to Edward Caswall, 10 February 1871.
[38] Letter of the Revd R. L. Ganter to Edward Caswall, 8 May 1871.
[39] Letter to Edward Caswall, 3 August 1871.
[40] Frederick's first wife had died and he had remarried and thus had two families.

much to bail out someone whose predicament was largely his own fault[41] as to ensure that the children did not suffer for their parents' largely self-inflicted misfortunes.

Caswall joins the Oratory

By the end of February 1850 it was clear that Caswall the generous benefactor – he had by then made the Oratory a further gift of £5,000[42] – would become a member of the Oratory, though it was as yet 'not certain' when he would begin the novitiate.[43] Having 'pressed [the Oratory Congregation] earnestly for admission',[44] on 29 March 1850 – Good Friday – 'Brother Edward' was admitted on probation as a novice and put on the habit.[45] Three days later he received the tonsure and was admitted to Minor Orders.[46]

Reactions were, of course, varied. The Catholic peer Lord Shrewsbury wrote to Caswall: 'It has given us all the greatest pleasure to hear of your pious resolve. God grant that you may persevere and be proved to have a true vocation for so holy and useful career!'[47]

Alfred Caswall, as was to be expected, had a quite different perspective, which he communicated in two letters. 'My dear Edward', he wrote on 16 April 1850, 'I have been bothered with the presentiment of approaching evil, and it seems always connected with you. I am not much given to superstition, but I should be really glad to hear how you are.' Three days later he wrote criticizing a number of supposed Roman Catholic converts, including Charles Marriott[48] and William Maskell,[49] suggesting that the former would be judged in the next life for the misery he had

41 Apparently Frederick not only persisted in involving himself in business speculations when he clearly had no head for business and should have sought gainful employment instead, but also, as Edwin Green delicately put it to Edward, Mr and Mrs Caswall lacked the ability to live within their means.

42 Letter of Newman to Mrs J. W. Bowden, 27 February 1850; (*LD*) XIII, p. 432.

43 Letter of Newman to John Edward Bowden, 27 February 1850; (*LD*) XIII, p. 431.

44 Newman, journal entry, 29 March 1850; (*LD*) XIII: p. 451.

45 Ibid.

46 Bellasis, 'Biographical Preface', p. 13.

47 Judging from Shrewsbury's reference to Caswall's cousin, a Mr. Jackson, who had called on him, members of the Caswall family must have been acquainted with the Shrewsburys.

48 Charles Marriott (1811–58) had been a leading Tractarian and was one of Newman's dearest friends. He never became a Roman Catholic, however.

49 William Maskell (1814–90), an authority on ancient liturgies, became a Roman Catholic after the Gorham judgment (1850).

created in his own family. Alfred never passed up the opportunity for an acidic comment: 'You are a precious lot', he wrote, 'in the same boat, who strive hard to keep each other's courage up. The time will probably come to all, though you struggle to keep in a corner, when the memory of ancient truth will sing in your ears like a long forgotten tune which had been loved in childhood. *Apostatis not sit spes*.' Undoubtedly possessed of a Type A personality, Alfred, a lawyer by profession, remained staunchly and rabidly anti-Roman right up to his death in his early forties. Having been diagnosed with heart disease in December 1853,[50] he was dying by May 1855 and yet still had enough strength in him to remain 'sharply opposed' to Roman Catholicism and to insist to Henry, 'No Mass for me, living or dead' and to desire Edward to pray for him 'as a brother though not as a priest'.[51] Alfred died on 23 May 1855. Edward wanted to resign as his brother's trustee but not as co-executor of his father's will, for he feared that such a step 'would not be safe ... , considering that two of us are Catholics, and that our interests might suffer in some way'.[52]

Undaunted by family reactions, Edward persisted in what he had discerned to be his vocation, and on 11 December 1850 he and Stanislas Flanagan, an Irishman and fellow novice whose life would be bound up with Edward's in the establishment of the Oratory mission in the neighbouring village of Smethwick, embarked upon the retreat that would prepare them for ordination to the subdiaconate, which Newman, in an address to the Congregation and to the ordinands in particular, called 'that great step which for ever unites them to the ministry of the Catholic Church'.[53] At that time it was at their ordination as subdeacons that candidates for orders in the Roman Catholic Church took the vow of celibacy. Caswall was ordained to the subdiaconate on 21 December 1850[54] – the anniversary of his wedding to Louisa. The irony was not lost on Alfred. When Edward emerged from his retreat on 20 December he found waiting for him a letter from his brother[55] recalling Edward's wedding day and how the entire family and 'a long list of friends all united in one happy feeling of hope and joy. I cannot describe the deadness of my very soul when I think of its probable anniversary'. Accusing him of 'so perseveringly & needlessly add[ing] to the

[50] Letter of Alfred Caswall to Edward Caswall, 7 December 1853.
[51] Letter of Edward Caswall to Newman, 6 May 1855.
[52] Letter of Edward Caswall to Newman, 26 May 1855.
[53] Newman, 'From the Decree Book of the Birmingham Oratory, 25 January 1869', in Murray, *Newman the Oratorian*, p. 232.
[54] Newman, diary entry, (*LD*) XIV, p. 171.
[55] Letter of Alfred Caswall to Edward Caswall, 17 December 1850.

bitterness of our Mother's old age', Alfred herewith lodged his 'formal & distinct protest against this wretched step of yours which I trust you may yet be spared to repent of in this life', and, as his 'elder brother who has loved you more than you are perhaps willing to credit', he warned Edward 'against joining more closely the false church who carries blasphemy on her very forehead'.

Alfred challenged Edward, should he present himself for Roman Catholic Orders, 'to think of our Fathers holy memory or our Mothers age blighted by you – of our happy Home destroyed by you ... & you must be more or less than man if you can with unfaltering lips pledge your broken faith to this foreign Church which be assured is doomed ... '

Edward's reaction to this last-minute attempt at dissuasion has unfortunately not survived, but at any rate, he was undeterred, and proceeded, one year later, to his diaconal ordination.[56] An unusual and somewhat amusing glimpse into his character around this time is provided by a situation that occurred in the autumn of 1851. Suffering from an otherwise unidentified serious illness, Edward had been sent to recuperate at The Priory at Little Malvern[57] and Stanislas Flanagan was looking after him. On 24 September Flanagan reported in a letter to Newman that Edward's health was

> improving rapidly ... Dr. was here this morning, and told him he might go downstairs. He is now sitting in Fr. Scott's huge easy chair beside the parlour fire – I have been giving him a refreshing draught in the shape of half an hour's reading of Robinson Crusoe – he relished it much, and laughed once or twice, which I consider to be one of the best indications of his improvement.

Flanagan could not get a minute to himself until Edward was 'made up for the night', around nine o'clock, and he requested that Newman please pack and send Edward's pillow, as he complained of the ones at The Priory being too soft and thus he could not sleep: ' ... waiting upon him will do me some spiritual good – for it is astonishing the number of whims he has, which one must gratify ... he obeys everything [the doctor] tells him with the most scrupulous exactness.' It was upon recuperating from this illness that Edward requested and took advantage of Newman's permission to accept his mother's invitation to visit her at her home.

The year 1852 was a significant one for the Oratory. The building in Edgbaston had been completed and by April the last of the

[56] 20 December 1851: Bellasis, 'Biographical Preface', p. 13.

[57] This is in the West Midlands, some forty miles south-west of Birmingham.

Oratorians had left the gin mill in Alcester Street for good to take up residence in the new, permanent location. On 18 September Caswall and Henry Bittleston, a convert whom Newman had received into the Church of Rome in 1849, were ordained priests.

During his address to the subdiaconate ordinands in December 1850 Newman had spoken of the necessity of 'perform[ing] well the duties of the day' if one is to aim at perfection:

> I do not know any thing more difficult, more sobering, so strengthening than [*sic*] the constant aim to go through the ordinary day's work well. To rise at the exact time, to give the due time to prayer, to meditate with devotion, to assist at mass with attention, to be recollected in conversation, these and similar observances carried duly through the day, make a man, as it is often said, half a saint, or almost a saint.[58]

The next chapter will describe how Edward Caswall became 'half a saint, or almost a saint', not through groundbreaking intellectual achievement, or through significant contributions on the national scene, but through his extraordinary attention to 'go[ing] through the ordinary day's work well'. This would not be without its challenges and trials, as well as its triumphs: Victorian Birmingham and its environs were growing by leaps and bounds, and there were people of all class levels to be ministered to and educated. The Roman Catholics needed churches and schools; indeed, as Newman saw, new conversions would have to be made among the better-off classes if Roman Catholicism was to thrive. The fledgling Oratory band would need a firm but gentle hand to organize it, particularly during the years of Newman's absence in Dublin. As Caswall would soon learn, there was indeed 'a work to be done'.

[58] Murray, *Newman the Oratorian*, p. 235.

Caswall was Perpetual Curate at the Church of St Lawrence at Stratford-sub-Castle before his conversion to Roman Catholicism.

In 1849 the Oratory took possession of its first Birmingham home in Alcester Street, 'on premises formerly occupied as a distillery', as Caswall noted with a glint of humour.

John Henry Newman, Caswall's mentor and Father Superior, regarded Caswall as 'one of my dearest friends'.

Caswall's timely donation of money to Newman's fledgling community enabled him to purchase the present site of the Birmingham Oratory.

Edward Caswall, described by Sir John Acton, visiting the Oratory in 1859, to a friend as 'the poet, also the politician of the house'.

A deeply prayerful man, Caswall considered his translations of the Latin Breviary hymns an important part of his pastoral vocation.

Caswall mentions wearing spectacles already in his early thirties. His poor eyesight undoubtedly gave him the 'dreamy' look, evident in this photograph.

Newman and his two closest friends, Frs Ambrose St John and Edward Caswall, are together in death as they were in life, in their graves at Rednal.

Chapter Five

Priest of the Birmingham Oratory

Victorian Birmingham

The middle years of the nineteenth century witnessed the crest of a wave of rapid growth in English towns. Spurred by the Industrial Revolution, this development began in the late eighteenth century, when workers, attracted by the higher wages offered by industry, started to migrate from rural areas to the towns, thereby swelling the populations of the latter at enormous rates.

Inevitably, the rapid growth led to health and other problems in the industrial towns, which were 'eventually almost overwhelmed by congestion, smoke, and squalor'.[1] Thus circumstances were ripe for the spread of social injustice and, consequently, mass discontent. The Poor Law had been enacted in Elizabethan times and was administered by parish overseers to provide relief for the aged, the sick, and infants, and work in the workhouses for the able-bodied. In 1834, however, the much harsher Poor Law Amendment Act was passed, which viewed poverty among the able-bodied as a moral failing; thus for the latter it offered no assistance except the misery of the workhouse, in hopes that this would motivate them to seek proper employment. Care for the poor was removed from the responsibility of the parish and its minister and assigned instead to the Board of Guardians, a new body of elected officials.[2] Soon after-

[1] Asa Briggs, *The Making of Modern England 1783–1867: The Age of Improvement* (New York: Harper Torchbooks, 1965), p. 45.

[2] See, e.g., Geoffrey Best, *Mid-Victorian Britain 1851–1875* (New York: Schocken Books, 1972), p. 36. This amendment effectively detached Poor Law philosophy

wards the economic depression of 1837–8 and the high unemployment that followed in its wake generated a desire for reform that crystallized in the nationwide working-class movement known as Chartism, after the 'People's Charter' or reform bill drafted in 1838. '... behind the specific demands was a deep ... revulsion of feeling against the bleakness and monotony of the industrial towns, for most of the urban workers still had memories of the countryside, and of a peace and beauty which no longer entered into their lives.'[3]

It was not the actual growth of the towns but its unprecedented rapidity which, along with other factors, 'darkened the future of communities which often began their history with bright promise'.[4] Birmingham was no exception to this growth spurt. During the last forty years of the eighteenth century Birmingham's population doubled,[5] and between 1831 and 1871 it increased again from 144,000 to 344,000.[6] In this industrial West Midlands city the phenomenon owed not a little to its canal system, crucial to a region farther away from a coast than any other industrial area in England. Birmingham's first canal, designed expressly to unite 'the numerous hearths and furnaces of industrial Birmingham with prolific coal-works of the contiguous mining districts of South Staffordshire',[7] had been completed in 1769. 'By the end of the eighteenth century, the canals had already transformed the Birmingham neighborhood, and factories and workshops clustered along their banks.'[8]

Thanks to its well-drained and maintained main streets, Birmingham was, according to the three reports on the town's health issued in the 1840s, considered 'perhaps one of the most healthy of our large towns'.[9] The city's smaller streets and courts were, on the other hand, 'much neglected'.[10] Most were undrained and many were also unpaved; thus it would have been impossible

---

from its original Christian and Gospel foundations, which enraged many Tractarians. (For this information I am indebted to Mr Gerard Tracey, private communication.)

3 Conrad Gill, *History of Birmingham*. Vol. 1: *Manor and Borough to 1865* (London and New York: Oxford University Press, 1952), pp. 242–3.

4 Briggs, *Making of Modern England*, p. 46. Among the other factors listed by Briggs are 'lack of efficient administrative machinery, ... the inadequate development of civil engineering, ... the dominant individualist outlook of busy manufacturing groups, and the social division of the towns between the well-off and the "masses"'.

5 Ibid., p. 44.

6 Gill, *History of Birmingham*, p. 363.

7 Briggs, *Making of Modern England*, p. 56.

8 Ibid.

9 Gill, *History of Birmingham*, p. 368.

10 Ibid.

completely to clean away the accumulated filth. Houses had been cheaply built. Initially easy to rent due to their cheerful appearance, they quickly revealed their defects – the cracks, leaks, and the damp – and thus were abandoned and became slums.[11]

These conditions in turn adversely affected the physical health of Birmingham's people. Although the town managed to avoid the worst effects of cholera epidemics and fared better than other towns of comparable size in escaping the ravages of infectious diseases, it was visited by 'persistent epidemics of various fevers'. Typhus, for example, was very common.[12]

Not even the best parts of town were exempt from the poor health that flourished in the unsanitary conditions. Edgbaston to the south-west had its share of inadequate drainage: for example, houses in the Hagley Road, where John Henry Newman came to establish his permanent Oratory foundation in 1852, were drained into open ditches, with not even an attempt made to reach a sewer.[13]

Not unexpectedly, the moral health of the town also experienced negative repercussions. 'Some of the worst areas of housing', in the town centre around what is now Corporation Street, 'were also the worst from the point of view of the police: full of haunts of vice and the resorts of thieves'.[14] Contemporary observers, claiming that the bad conditions 'drove men and women to the public houses, and so aggravated the greatest social evil of the time', called urgently for reform, because drinking was 'an infinitely more frequent cause of disease and death among workers than all of the trades and jobs combined'.[15] It was in 1849 and 1850 that two municipal institutions, both designed by the architect D. R. Hill, opened in response to these problems: the Birmingham jail and the lunatic asylum, respectively. The former housed both male and female criminals and had separate wings for juveniles and debtors. It originally contained cells for 321 prisoners, but within a short time this number proved to have been underestimated: within two years the jail was more than full.[16]

Newman's establishment of the Oratory in Birmingham

This, then, was Birmingham as Newman found it when he arrived to establish England's first Oratory in the 1840s. Religions of a

[11] Ibid., pp. 368–9.
[12] Ibid., p. 369.
[13] Ibid., p. 370.
[14] Ibid.
[15] Report of the Medical Committee, 1841, p. 32; quoted in ibid.
[16] Gill, *History of Birmingham*, p. 277.

variety of denominations appeared to be thriving.[17] Noting the 'evident desire' to ensure that the number of houses of worship would keep pace with the town's growing population, Gill observes that 'the new churches ... were generally placed at the very edge of the built-up area, anticipating the spread of population, which never failed to follow'.[18] This is precisely what was to happen with Newman's permanent Oratory foundation in the then-suburb of Edgbaston,[19] following the original, temporary establishment in the 'squalid wretchedness'[20] of Alcester Street in central Birmingham.

By the powers conferred on him in a papal brief dated 26 November 1847, Newman formally constituted the Birmingham Oratory at Maryvale, the site of the old Oscott College near Birmingham, on the Feast of the Purification, 2 February 1848. In addition to Newman himself the original band of Oratorians consisted of nine members, followed, in the course of a few months, by several others, including the poet and hymn writer Frederick William Faber (who had become a Roman Catholic one month after Newman) and his community of Wilfridians, so that by the end of that year the Oratory members numbered some thirty to forty persons, all housed at St. Wilfrid's in Cotton, Staffordshire, some forty miles north of Birmingham. From out of this remote moorland setting enquiries were made in search of a temporary home in Birmingham, and one year after the Oratory's original institution, on 2 February 1849, Newman opened a chapel in Alcester Street, 'on premises formerly occupied as a distillery', as Caswall, undoubtedly with a glint of humour, noted in his 1855 state-of-the-Oratory report. Caswall continues: '... almost from the first our chapel, poor as it was, began to fill, nay, more, to become a place of cherished resort. In an incredibly short period of time, a large Catholic body showed itself all round us, and during the period of our residence, several hundreds of Protestants were received into the Church.'

The brief of Pius IX characterized the Oratory's mission as extending primarily to the *nobiliores* and *doctiores* among the population, and the premises in Alcester Street were not suited to such outreach. It thus became necessary to seek new accommodation, and Edgbaston came to the community's attention as a spot 'well

[17] Gill, *History of Birmingham*, p. 374, gives census statistics for adherents of religious denominations.

[18] Ibid.

[19] Ironically, it was in Edgbaston that the needs of Birmingham's Roman Catholics had been served a century earlier by a chapel provided by the Middlemore family. Ibid., p. 375.

[20] Edward Caswall, Oratory report, 1856.

adapted to this end. It lay in that part of town which might be supposed to include the *nobiliores* and *doctiores* of whom the Brief speaks'.[21]

Now a bustling part of metropolitan Birmingham in which crumbling old residences and shops jostle side by side with some of the most valuable real estate in Britain outside London, Edgbaston in the mid-nineteenth century was an aesthetically appealing suburb 'affording a fine variety of scenery'[22] and home to many Birmingham businessmen. A 'fine example of the benefit of enlightened planning', it was an 'outstanding exception' to the haphazard development that characterized most of the growth of Birmingham.[23] The Oratory developed its permanent home along and around the main artery known as the Hagley Road. Gill notes that here Newman 'carried out for forty years St Philip's principle of drawing people to religion by means of example and teaching, quietly and steadily exercised'.[24] He goes on to state, however, that '[t]his principle restrained [Newman] from taking an active part in local affairs: he was rather a national leader of religion and thought than a builder of the community in his adopted town'.[25]

Gill's statement should not be misconstrued, however, to mean that the Oratorians did nothing but celebrate Mass and administer the sacraments while their Father Superior occupied himself with literary work and events on a national scale. In fact the Oratory became a vital force for social and educational improvement in Birmingham. Newman must be credited with allowing and empowering the Oratory Fathers and Brothers to organize an extensive apostolate to the Catholics of Birmingham and the outlying areas for some miles to the west – indeed, to the needy as well as to the well-off, educated classes mentioned in the papal brief – and this chapter will not only describe that outreach, but will also demonstrate Edward Caswall's crucial role in the process.

Caswall as Acting Superior of the Birmingham Oratory

In April 1859 Sir John Acton, visiting the Birmingham Oratory, wrote a letter to his friend Richard Simpson in which he described Edward Caswall as 'the poet, as also the politician of the house'.[26]

21 Ibid.
22 Gill, *History of Birmingham*, p. 366.
23 *White's Dictionary*, 1855; quoted in ibid.
24 Gill, *History of Birmingham*, p. 375.
25 Ibid., pp. 375–6.
26 Newman, *Letters and Diaries* (*LD*) XIX, p. 16, n. 2.

Perhaps it was Caswall's skill at negotiation; perhaps his talent for organization and his meticulous attention to detail; or perhaps Newman had already sensed the unswerving loyalty that would keep Caswall at his side for the rest of his life (and indeed, afterward as well[27]). Whichever of Caswall's qualities had impressed Newman, when Newman officially assumed his duties as Rector of the new Catholic University of Ireland in 1854, seeing the necessity of appointing someone 'to take the duties of Father Superior [of the Oratory] during his absence in Ireland',[28] his choice fell upon Caswall.[29] Caswall recorded his own reaction in the Oratory Journal: 'This decision was received by the said Father in silence because he really felt astonished at the choice and did not know what to say.'[30] The appointment, renewed at least once,[31] lasted until Newman's eventual release from his obligations in Ireland in 1859.[32] It involved Caswall in decisions, and their implementation, concerning every aspect of the Oratory's activities. The two chief projects for which Caswall was directly responsible in his capacity as Acting Superior were the establishment of the Poor Schools in Edgbaston and the establishment of the mission (eventually the parish) and schools at Smethwick.

Caswall and the Oratory's mission schools in Edgbaston

Education in Mid-Victorian England

A survey taken in 1838 found that less than half of Birmingham's 45,000 children aged between five and fifteen years had attended any school at all.[33] Education in mid nineteenth-century England

27 According to Newman's directions he himself was eventually buried in the same grave as Ambrose St John, while Caswall was buried to the right and Joseph Gordon to the left, the idea being that Newman and the three men who had unreservedly thrown in their lot with him should form a cruciform company in death, with Newman as head and St John, Caswall, and Gordon the feet and arms. I am indebted to Mr Gerard Tracey for this information (personal communication).

28 Caswall, Oratory Journal, 22 August 1854.

29 Ambrose St John had originally been appointed Rector, but after a few months his handling of certain events suggested to Newman that he was not temperamentally suited for this post, and so Caswall was put in to replace him. (Private communication from Mr Gerard Tracey.)

30 Caswall, Oratory Journal, 27 August 1854.

31 Cf. Letter from Caswall to Newman, 19 February 1855.

32 Cf. Caswall's 1859 Oratory report expressing the community's 'joy' over the release, for which they had been praying so long.

33 Published by the Statistical Society (of London) in its *Proceedings* (1840); cited in Gill, *History of Birmingham*, p. 383.

was a haphazard sort of affair: the manner of organization was far from uniform and no regulations existed to ensure a minimum standard of quality. The commonest types of schools were:[34]

(1) the so-called *dame schools*, each run by an individual woman who was motivated chiefly by the income opportunity it presented. Little if any real teaching took place, the school's main function being to keep the children off the streets for a time.
(2) the privately owned *common day schools*, in which the children of artisans and shopkeepers sat in dirty, ill-ventilated rooms and learned chiefly by rote. Some pupils learned a smidgen of history and geography and some of the girls needlework.
(3) the *endowed schools*, of a considerably higher standard than the previous two, with an average of one hundred pupils each. Some operated in connection with religious establishments. In general the surveyors were 'favourably impressed' with these schools.[35]
(4) the *evening schools*, which mainly taught reading, writing, and arithmetic, along with some grammar, geography, drawing, and more advanced mathematics. The surveyors approved of these schools and 'hoped to see the system extended'.[36] Their drawback was that more than half the pupils were between five and fifteen years old, many of whom must have been working for long hours before beginning their school 'day'.
(5) the *Sunday schools*, which provided another form of part-time schooling. Since they aimed principally at religious instruction they spent a good deal of time on Scripture, but they also taught reading in hopes of forming in the pupils the habit of private Bible reading. Some of the teachers realized that more general learning would encourage regular attendance; thus half the schools also taught writing, while some taught grammar, geography, and history as well, while a few taught some arithmetic. These schools met with general approval in the survey. They had a large attendance, but for three-fourths of their pupils this was the only form of schooling they received.

Clearly, some kind of reform was urgently needed. In 1839, one year after the survey was taken, a Committee of Council for Education was created as an 'embryo Education Department' with education pioneer Dr James Kay-Shuttleworth as Secretary. The

[34] I am indebted to Gill, *History of Birmingham*, pp. 383–5 for this information.
[35] Ibid., p. 383.
[36] Ibid., p. 384.

Committee immediately set about establishing a system of inspection for the schools and announced that all schools wishing to qualify for government grants must submit to the inspection. Not even church-run schools were to be exempt; however, in 1840 a Concordat was negotiated that gave the Archbishops of Canterbury and York the right to be consulted about the appointment of inspectors for Church of England schools and stipulated 'that no person be appointed without their concurrence'.[37] In 1847, once it was accepted that the government had a duty to educate the people, the same procedures for the appointment of inspectors were extended to other denominations, including the Roman Catholics,[38] who had previously been excluded by the implied requirement that the Authorized Version be used for daily reading of Scripture.[39]

The inspectors' duties were formidable. Inspectors were to pay occasional visits to the state-aided schools in order to determine whether the grant had been 'duly applied' and to amass correct information on the 'discipline, management, and methods of instruction' in each school. They were not to exercise control, not to restrain, but to assist and encourage local efforts.[40] The inspectors 'went forth armed with ... forms to fill up over the most extraordinary minuteness ... The information they were to gather was to be exhaustive' and included details of the physical plant and equipment as well as of such matters as numbers and ages of pupils, subjects taught, and qualifications of the teachers.[41]

Indeed, the quality of teaching was soon to feel the Committee's reforming hand. In the late 1830s England's elementary schools were still being run chiefly on the so-called mutual or monitorial system, in which somewhat 'older' children (who might still be as young as eight or nine) called monitors were 'employed', in a sense, to teach the younger children – that is, to pass on to them what they had learned. The defects of this system, already obvious, were aggravated by the poorly qualified schoolmasters and -mistresses who oversaw the monitors' activities:

> As a rule, these adult practitioners were persons of scanty knowledge

[37] Quoted in Mary Sturt, *The Education of the People: A History of Primary Education in England and Wales in the Nineteenth Century* (London: Routledge & Kegan Paul, 1967; repr. 1970), p. 97.

[38] J. Stuart Maclure, *Educational Documents: England and Wales 1816–1968* (London: Methuen Educational Ltd., 1965; 2nd edn 1968; repr. 1969, 1971), p. 46.

[39] Sturt, *Education of the People*, p. 185.

[40] Maclure, *Educational Documents*, pp. 48, 49.

[41] Sturt, *Education of the People*, p. 97.

> and no great force of character. As Kay-Shuttleworth pointed out, nothing but a sense of religious vocation could ensure the presence of suitable men and women in the schools. There were no material attractions. The schoolmaster had no social standing, his income was scanty and precarious, dependent upon fluctuating fees and a contingent share in voluntary subscriptions. Even though he sought and found other posts and occasional jobs to supplement his income from the school, he could only look forward to 'hopeless indigence' (Shuttleworth's phrase) in old age.[42]

As Kay-Shuttleworth stated, 'To entrust the education of the labouring classes to men involved in such straits is to condemn the poor to ignorance and its fatal train of evils.'[43] And the time was now ripe to act: 'the nation had ... recognized that even the working man had a right to live as a human being. The attitudes to education [as a privilege of the elite classes] had changed.'[44]

Accordingly, the Committee tackled the challenge of elevating the level on which the teaching profession was held and providing assistants to facilitate their work. In 1846, building on the monitorial system and adapting from models Kay-Shuttleworth had observed in Holland, they established a plan for the apprenticeship of pupil teachers designed to create a professional teaching corps. Boys and girls at least thirteen years old and of good moral character, who showed an ability to teach and passed certain required elementary examinations, would be indentured for five years as apprentices to Head Teachers.[45] The pupil teacher was considered 'indentured' for one year at a time and had to take an examination at the end of each year.[46] The Government would give grants to the pupil teachers' instructors and would increase the rate of pay if the masters or mistresses taught the apprentices gardening or mechanical art (for boys) or sewing, knitting, cooking, or laundry work (for girls). Once they had completed their apprenticeship, the pupil teachers would sit for a competitive examination. The successful candidates or 'Queen's Scholars' would be awarded exhibitions of £20 to £30 toward their fees at a teacher training college.[47] The

[42] John William Adamson, *English Education 1789–1902* (Cambridge: At the University Press, 1930), p. 134.

[43] *The Minutes of 1846*, quoted in Sturt, *Education of the People*, p. 178.

[44] Sturt, *Education of the People*, p. 177.

[45] The examinations would cover arithmetic, English grammar, composition, and history, geography, religion (including Scripture), vocal music, teaching, and school lesson organization. (Adamson, *English Education*, pp. 143–4.)

[46] Sturt, *Education of the People*, p. 206.

[47] Kay-Shuttleworth founded the first teaching training college in England, St John's College in Battersea, in 1839–40. *Encyclopedia Britannica*, 15th edn (1991), vol. 6, p. 772.

course at this training college would last one, two, or three years. At the end of each year an examination would be given and certificates awarded, thereby qualifying the successful Queen's Scholars as certified teachers.[48] Since these certificates 'conferred status, and carried considerable pecuniary rewards, they were eagerly desired'.[49]

The lot of the schoolmaster and schoolmistress was also to be improved. Each schoolmaster who headed a school eligible for inspection and who had studied at a teacher training college would be granted, as a supplement to his or her salary, between £15 and £30 annually depending on the length of study at teacher-training college, provided that: (1) the school give the schoolmaster a rent-free house and a further salary equalling at least twice the grant amount; (2) the schoolmaster's character, conduct, and 'attention to his duties are satisfactory'; (3) his or her school receive a favourable report from the inspector.[50]

The Oratory's mission schools in Edgbaston

In early February 1855 the Oratory Congregation passed a decree agreeing, in principle, to proceed with building a mission school in Edgbaston and authorizing £200 to be spent on it. The proposed school building project would not be the Oratory's first venture into education: a mission school was already in operation, housed in *ad hoc* premises a few blocks from the Oratory and managed by Fr Nicholas Darnell in merely a private capacity 'with casual help from pious ladies'.[51] Now, however, the Congregation wished to formalize the school's status as a regular part of the Oratory's missionary work. Thus they charged Caswall, as 'head Missioner', with asking Newman to appoint someone who might 'do all that could be done towards getting help from the [Committee of Council on Education] ... with the view of establishing the Edgbaston school on a better footing'.[52]

48 Adamson, *English Education*, p. 144.

49 Sturt, *Education of the People*, p. 182. The visionary Kay-Shuttleworth anticipated that the benefits of this system would extend beyond the immediate goal of improved education in that the new pupil teachers would most likely come from 'families supported by manual labor; there will thus open to the children of such families a career which could otherwise be rarely commenced'. (James Kay-Shuttleworth, *The School in Relation to the State, the Church and the Congregation 1862*, chap. IV, n.p.; quoted in Sturt, Education of the People, p. 180.)

50 *Minutes of the Committee of Council on Education Dated 21 December 1846: Regulations Respecting the Education of Pupil Teachers and Stipendiary Monitors*; cited in Maclure, *Educational Documents*, p. 55.

51 Letter from Caswall to Newman, 21 February 1855.

52 Ibid.

Although Newman thought it 'a very good plan to have some Father to undertake the schools', he declined to make the appointment himself as he did not know the Fathers' 'respective engagements and wishes enough to do so'; instead, he agreed to acquiesce to the nomination made by the Congregation of Deputies.[53] In early March, therefore, the Congregation expressed the wish that Caswall himself 'undertake the office ... of superintending the temporal concerns of the Edgbaston School and endeavouring to put it on a solid basis',[54] charging him 'to discover all that could be got towards such a school from government, or from the Catholic Committee, and so to ascertain all the preliminaries before attempting to *do* anything'.[55] As Caswall explained to Newman, who was pleased to learn of the decision,[56] this was an opportune time for this project: new roads then being built in the immediate vicinity of the Oratory[57] would make the Oratory and especially its schools accessible to a well-populated and, thus far, inadequately served part of town.

After passing the original Decree authorizing the project, the Fathers asked an Edgbaston builder named Nowell to submit an estimate for erecting a schoolroom to adjoin the Oratory. Caswall, as Rector, forwarded the estimate and plans to Newman for his approval and received in reply a caution to 'keep quite close to the Decree about it'.[58] Very shortly thereafter he had to report to Newman that 'matters seem[ed] to be at a fix again',[59] since the Congregation of Deputies had their reservations. Nowell's estimate did not allow for the plumbing for the water closet; the porch, which they considered essential, would exceed the amount permitted by the Decree; and the walls would only be whitewashed and not plastered. The Congregation, therefore, viewed this plan as less than satisfactory and was inclined to set it aside; thus progress was suspended for several months.

53 Letter from Newman to Caswall, 27 February 1855 (*Letters and Diaries* [*LD*] XVI, p. 392).

54 Letter from Caswall to Newman, 5 March 1855; see also the Oratory Journal for the same day.

55 Letter from Caswall to Newman, 14 March 1855.

56 Letter from Newman to Caswall, 14 March 1855 (*LD*) XVI, p. 413.

57 A new road that would connect the road behind the Oratory with Lady Wood Lane would be entirely finished in three months. Newman was very glad to hear of this in a letter from Caswall (5 March 1855).

58 Letter from Newman to Caswall, 16 February 1855 (*LD*) XVI, p. 381. Nowell had estimated a cost of £185 without a ceiling and £200 with, plus £9 for a porch to connect the school with the church: letter from Caswall to Newman, 14 February 1855.

59 Letter from Caswall to Newman, 19 February 1855.

In June Caswall broached the subject again and had Nowell draw up revised plans, with a new estimate of £400; this time, all the Fathers approved. Of the costs £245 would be met by various donors[60] and Caswall had begun soliciting subscriptions, which he hoped would produce £50. He anticipated that he would have to advance the remaining £100 from his own funds. On 26 June he sent the plans and estimate to Newman for his approval, suggesting also that they attempt to get the estimate reduced, for example by having fewer windows. Newman asked whether the proposed building would be on the ground of the Oratory church;[61] Caswall replied that a portion of it would be on the churchyard ground.[62] While Newman did not consider this 'a great difficulty', he did express concern that the £400 would eventually inflate to the 'prodigious sum' of £500; more seriously, he had his reservations about Nowell, whom he had 'never liked' because of some substandard work he had done on their cottage at Rednal. Accordingly, at Newman's suggestion Caswall approached another builder he knew, a Mr Heywood.[63] Heywood's estimate was accepted and he built the school at a cost of £500, 'partly on the land belonging to F. Ambrose St John's Houses; and partly on Oratory land, facing the Plough & Harrow Road'.[64] Among the major donors were the Misses Farrant (£220), Caswall himself (£50), and Miss Munro, a protégé of Newman's (£16 15s 5d).[65]

The new school was ready for use by December 1855.[66] On 4 December Caswall informed Newman that the schools were furnished and would be used the next Sunday for Sunday school and that they 'seem to give great satisfaction'. He also asked Newman whether he would be willing to sell him six card tables, currently in the Oratory and previously in the refectory, for the new school, assuring him that they could still be used 'in the event of their being wanted for any party'.

60 These included £200 from the Misses Farrant originally offered for the mission at Smethwick, and £45 from another donor.

61 Newman to Caswall, 27 June 1855 (*LD*) XVI, p. 495.

62 Caswall to Newman, 28 June 1855.

63 The name is sometimes spelt Haywood.

64 'Some Account of Properties Owned, Held in Trust, Rented, or Otherwise Held, by the Birmingham Oratory. By E. Caswall, F. Treasurer,' p. 195. Caswall kept this notebook, and others after him added updated information as appropriate. The area on which Heywood built his school rooms is now occupied by the apse and sanctuary of the present Oratory church.

65 Ibid., p. 115.

66 Fr Austin Mills wrote to Newman on 27 November 1855 that 'Edward's schoolroom' would be ready for use next Saturday.

In his 1856 report to the Oratory community Caswall had this to say about the recently opened mission schools:

> our schools, both of boys and girls, have been maintained more than efficiently, by teachers who have voluntarily devoted themselves to the work without fee or reward, and the unusual sight has been seen of between thirty and forty boys entirely obedient to the firm but gentle control of a lady's hand. Whatever engagement it may be ultimately necessary to make with regard to the teaching of our schools – of one thing I am convinced – that in after life on looking back upon this year just past, those children both boys and girls will feel what now they perhaps little comprehend – the extraordinary advantages which they have enjoyed ... by the contact into which they have thus been brought ... with the minds of persons belonging to a sphere above their own.

Caswall's fellow-convert Thomas Allies, 'who as a layperson was doing great work in Catholic elementary education',[67] had recommended to Caswall that he apply for a government grant toward the building of the school. Caswall never acted on this suggestion, and the building of the new school was funded with private means as listed above. In December 1856, however, Newman informed Bishop Ullathorne that they hoped to apply for government assistance for maintaining the girls' school during the next half year.[68] In mid Victorian England Roman Catholics, feeling themselves to be a beleaguered lot in the midst of a hostile majority, naturally hesitated before becoming involved with anyone that represented 'an heretical power';[69] thus Catholic school managers found themselves in a dilemma with respect to applying for government grants. But Ullathorne replied his approval, adding that he had no objection to the clergy 'availing themselves of Government aid'.[70] In this case the grant would allow the Oratory to engage a qualified schoolmistress rather than relying on volunteer help. The person they had in mind was Newman's sometime spiritual directee Catherine Anne Bathurst, a certificated teacher and member of the Sisters of Charity of the Precious Blood, who was well acquainted with the Oratory. 'She would come with a trained pupil teacher and assistant for the cooking and other household work,' Newman had told Ullathorne.[71]

[67] Owen Chadwick, *The Victorian Church*, vol. 2 (London: Adam & Charles Black, 1970), p. 416.
[68] Letter from Newman to Ullathorne, 11 December 1856 (*LD*) XVII, p. 475.
[69] Caswall had originally written this phrase in his Oratory report for 1857 but then crossed it out and wrote 'a power which is not Catholic'.
[70] Letter from Ullathorne to Newman, 12 December 1856.
[71] Letter from Newman to Ullathorne, 11 December 1856 (*LD*) XVII, p. 475.

Thirty-year-old Catherine Bathurst, a convert to Roman Catholicism, had begun a parish girls' school when Newman and his fledgling community were still in Alcester Street. She then left Birmingham to join the Sisters of Charity of the Precious Blood, a community based in London. Now, she and other members of that community were sent back to Birmingham to help with the Edgbaston girls' school.[72] In April 1857 a young woman named Ellen Hennessey was apprenticed to her as pupil teacher. Hennessey's official Certificate of Indenture survives, signed by herself and her father on one hand and Ambrose St John, Edward Caswall, and Catherine Anne Bathurst on the other, telling proof of the seriousness with which the Committee of Council on Education took such arrangements.

In his Oratory report for 1857 Caswall expressed his happiness at the 'inauguration' of the Sisters of Charity of the Precious Blood into the Oratory community. The Sisters, he related, 'have most kindly undertaken the management of our girl and infant schools, and under their devoted superintendence leave us nothing to desire'. The boys' school, meanwhile, had 'been placed under a schoolmaster whose heart is truly in his work, and whose discipline at once firm and mild is the guarantee of cheerfulness, order, and good conduct'.[73]

In relating that the schools had now been put 'in connection with goverment' (*sic*), Caswall assured his audience that this arrangement was 'simply annual, and dissolvable at pleasure'.[74] He felt constrained to add, however, that 'the government aid, in obliging us to maintain our schools in a high state of efficiency', in some senses tended 'rather to increase than diminish our expenses'.[75] The regular weekly collections were 'decidedly inadequate' to cover these expenses and he feared that in the near future the Oratory would be compelled 'to make application in some form to all the resident Catholics of the district'.

[72] Caswall's Oratory report for 1856 relates that in that year the Sisters of Charity of the Precious Blood took over the management of the girl and infant schools. Joyce Sugg (*Ever Yours Affly: John Henry Newman and His Female Circle* [Leominster, England: Gracewing, 1996]) observes, 'In work for young people [Bathurst] was extremely efficient, cared for them tirelessly and had an excellent head for management. Outwardly she was more than ordinarily competent and inwardly she was very tender ... Her help was invaluable in the big Oratory parish' (pp. 194, 195). Letter from Newman to Ullathorne, 11 December 1856 (*LD*) XVII, p. 475.

[73] This schoolmaster was probably Benjamin Wilson, a friend of Caswall's from his youth and, like him, a convert to Roman Catholicism, whose married state, however, prevented him from seeking ordination.

[74] Caswall, Oratory report for 1857.

[75] Ibid. This was due to the exacting standards that the schools had to meet in order to qualify for government grants.

The year 1857 also saw Caswall supervising an addition to the boys' school, which was completed in July 1857.[76] A short time later Fr Frederic Bowles proposed still further alterations which Caswall considered to be 'a natural part' of the work carried out during the summer. It involved removing a wall that divided the boys' schoolroom in half and would improve the premises both for day and Sunday school purposes. Heywood had assured them that it was quite a simple matter that could be done in a few days; Caswall and Fr Frederick themselves would meet the 'trifling expense'.

By 1858[77] the girls' day school had nearly 90 children and the night school nearby had 25 young women. The following year showed a steady increase in numbers: the day schools had 81 boys and 120 girls and infants, the Sunday schools 85 boys and 65 girls, while the evening school had 50 girls and young women.[78] The boys' evening school, however, shared the fate of so many of its kind, having gradually dwindled away after a three-year attempt to keep it going: 'It was found by a long experience', Caswall related, 'that after a regular day's work in Birmingham, boys will not permanently undertake the toils of an evening school. In fact they are too wearied out when evening comes to be able to give their minds to instruction, unless they are simply compelled, as in some factories.'

In 1867 the Edgbaston mission schools relocated to a new site that had been purchased by Fr Austin Mills for the orphanage, and here new school buildings were erected to hold 160 children.[79] A financial statement issued in 1870[80] reported that both the boys' and the girls' schools 'have passed creditable examinations under the Catholic Inspector appointed by government, and are entitled to the annual Government Grants'. The Fathers had incurred a deficit of £228 in building the new schools and it was hoped that 'all who are attached to the Oratory' would 'continue their exertions' toward making it up. The statement was signed by Caswall as 'Missioner' and Henry Bittleston as 'School Manager', evidence of Caswall's continued involvement with the Oratory's mission schools.

76 Letter from Caswall to Newman, 16 July 1857. Presumably the work was being done during the school's summer vacation.

77 Oratory report for that year. Newman rather than Caswall gave the report in 1858 (as was customary, at Michaelmas) because he wished to insert a word of praise and gratitude to Caswall for his newly-published book of Hymns and Poems (see chapter 6).

78 Caswall, Oratory report for 1859.

79 The new property was quite sufficiently large enough to house both the mission school and the orphanage. (Personal communication from Gerard Tracey.)

80 'Oratory New Poor School Buildings', 12 March 1870.

In 1870 the Birmingham Diocesan Schools Crisis Committee,[81] of which Caswall was, at the bishop's invitation, a member as well as serving on its Executive Board, published a statistical report that included a list of 'Missions deficient in School accommodation'. The Oratory was not among them.

Establishment of the Oratory mission school at Smethwick

Smethwick: village of dark Satanic mills

Smethwick today is a bustling, crowded, intensely multicultural community near the outskirts of Greater Birmingham. A detailed sketch of the 'aspects and prospects' of Smethwick in 1850, the year in which Edward Caswall first came to Birmingham, was written by one Charles Hicks. According to Hicks the aspects were, on the whole, far from positive, but the prospects were good. The great potential of this village badly needed to be tapped.

The housing was scarcely fit for human habitation. The poorly drained and ventilated 'common tenements and workmen's dwellings, ... continued to yield to their occupants the smallest quantity possible of convenience and comfort, [were] not made to live in, but to get rent for'.[82] As for the 'promotion of knowledge or intellectual culture', this was left to the various churches and their schools. Clearly, it was time for public institutions to remedy their neglect of the large population, who exhibited 'so much rudeness of speech, unrefinement of manners – so much superstition and credulity, and other and worse evils, the brood of ignorance'.[83] The level of reading matter enthusiastically consumed by the scantily educated populace was deplorably low and included not only such 'noxious publications' as adventure stories and romances, but also, to some extent, socialist, communist, and atheist publications.[84]

[81] This committee was convened by the bishop of Birmingham in response to 'the present crisis affecting Catholic schools', namely, at the close of that year the government would discontinue giving building grants, so that, if funds were not raised in some other way, Catholic children in those areas with more children than the local Catholic schools could accommodate would be compelled to attend non-Catholic schools.

[82] Charles Hicks, *A Walk through Smethwick: A Sketch of Its General Aspects and Its Prospects*. A Lecture delivered April 1850 in the British School Rooms, Smethwick (Birmingham: Guest, Allen), p. 18.

[83] Ibid., p. 22.

[84] Ibid., p. 24.

While Smethwick fortunately could not boast 'many notorious dens of vice and infamy', nonetheless there were 'a preponderance of households in which even the lower class of virtues are scarcely found, such as cleanliness, sobriety, industry, prudence, or honesty'.[85] The pauper population was 'relatively small' but varied seasonally. The number of destitute and disabled poor then receiving relief was fifty-six heads of families or 125 persons, while 'only' about thirty casual poor were on the Receiving Officer's list.[86]

Hicks decried the absence of anything aesthetically appealing or uplifting in Smethwick, lamenting that the local gardens more often contained cabbage plants and onion beds than flower plants and tulip beds. We can contend that tulip beds were a luxury while onion beds served to fend off starvation; but we cannot deny Hicks's insight that 'objects of beauty, whether in nature or in art, ... do at length conform the subjective, the inner feelings, aye, and the outer deportment to corresponding grace, sweetness, and refinement. There can be little enjoyment of life, in any pure sense, where aesthetics are disregarded – where objects of art, taste, and beauty are altogether absent.'[87] Not surprisingly, many of the inhabitants used drink as a means of escaping their daily drudgery. The 'most crying evil' in the town was intemperance,[88] and what a blessing it would be 'if one half the sixty Beershops in our Parish were shut up'.[89]

On the positive side, Smethwick's highways and byways had undergone 'considerable improvement of late'[90] and new building was constantly taking place. The two railway lines, when completed, would give impetus to local trade and manufacture. Smethwick's nearness to Birmingham and its advantages to 'enterprizing capitalists and heads of iron factories, for whom Birmingham itself affords less and less room and facility', would ensure its growth. Indeed, Smethwick would soon triple its present size.[91]

The Oratory mission at Smethwick

Another person who was visionary enough to recognize the potential of Smethwick was Edward Caswall. In the Oratory report

85 Ibid., p. 29.
86 Ibid., p. 21.
87 Ibid., pp. 28–9. Cf. Gerard Manley Hopkins, after his pastoral experiences in Liverpool and Glasgow, commenting on the degrading effect of industrial towns on the human spirit.
88 Ibid., p. 30.
89 Ibid., p. 22.
90 Ibid., p. 18.
91 Ibid., p. 32.

delivered in 1857, in which he recorded that the Oratory had just purchased its first plot of land in the village, he alluded to Smethwick's past history as well as to the work to be done there in the future.

Smethwick lay, he said, 'between Birmingham proper and those vast mining districts, the dismal abode of flames and desolation, commonly called the Black country'. The village owed its development to the Industrial Revolution. Here 'was constructed the first of those wonderful engines of modern times which are fast revolutionizing the world – I mean the steam engine'.[92]

> There are carried on those vast operations of forging and foundry works for which Birmingham cannot find sufficient space and there accordingly congregate large shifting multitudes of persons employed on the various works in progress. No sooner is a new forge or foundry raised than at once as by magic there spring up round it long lines of houses as habitations for the work man – and thus, what with building speculations, allotments and the like, Smethwick, amidst much misery, drunkenness, and filth, is rapidly pushing itself forward into a most important and peculiar position.[93]

In this situation Caswall perceived a clear challenge to religious organizations, and above all to Roman Catholics, to preserve or, perhaps, instil some sense of morality and decency. Already Smethwick 'has three Protestant Churches of the establishment, already it has its independent, its wesleyan its Presbyterian and its Baptist chapels, and alas its Mormonites too and scoffing infidels, and in the midst of this mingled mass of heresy and atheism some three hundred Catholics with difficulty preserve the spark of faith.'[94] Three hundred Catholics does not sound a lot when one considers that the 1851 census set the population of Smethwick at 8,379. In the absence of a church of their own, the Roman Catholics of Smethwick had been attending the Oratory church in Edgbaston since its opening in 1853.[95] A Catholic school of sorts was already in operation in Smethwick; consisting of two small rooms in one, it was run as a mixed boys' and girls' school by a Mrs Catton from her home in Cranford Street. It is unclear as to who was ultimately

[92] In 1774 James Watt joined Matthew Boulton in his mill in Soho; in 1796 the famous Soho foundry was built. *Church of St Philip Neri Smethwick: Souvenir Booklet of Consecration Day* (25 June 1936), p. 3.

[93] Caswall, Oratory report delivered 29 September 1857.

[94] Ibid.

[95] In a letter dated 2 November 1854 Caswall could still inform Newman that 'at our Sunday school [in Edgbaston] we have some quite small boys from [Smethwick]'.

responsible for the education offered at the school. One source names Mrs Catton as 'the lady who superintended the teaching there'.[96] In a letter to Newman in November 1854 Caswall mentioned that the school had then been 'managed for some months by Mrs Wootten and Miss French going over there on alternate weekdays and coming back in the evening'. Frances Wootten and Elinor French, both dedicated to helping the Oratory mission in any way they could, were later associated with the Oratory School, Mrs Wootten as 'Chief Dame'[97] and Miss French as her second in command.[98] In any case, the Smethwick Catholic school in this early stage of its existence appears to have been run along the lines of the so-called 'dame schools'. While one cannot make any definite claims as to the quality of the teaching at Smethwick's Catholic school at this time, one can be sure that, unlike many of the dame schools, hope of income played no role in the motivation of the ladies in charge. Attendance at the school seems to have fluctuated, the number of pupils being variously given as sixty in 1854,[99] forty-six in 1855,[100] and nearly forty in 1857.[101]

The decisive catalyst for the Oratory's development of Smethwick was the offer, in the autumn of 1854, of a £200 donation toward that mission. The offer came from two sisters, the Misses Farrant, who over the course of time proved to be generous benefactors of the Oratory's work: a leaflet tribute to Frances Farrant at her death in 1869 described her as 'a Lady who endeared herself to hundreds of the Catholic poor'.[102] Even though ultimately the money was not used for Smethwick, the process of discernment concerning this offer brought to the fore the question of the nature and extent of the Oratory community's involvement in the Smethwick mission.

With Newman occupied in Dublin it fell to Caswall as Acting Superior to moderate discussions on the Farrants' offer and to report them to Newman for his comments or approval. Three of the Fathers favoured the idea of making Smethwick a centre of Oratory activities while three opposed it. Caswall himself favoured 'not making it a centre at once, but gradually nursing it towards

96 *Souvenir booklet*, p. 9.
97 Sugg, *Ever Yours Affly*, p. 252; Mrs. Wootten's role was what today we would call matron or 'house mother'.
98 Ibid., p. 236.
99 In his letter to Newman of 2 November 1854, Caswall gives this figure as reported in the Oratory's return to the bishop.
100 Caswall, Oratory report for 1855.
101 Caswall, Oratory report for 1857.
102 Anonymous leaflet, quoted in Sugg, *Ever Yours Affly*, p. 239.

becoming a future centre'.[103] All agreed that some day it must become an independent mission in its own right;[104] no one had any difficulty with the questions of carrying on the school at Smethwick or about the locality.[105] As to what to do with the money, the general consensus was that the Farrant sisters did not wish to bind the Oratory to any specific application of the money,[106] and three weeks into the discernment process the Fathers voted not to spend the Farrants' donation on Smethwick.[107]

One question that arose in the course of the discussions concerned what would actually be involved in making Smethwick a centre in its own right. Newman was consistently opposed to making Smethwick a centre if it were to entail celebrating masses, administering the sacraments, and preaching on a regular basis. While he left open the question of a school, he believed that the Oratory should be directing all their efforts toward a school in their own immediate neighbourhood in Edgbaston, where a school would be more useful.[108] Caswall tended to agree with Newman on according priority to Edgbaston above Smethwick in all matters. He did, however, admit to a concern for the education in Smethwick because the school in Mrs Catton's house was a 'poor little affair'.[109] Thus when he reported, in September 1857, that the Oratory had just secured a piece of land in the centre of the village, he described the plot as large enough for a church later, 'and where now a school might be erected with great advantage'.[110]

The Oratory property in Smethwick was acquired from a Mr Robert Dolphin in stages between 1857 and 1861 and initially consisted of a Poor School Trust and private property purchased by Caswall with his own personal funds. Caswall's private property, bought in three parcels in 1857, 1858, and 1861, was the largest piece of land, with an area of 7,243 square yards. He purchased it freehold at a total cost of £908 16s 3d and then built a house on it that cost £632 8s.

The Poor School Trust, which adjoined Caswall's property,

[103] Caswall to Newman, 1 November 1854.
[104] Ibid.
[105] Caswall to Newman, 2 November 1854.
[106] Caswall to Newman, 1 November 1854.
[107] Caswall to Newman, 21 November 1854.
[108] See, e.g., Newman to J. D. Dalgairns, [4? November 1854] (*Letters and Diaries* XVI, pp. 286–7); Newman to Ambrose St John, 7 November 1854 (ibid., pp. 289–90); Newman to Caswall, 15 November (ibid., p. 295) and 17 November 1854 (ibid., p. 300).
[109] Caswall to Newman, 2 November 1854.
[110] Caswall, Oratory report for 1857.

consisted of 1,200 square yards and was acquired in April 1858 with the specific purpose of erecting a school house on it. The total cost of this project was £1,103 8s 2d – £165 for the land and £938 8s 2d for the buildings. To finance it, subscriptions and grants had to be solicited from a variety of sources; it was probably necessary to constitute this property as a Trust in order to be eligible for some of these funds. It took some three years for the full amount to be realized, and even then only after Caswall himself had covered the deficit with his own contribution of £128 4s 11d.[111] Grants of £220 and £85 were received from the Privy Council (Committee on Education) and the Catholic Poor Schools Committee respectively. The Privy Council grant was government aid intended to 'promote the education of children belonging to the classes who support themselves by manual labor' and was given to schools founded and maintained by 'voluntary local exertion'.[112] Caswall, on the Oratory's behalf, would in this instance have applied for aid to *establish* a school, that is, a grant toward the actual construction and furnishing of the school. A variety of donors contributed the rest of the money, including Miss Farrant (£50) and the three lay trustees (John Hardman £70; John Poncia and Robert Fletcher £25 each).[113] In 1859 Caswall reported[114] that before construction could begin they would need £200 above the subscriptions already received and that they were hoping for a grant from the Society for the Propagation of the Faith. By autumn 1861 this grant was in hand.[115]

Because of his initiative and commitment to Smethwick Caswall became *de facto* the person responsible for the development of this mission, particularly for superintending its physical and financial affairs. That he was formally recognized as such is indicated by his being named as Treasurer of the Smethwick Catholic Poor Schools on two documents dating from 1861, a statement of subscriptions and expenditures and a paper signed by Newman and Ambrose St John authorizing the payment of the government grant to Caswall as Treasurer for building the Smethwick school.[116] From 1860 there survive, carefully preserved and pinned and folded together,

111 Caswall initially donated £50 and then added £78 4s 11d to make up the deficit.

112 Rt. Hon. The Lords of the Committee of the Privy Council of Education, Revised Code of Regulations, 1862.

113 Edward Caswall, notes on Smethwick, recorded between June and December 1876 in 'Some Account of Properties Owned, Held in Trust, Rented, or Otherwise Held, by the Birmingham Oratory'.

114 Caswall, Oratory report for 1859.

115 A statement of subscriptions and expenditures dated 20 October 1861 lists this donation.

116 The statement is dated 20 October; the authorization is not dated except for the year.

various expense receipts, made out to Caswall and kept with his papers, thus indicating that it was his personal outlay. They include fees for the surveyor, architect, and solicitor, building materials and labour, and over £47 for school furniture. In 1864 estimates for further building work, including £80 for a school bell turret, £17 7s for the bell, and £38 for unspecified work, were sought and received, all addressed to Caswall.

No records survive indicating precisely when the new Smethwick school opened. The amount of £774 for Heywood the builder listed in the expenditures for 1861 suggests that it must have been 1861 or 1862. Caswall endeavoured to secure properly qualified teachers in order to raise the standards above the 'poor little affair' that he had observed at Catton's and thereby to ensure the school's eligibility for government aid toward maintaining the school. Such aid, known as an Annual Grant, was conditional on the attendance records, proficiency of the pupils, qualifications of the teachers, and the general state of the school. To be eligible for the grant a school had to be open to periodic inspection by the government-appointed School Inspector who would certify that the conditions had been met, and it was due to Caswall's efforts that the Oratory school in Smethwick met the government's criteria and thus qualified for the grant.

Once the school building was complete, the next step was to employ qualified teachers. Caswall must have been making enquiries, for in November 1862 he received from a nun in a Liverpool convent a letter of recommendation for two sisters, Matilda and Mary McGarvey, prospective school teachers who wished to secure employment together. They would be very glad to go to Smethwick 'and do all they can to prove themselves worthy of [Caswall's] kindness'. It was proposed that they have a fixed salary of £60 between them and, in the first year, receive nothing out of the capitation grant; but if the grant were to increase, Caswall should, at the end of the second year or rather after the second examination, allow a gratuity of £5–10 to the certificated sister.

The McGarvey sisters were hired and apparently lived up to their promise: in 1865 the Privy Council Office in London advised Caswall[117] that Matilda, Teacher in St Philip's School, Smethwick, had 'passed a successful examination'. Flanagan, the priest at Smethwick, commented to him, 'it is a comfort to know we are sure of one condition for next year's grant, viz. – Miss McGarvie's [*sic*] certificate'.[118]

[117] Letter, n.d.

[118] Letter, n.d. Some sources spell the name McGarvie. That her sister Mary was also certificated is indicated by a form signed by Fathers Caswall, St John, and Scott (then priest at Smethwick) and dated September 1866.

As early as 1863 the Smethwick school came in for official recognition, when H. M. School Inspector informed Caswall, 'I find reasons to place it high among the Catholic schools of Staffordshire. It is already superior to the schools in Wolverhampton, Bilston and Walsall ... considering its youth, I believe you have every reason to be satisfied with its progress and its prosperity.'[119] The news was not all positive, however: the Inspector expressed doubts about the two pupil teachers who had been apprenticed to the McGarveys. While acknowledging their 'good conduct and respectable attainment', he observed that

> they appear – and here I refer especially to E. Hughes – to be settling down into a listless, slovenly mode of instructing their classes, which must certainly reduce them to a low rank among teachers and perhaps destroy their usefulness altogether. They need ... to see daily before them models of teaching of a high order. To you then, ... I should say, endeavour to find these two girls vacancies in some first-rate school where the numbers are large and the teachers numerous and transfer their indentures to the mistress of that school. If they do not propose hereafter to teach school you will be doing them a kindness by releasing them at once from service while yet young enough to enter upon some other way of life.[120]

Caswall and the school managers appear to have retained the pupil teachers, for Emily Hughes again figures in the correspondence the following year. This time the Education Department refused to recognize her as teacher, removed her name from the register, and discontinued further payments on her account.[121] There ensued further correspondence between Flanagan and the Education Department, Flanagan expressing surprise that she would be removed at the very moment when she was preparing to present herself to H. M. Inspectors for the examination.[122] The Education Department then inquired whether the School Managers wished Hughes to be engaged and whether the girl and her parents were also agreeable,[123] to which Flanagan replied in the affirmative. Consequently the Education Department reinstated Emily Hughes's name on the Official Register of Pupil Teachers.[124]

[119] Letter, 25 July 1863.
[120] Ibid. The phrase 'appear ... to be settling down' suggests that the Inspector had visited the school the previous year and thus had a point of comparison.
[121] Letter from Education Department to Flanagan, 16 July 1864.
[122] Letter from Flanagan to Education Department, n.d., reply to letter of 16 July 1864.
[123] Letter from Education Department to Flanagan, 22 July 1864.
[124] Letter from Education Department to Flanagan, September 1864.

In April 1865 a Charitable Trust was established by Caswall's sale of part of his own land for £132 8s to the persons who held the Poor School Trust, 'it being judged right, that owing to the complications involved, the same persons should hold both'.[125] The property consisted of 102 square yards at the back of the Poor School Trust and 295 square yards at the side of it. As with the Poor School Trust, the purpose of the Charitable Trust was to make land available for institutional use and thereby ensure its eligibility for funding: specifically, in Caswall's words, the property would now be intended 'for a Roman Catholic Church or Schools or other religious educational or charitable purpose according to the rites and teaching of the Roman Catholic Church, and under the authority of the Right Revd William Bernard Ullathorne or other person exercising episcopal jurisdiction in Birmingham and its neighbourhood'.[126] Thus a portion of the land that adjoined the house that Caswall had built was set aside for a chapel and sacristy, and these were erected at a cost of £431 8s 6d, thus bringing the total cost of this project to £563 16s 6d. Again donations were solicited from various sources and included £30 from Bishop Ullathorne, £50 and £20 from trustees Poncia and Fletcher respectively, and £164 3s 4d from the Earl of Dunraven, a wealthy convert who became a close friend of Stanislas Flanagan, the priest then in charge of Smethwick's pastoral affairs. The Smethwick chapel was opened on the first Sunday in July 1865.

That same year a new priest, Fr Thomas Scott, replaced Flanagan in Smethwick. Scott thoroughly understood the obligation he was under to raise the deficit for which Flanagan and Caswall had made themselves liable on account of the new buildings and the attached land.[127] He promised that he would not attempt to raise subscriptions for any other purpose until this deficit was made up, and that he would 'lodge [the money raised] in the hands of Fr Caswall'. The thirty-year-old Scott was faced with a formidable challenge; Fr James A. Ellis, who was a boy in Smethwick at the time, related that owing to the poverty of the congregation, Fr Scott 'had a very hard time'.[128]

Caswall never ceased his interest in the Smethwick mission:

[125] Caswall's Smethwick notes, p. 183. In addition to Caswall himself the trustees were Newman, Ambrose St John, John Hardman, John Poncia, and Robert Fletcher.

[126] Caswall's Smethwick notes, p. 185.

[127] Letter from Scott to Flanagan, n.d.

[128] *Souvenir Booklet*, p. 13.

> He would come sometimes on Sundays and say Mass, and he often visited the schools, to the delight of the boys, for he would organize races and sports, or inspect the small plots of land which the lads cultivated while he paid for the seeds and plants.[129]

Caswall also proved himself a proponent of environmental and social concerns:

> Primarily to dissipate the fumes that came from a neighbouring chemical works he conceived the idea of raising a mount at the side of the Presbytery. He promised to pay all expenses; and when Father Scott agreed to the suggestion, the men of the congregation set to work. Many gave their services free, and Mr. Ellis (father of Father J.A. Ellis) lent horses and carts to bring ashes and soil from the surrounding district. But another object of the work was to give employment to men who were out of work owing to trade depression: these were paid by Father Caswall, and many a family had food and clothing through his charity, at a time when the 'dole' and 'relief' were unknown.[130]

In 1876 Fr Scott proposed to build a church and a priest's house. Accordingly the bishop asked Caswall what his intentions were regarding the Smethwick property. On 10 October 1876 Caswall met with the bishop and informed him that he intended to sell from his land what would be needed for the church and the priest's house, but to reserve his own house to be let for the Oratory's benefit. The bishop was satisfied and remarked that the house would do for a convent of sisters for the school, who would pay rent. Accordingly, in December 1876 Caswall sold to the bishop and 'certain priests of the Diocese', for the 'nominal sum' of £279, a corner piece of his property on which the diocese could build a church and priest's house. In fact Caswall only received £132, 'ceding the remainder £142 as a donation to the future church'.[131] Since only Newman and Caswall survived of the original trustees of the School and the Charitable Trusts, four new trustees, all priests of the Birmingham diocese, were added to both the Trusts.[132]

Caswall had been letting his Smethwick house to Fr Scott on a yearly basis, though he reserved the right to let it, along with the land, at any time 'to a layman who can pay better'.[133] He willed the house to Newman and Fr Austin Mills 'for their own private use

[129] Ibid.
[130] Ibid.
[131] Ibid.
[132] Caswall's Smethwick notes, p. 161.
[133] Ibid., p. 173.

and benefit', anticipating that they would 'probably make of it an endowment for maintaining by its proceeds a priest of the Oratory who may need the income', and hoping that 'with the improvement of the mission the priest of the mission may be able to pay a good rent'.[134] In December 1876 Caswall excused Fr Scott from paying the rent but 'strongly advise[d his] heirs and executors to obtain a just payment'.[135] A valuer, he surmised, would surely value the rent at £40 per annum. 'That might be too much to insist on at first', he admitted, 'but as the house is left and intended for the good of the Oratory I earnestly recommend beginning at once with definite payments for rent.'[136]

In all his financial and legal dealings Caswall strove to ensure that all transactions would be in the Oratory's favour above all. In June 1876, aware that his health was failing and that he might not have much longer to live, Caswall wrote down his detailed history of his and the Oratory's involvement with the Smethwick mission. In order to prevent his own property there from ceasing to be private property and 'becoming ecclesiastical through some misconstruction of Fr Edward Caswall's intentions', Caswall sought and obtained a letter from the Bishop acknowledging this land to be private property. He did not specify precisely when he did this, but he did add that the property was 'thus so regarded by Fr Caswall' at the time of his writing these notes (20 June 1876).[137]

In 1912, on the death of Fr Charles Ryder, then Rector of Smethwick, that portion of the Smethwick property which still remained in the ownership of the Oratory was now sold to the diocese of Birmingham for £700. By this time Smethwick had become a populous mission in its own right, and the Oratory needed the money to finance the expansion of its church in Edgbaston.[138] The present church at Smethwick was built in 1893. St Philip's parish school at Smethwick survives, the spiritual descendant of the school begun by the Oratory under Edward Caswall's initiative and largely with his money. On the last page of his Smethwick notes Caswall gives the total cost of the land and buildings (house, schools, chapel and sacristy) as £3,076 1s 11d.[139] Some time later an unknown hand recorded that of this sum Fr Edward contributed £1,579, in other words, more than half.

134 Ibid.
135 Ibid., p. 175.
136 Ibid.
137 Ibid., p. 171.
138 Ibid., p. 177. This note was added in an unknown hand, Caswall having died in 1878.
139 Ibid., p. 191, dated 21 June 1876.

Conclusion

The Oratory parish school in Edgbaston still exists today, largely a legacy of the tenacity of Edward Caswall, who transformed the *ad hoc* educational effort run 'with casual help from pious ladies' to mission schools that complied in every way with exacting government standards, thus ensuring that they kept pace with the educational reforms then under way in England. Further, the Oratory mission at Smethwick, today St Philip's parish under the control of the Archdiocese of Birmingham, owes its existence to Caswall's material generosity and administrative talents. Caswall saw the potential of this industrial village and the challenge to the Oratory to minister to its inhabitants, and thus took the initiative to purchase property there. He superintended the finances, the acquisition and distribution of the property, and the building of house, school, and chapel, and he ensured that the schools would meet government criteria for educational standards. More than half of the cost of this operation came from his own pocket.

It is part of the Oratory's charism to contribute one's own resources to the community, and Caswall clearly lived up to this, even to the extent of ensuring that his own house and land in Smethwick would remain unequivocally under the control and thus for the benefit of the Oratory. Yet in another way Caswall appears not so much to have adopted Newman's Oratorian ideal as to have continued the pastoral orientation of his ministry as an Anglican clergyman. Pius IX's Brief of 1847 establishing the Oratory in England refers to the promoting of religion 'among those in the higher ranks, the more learned and generally among the more educated'.[140] Newman elaborated on this in a letter to Frederick William Faber, stating that '*if there* be a class in Birmingham of sharp intellects, who are the recipients of political power, and who can be made Catholics, I think we are fulfilling the Brief... .'[141] Thus while Newman indeed admitted that '[i]t would be a great thing if we were able to do anything permanent in and for Smethwick', he also maintained, 'much as I desire to encourage plans of conversion among the Protestant poor of Smethwick, I think distinctly we have prior duties to the Protestant rich of Edgbaston'.[142] Caswall, in his five-year tenure as Perpetual Curate

[140] Quoted in Placid Murray, *Newman the Oratorian* (Dublin: Gill & MacMillan, 1969), p. 426.

[141] Letter of Newman to Faber, 16 February 1849 (*Letters and Diaries* XIII, p. 50).

[142] Newman, 'Remarks on the Oratorian Vocation (1856): Rough Draft', quoted in Murray, *Newman the Oratorian*, pp. 312, 307.

at Stratford-sub-Castle, Wilts., strove both to educate and form the children of his flock in the Christian life and to alleviate their poverty, frequently giving them money from his personal funds to buy clothing. Thus Caswall's work with the Edgbaston mission schools and the Smethwick mission can be seen not only as a significant pastoral contribution to Newman's Oratory foundation but also as one important point of continuity between his Anglican and his Roman Catholic ministries. Another such point – his creativity as an author of verse – will be discussed in the next chapter.

Chapter Six

Hymns and Poems

Caswall's fundamental pastoral orientation was not the only locus of continuity between his life as an Anglican clergyman and his ministry as a Roman Catholic priest.[1] His creativity as hymn writer and poet – which, as will be shown, can likewise be regarded as another aspect of his pastoral work – also demonstrates such continuity. Caswall does not fit the cliché of an ivory-tower Romantic poet, if indeed such a figure ever existed. He wrote and published his hymns and poems during a flourishing period of poetical activity in the Churches of England and of Rome. Caswall's creative life spanned both the Anglican and the Roman Catholic halves of his life; thus he made a contribution to hymns, devotional poetry, and poetry in general that cut across denominational boundaries.

In tracing the fate of his hymns in the context of the cottage-industry-writ-large that was Victorian hymnal publishing, this chapter will illustrate the issues confronting the hymn text author in this milieu and describe how Caswall dealt with them, and will thereby also further illumine aspects of his personality. Further, it will discuss Caswall's poems as representative of the English and then the Tractarian poetical traditions and show how he brought his distinctive working methods to bear on crafting a peculiarly Roman Catholic poetic.

[1] Like Newman, Caswall lived approximately half his life as an Anglican and half as a Roman Catholic.

Background

The quarter-century from 1825 to 1850 witnessed a proliferation of poetical creativity accompanying and, indeed, intended to further the ongoing revival in the Church of England. This outpouring of hymns, poems, and other devotional and polemical material in verse – the lines of distinction among these forms are thin if not, frequently, blurred or nonexistent[2] – flourished throughout the heyday of the Oxford Movement and beyond and culminated in the poetic masterworks of Christina Rossetti and Gerard Manley Hopkins on the one hand, and in such great standard hymn collections as *Hymns Ancient and Modern* on the other.

Although published in 1827, six years before the event conventionally regarded as the inauguration of the Oxford Movement,[3] John Keble's *The Christian Year* can be identified as the starting point of this poetic tradition.[4] This 'work of the quintessential Tractarian poet priest "seeking the Deity in poetry or prayer"'[5] is a book of devotional poetry arranged according to the Book of Common Prayer and thus according to the liturgical year, and the poems themselves are structured as prayers. According to G. B. Tennyson, *The Christian Year* 'caused a quiet revolution in prayer and poetry in the Victorian age … The idea of a collection of poems organized in exact sequence of the order of worship in the Prayer Book turns out to be a strikingly original concept in devotional poetry. But it was an idea whose time had come'.[6] The volume achieved phenomenal popularity, appearing over the next several decades in numerous editions, often made to resemble prayer books.[7]

Lyra Apostolica, which followed in 1836, had a very different thrust from the gentle, lyrical *Christian Year*. John Henry Newman,

[2] This will be discussed later in this chapter.

[3] Newman always regarded 14 July 1833, the date of John Keble's Assize Sermon, as the 'official' start of the Oxford Movement.

[4] Margaret Johnson's comment, '[t]o limit the term 'Tractarian' to the years during which tracts were produced suggests a rigidification of terms rather than an awareness of the evolutionary character of the Tractarian Movement, and also restricts the application of a very useful adjective' – while meant for Gerard Manley Hopkins, is equally applicable to Keble (Margaret Johnson, *Gerard Manley Hopkins and Tractarian Poetry* [Aldershot, England, and Brookfield, VT: 1997], pp. 2–3).

[5] G. B. Tennyson, *Victorian Devotional Poetry: The Tractarian Mode* (Cambridge, MA, and London: Harvard University Press, 1981), p. 75.

[6] Ibid., pp. 75, 80.

[7] Johnson records that *The Christian Year* and *Lyra Apostolica* were 'ubiquitous in High Anglican circles, forming part of the regular worship of many families' (*Hopkins and Tractarian Poetry*, p. 17).

who contributed the majority of the poems to this collection,[8] indeed denied that he was writing poetry at all:[9] in the Postscript that he supplied for a later edition he stated that the *Lyra Apostolica* shared with *Tracts for the Times* and the *Church of the Fathers*, with which they were contemporaneous, the object 'of enforcing what the authors considered to be Apostolical or Primitive Christianity, at a time when its principles, doctrines, discipline, usages, and spirit seemed, in the length and breadth of the Anglican Communion, to be wellnigh forgotten'.[10] Accordingly, the authors assumed 'a more didactic and less meditative mode',[11] writing 'with the simple purpose of startling, of rousing, of suggesting thought, and of offering battle'.[12] As Newman recalled saying to a friend at the time, 'We are but bringing out ideas in metre'.[13]

Thus the poetry of the revival ran the gamut from the lyrical and doctrinal to the polemical. Still another dimension, probably the most influential in terms of subsequent history, incorporated both these aspects, acknowledging and claiming the legacy of the Apostolic Church by reviving its ancient Latin hymnody and making it accessible in English translation. Newman's indictment, in *Tracts for the Times* (1836),[14] of the Church of England for its neglect of Latin hymnody resulted in several Tractarian-inspired collections of translations of ancient hymns.[15] In 1837 there came *Hymns of the Primitive Church* by John Chandler, Fellow of Corpus Christi College Oxford and Vicar of Witley in Surrey,[16] and *Ancient Hymns from the Roman Breviary for Domestic Use* by Richard Mant, Bishop of Down and Connor.[17] *Hymns Translated from the Paris Breviary* by Isaac Williams, one of the principal Tractarian poets, followed in 1839[18] and, in

[8] The other contributors were John William Bowden, Richard Hurrell Froude, Keble, Robert Isaac Wilberforce, and Isaac Williams, all of whom were involved in the Oxford Movement.

[9] See LD vol. xi, p. 401.

[10] London: Rivingtons, 1879, p. vi.

[11] Johnson, *Hopkins and Tractarian Poetry*, p. 37.

[12] *Lyra Apostolica*, p. vi.

[13] Ibid.

[14] Tract 75, 'On the Roman Breviary as Embodying the Substance of the Devotional Services of the Church Catholic', in *Tracts for the Times by Members of the University of Oxford*, Vol. 3, *For 1835–6*, new edn (London: Printed for J.G.F. & J. Rivington, 1840).

[15] Ian Bradley, *Abide with Me: The World of Victorian Hymns* (London: SCM Press, 1997), p. 22.

[16] John Chandler, *Hymns of the Primitive Church: Now first collected, translated, and arranged* (London: John W. Parker, 1837).

[17] Richard Mant, DD, *Ancient Hymns from the Roman Breviary for Domestic Use, to which are added original hymns*, new edn (London: Rivingtons, 1871).

[18] Isaac Williams, *Hymns Translated from the Paris Breviary* (London: J.G.F. & J. Rivington, 1839).

1848, *Hymns for the Week, and Hymns for the Seasons* by William John Copeland,[19] Caswall's friend, Fellow of Trinity College Oxford, and Rector of Farnham in Essex.

Lyra Catholica

That Caswall would join his voice to the growing chorus of translators of the ancient hymns was, perhaps, inevitable. His Oxford training had, after all, instilled in him a familiarity with the classical world and, as *The Art of Pluck* had shown, a facility with the Latin language, and from his fascination with Newman it is reasonable to assume that he had read Tract 75 and taken it seriously.[20] But more than that, a pressing pastoral issue would have intensified a Tractarian predilection for antiquity to provide Caswall with the impetus for translating the ancient hymns. In his conversion journal he had articulated his concerns about the Latin liturgy, which he had observed in Ireland, being unintelligible to the laity, and in that same journal he also sketched his early efforts at translating some of the more popular hymns.[21] This suggests that a major motivation for his translations was a wish to compensate for the inaccessibility of the Latin ritual by making available, in the vernacular, a significant portion of the Roman Catholic liturgical tradition that laypersons could read and pray in private.

Accordingly, in 1849 – two years after his conversion to Rome – Caswall published *Lyra Catholica*, his first collection of hymns,[22] all translations of Latin texts. In its Preface he acknowledges 'the help he has received from existing versions'[23] and quotes extensively from *The Catholic Choralist*,[24] a collection chiefly of translations of Latin hymns as found in the Office of Vespers.[25]

Referring to the omissions of the Matins and Lauds hymns from *The Catholic Choralist*, Caswall expresses the intention now to

19 William John Copeland, *Hymns for the Week, and Hymns for the Seasons translated from the Latin* (London: W.J. Cleaver and John Henry Parker, 1848).

20 This Tract had appeared in 1836, while Caswall was still at Oxford.

21 E.g., an attempt at a blank-verse rendition of *Salve Regina*.

22 Edward Caswall, *Lyra Catholica: Containing All the Breviary and Missal Hymns with Others from Various Sources* (London: James Burns, 1849).

23 Ibid., Preface, p. xii.

24 Ibid., p. v.

25 [William Young, ed.,] *The Catholic Choralist. For the Use of the Choir, Drawing Room, Cloister, and Cottage*, harmonized and arranged for voice, band, piano forte, organ (Dublin: Catholic Choralist Office, 1842). It also contained a selection of twenty Temperance Hymns intended to combat a 'great evil' besetting the world (Preface, p. xi).

remedy this lack.[26] Notable for being the first complete translation of the Latin hymns,[27] *Lyra Catholica* represents Caswall's

> attempt to exhibit, for the first time in English form, the entire series of those divine Hymns, which, in their Latin originals, have through the years been, and still continue to be, to countless saintly souls, the joy and consolation of their earthly pilgrimage ... There is reason to believe that nearly half the hymns here given have never before appeared in the English tongue.[28]

The volume comprises all the hymns from the Roman Breviary, including those from the Office of the English saints, the hymns and sequences of the Roman Missal, and 'Hymns from various sources'.[29] Among the latter are hymns for various feasts and saints' days from the Breviaries of Cluny and Paris and from the *Raccolta delle Indulgence*.[30]

A laudatory review of *Lyra Catholica* by one Dr Russell appeared in the *Dublin Review* shortly after the book's publication.[31] Opening with a brief discussion of earlier collections, which had only contained selections, the reviewer asserts that violence is done to the integrity of the liturgical year and to the essential Catholicity of the Breviary by making an arbitrary selection of hymns for translation; thus he praises the completeness of Caswall's collection.

> Mr. Caswall [could not] have earned a stronger title to the gratitude of the Catholic body in England, than that which he may rest upon the volume now before us. His collection ... is complete, supplying a metrical version of every hymn in every office and mass throughout the year; it is free from those arbitrary and capricious mutilations which destroy the unity and pervert the character of the original; it

[26] Caswall composed his translations during 1847 and 1848, 'circumstances having afforded him, during the past year, an unlooked-for amount of leisure' (*Lyra Catholica*, Preface, p. vi). Here he refers to the loss of his living as an Anglican clergyman due to his conversion; thanks to his independent financial means he had no urgent need to seek paid employment.

[27] The earlier translation collections had only contained selections.

[28] Ibid.

[29] Ibid., p. vii.

[30] The *Raccolta* was a special collection of indulgenced prayers first published in 1807 and specially approved by the Sacred Congregation of Indulgences in 1849 (cf. Mary Heimann, *Catholic Devotion in Victorian England* [Oxford: Clarendon Press, 1995], p. 73). It was first translated into English by Newman's good friend and fellow Oratorian priest Ambrose St John and published in 1857 as *The Raccolta: or, Collection of Indulgenced Prayers*, Authorized Translation by Ambrose St John (London: Burns & Lambert, 1857). Caswall had contributed most of the verse renditions to Fr Ambrose St John's translation.

[31] *Dublin Review* 26, no. 52 (June 1849): pp. 300–15.

> is, above all, fully and fearlessly Catholic in its spirit, in its tone, in its imagery, and in its language. And, in addition to these negative, but yet very important excellencies, its positive merits, in a literary point of view, are of the very highest order.[32]

Calling the translations of the 'great and striking' hymns 'eminently successful', the reviewer adds that 'in the most plain and unpoetical of them all, he has ... succeeded in preserving all the plainness and simplicity of the original, without permitting it to degenerate into commonplace, or, at least, into inelegance'.[33] Even with the proper hymns of saints, as a rule the least poetical of all the Breviary hymns, Caswall has, in many instances, 'succeeded in working up ... these simple materials into no inconsiderable degree of poetical beauty'.[34]

Caswall had sent Newman a copy of *Lyra Catholica* while it was still in proof stage. In Newman's opinion Caswall 'succeed[ed] better with the tranquil and the gentle than the more vigorous',[35] otherwise most of Newman's criticisms concern Caswall's choices of metre. What is especially interesting is that Newman feels that he could have made more valuable comments had he been clear as to the purpose of Caswall's translations. Still, he says, 'If I did not think your translations on the whole very happy, I should not criticize so much in detail'.[36]

Caswall's poetry collections

Unlike his hymn translations, many of Caswall's original poems were written during his Anglican days, some as early as his first year at Oxford – that is, when he was eighteen years old.[37] The early poems were conventional for their time – for example, drawing on some aspect of nature for a moral lesson, frequently on the theme

32 Ibid., pp. 304–5.
33 Ibid., p. 306.
34 Ibid., p. 313. He reproduces the Vesper Hymn of St Hermenegild, martyr, as an example.
35 Letter from Newman to Caswall, 21 May 1848 (*Letter and Diaries* XII, p. 207).
36 Ibid., p. 208.
37 This is evident from a manuscript that Caswall titled *Peritura*, which includes all the poems written up to and including 1849 with their dates. Caswall is not likely to have written, or at least completed, any poems before 1833, the date of the earliest poems in this manuscript; his thoroughness would have led him to include all complete poems in this, his earliest deliberate compilation of his poems, for it does indeed include a number of poems that he has marked 'not for publication'.

of the transience of earthly life. Some of them had 'appeared already in magazines, songbooks, and works of devotion', [38] he mentions in a 'Notice' appended to the front of a manuscript collection of his poems that he completed in 1852. The Notice states clearly, in the event of his 'dying unexpectedly', that he had 'prepared these poems with a view to publication'.[39] Although he does not explicitly give reasons for publishing his poetry, presumably two motives were operative: a wish, arising from his pastoral sensibilities, to provide hymns and devotional poems for Roman Catholics, and a desire to fulfil, in part, his youthful ambitions for a literary career. Thus the young satirist who twenty years earlier had aspired to fame as an author was now embarking on a new vocation as poet–priest who would channel his muse to nourish the souls of a widespread flock.

The realities of priestly life and its responsibilities in the burgeoning industrial mission area of Birmingham – he was ordained priest some seven months after penning this Notice for his manuscript compilation – must have laid a major claim to the time and energy of the new Father Caswall, for it would be still nearly six years before his collection of poems was published. Titled *The Masque of Mary and Other Poems*[40] and issued in 1858, it was Caswall's second book of verse and his first to include original work.[41] This volume contains a selection of the *Lyra Catholica* translations plus a few new translations that had been composed for an English version of the *Raccolta*; the bulk of the collection, however, consists of original compositions, some as much as twenty-five years old, for in it Caswall included all of the poetry written since the early 1830s that he considered worthy of publication. These include the title work, two other extended poems, sixteen odes, and ninety-nine shorter poems categorized under either 'Miscellaneous Pieces' (forty-eight) or 'Hymns and Meditative Pieces' (fifty-one). The lengthy verse drama from which *The Masque of Mary* takes its name, 'A Masque of Angels before Our Lady in the Temple', was composed in response to a suggestion from Newman that Caswall write a drama, although

[38] He does not give names or dates of the periodicals, and does not appear to have saved any copies of them.

[39] Should that event occur, it was up to 'the Superior of the Oratory ... to publish or not, wholly or in part, at his discretion'.

[40] Edward Caswall, *The Masque of Mary and Other Poems* (London: Burns & Oates Ltd., 1858).

[41] It was reissued simply as *Poems* in 1861. The publisher had suggested the title change to Caswall to increase sales; the elimination of the mention of Mary in the title would certainly have made the book more palatable to non-Catholics and thereby furthered the ecumenical influence of his original hymns.

Newman 'did not fix any subject'.[42] It portrays a pageant presented as a gift to Mary on her seventh birthday in which the angels assume all the roles – for example, various prophets, choirs of virgins and priests, Adam and Eve. Lavish praise is heaped on the young girl, but amid all the exuberance it is clear that her worthiness of such adulation depends on her role as mother(-to-be) of the long-awaited Saviour.

In 1865 Caswall issued a smaller collection called *A May Pageant and Other Poems*,[43] which contained the ambitious epic of the title, a verse drama in three scenes titled *The Minster of Eld*, and ten miscellaneous hymns, seven original and three translated. The lengthy title poem on its own went through several reissues in different versions; Caswall seemed to have felt the need to experiment with revisions of this work.

The last collection of Caswall's verse to appear in his lifetime was published in 1872.[44] It comprised a kind of 'omnibus edition' of the *Lyra Catholica* translations along with most of his original works, including some newer ones not previously published.[45] A new edition of the hymns and poems, published in 1908, included the 'Biographical Note' by Edward Bellasis.[46]

Hymns, poems, and meditative pieces: distinctions

While Caswall labelled about half of his original works 'Miscellaneous Pieces' and the other half 'Hymns and Meditative Pieces' in his 1858 collection, in the lengthier 1872 volume the 'Miscellaneous Pieces' had been rechristened 'Poems'. This gives rise to several questions: Can one distinguish clearly between Caswall's 'hymns' and his 'meditative pieces'? Is his distinction between 'Hymns and Meditative Pieces' on one hand and

42 From a 'Notice' prefacing *Poems Original and Translated*, a manuscript of Caswall's works compiled by him in 1852. Bellasis reports that the 'Masque' 'was chiefly taken from the writings of "the last of the Greek Fathers," St John Damascene, to illustrate Our Lady's place in the Church' ('Biographical Note', 11). I am grateful to Dr John McGuckin for pointing out the parallel to the Orthodox feast of the Entrance of Mary to the Temple (personal communication).

43 Edward Caswall, *A May Pageant and Other Poems* (London: Burns, Lambert, & Co., 1865).

44 Edward Caswall, *Hymns and Poems Original and Translated*, 2nd edn (London: Printed by Spottiswoode & Co., 1872).

45 *A May Pageant* was omitted from this collection.

46 Edward Caswall, *Hymns and Poems Original and Translated*, New Edn with Biographical Preface by Edward Bellasis (London: Burns & Oates, 1908).

'Poems/Miscellaneous Pieces' on the other an arbitrary one, or can certain characteristics be discerned that differentiate one category from the other?

The failure to differentiate clearly between hymns and other forms of religious versification[47] was common among authors, compilers, and publishers in nineteenth-century England. Several factors contributed to the blurring of this distinction. First, the myriad hymnal compilers in Victorian England frequently included in their collections, and set to music, selections from the flourishing devotional and other poetry of the period that the authors never intended to be sung.[48] Second, a large number of hymn collections – ranging from books of translations by one author to compilations of original and translated works by many different authors – were published in which it was unclear whether the contents were primarily intended to be sung at worship or read for private devotion. William Copeland, for example, while he seems to express the hope that the ancient hymns, plainly superior to 'all modern Hymns', would replace or at least supplement the latter in worship services, does not actually specify whether he intended his translations primarily to be sung at public worship or read at home for private devotion.[49]

Yet other hymnals appeared that were explicitly meant to serve the dual purposes of public worship and private devotion. As its full title implies, *The Catholic Choralist. For the Use of the Choir, Drawing Room, Cloister, and Cottage*, was one of these. The Preface suggests that the hymns and canticles of the Office 'might ... be frequently ... *recited* by [the laity] with great spiritual benefit and fruit'.[50]

Finally, hymn collections were published that were intended principally, even exclusively, for personal devotional use even though most of their contents were originally meant to be sung, while the entire original contents of still other hymnals, though

47 Recall Newman's claim that *Lyra Apostolica* was not poetry at all but 'ideas in metre'.

48 Newman's 'Lead, Kindly Light' is probably the most famous example.

49 Copeland, *Hymns for the Week*, Preface, p. iv. Copeland encourages his readers to 'trust that there is that spirit amongst us which may discover and appreciate the characteristics which distinguish the ancient from all modern Hymns, and which will be more or less discernible through the poorest translation, their dogmatic precision, their reverential fervour, and sympathetic tendencies'.

50 Italics added. This collection also had a polemical purpose and harboured aspirations of moral reform. The compiler hoped that other Christian denominations would 'feel gratified in being disabused ... of many erroneous notions which they had been taught to entertain respecting Catholic doctrines and practices' (Preface, p. viii).

titled 'hymns', were destined primarily for private consumption.[51] In his Preface to *The Book of Praise from the Best English Hymn Writers*,[52] Roundell Palmer makes clear that he did not intend to add to 'the multitude of congregational hymnals' but rather to present 'a collection of such examples of a copious and interesting branch of popular literature, as ... have seemed to the Editor most worthy of being separated from the mass to which they belong'.[53] Thus Palmer's book took its place among a 'booming market [of hymn anthologies] solely designed to be read at home as devotional poems'.[54] As we have seen, Keble's *Christian Year* was the book that launched the popularity of devotional poetry for home use. Although some of the poems in Keble's collection were eventually set to music and achieved success as hymns,[55] Keble set out to write not 'hymns' but, as he called it in the subtitle, 'Thoughts in Verse'.

Among the hymn collections consisting entirely of original 'hymns' destined principally for the private market the sick-bed proved an important and successful 'niche market': Charlotte Elliott's *The Invalid's Hymn Book*, for example, which first appeared in 1835, sold over 13,000 copies in twenty years, and the noted Anglican hymnologist John Mason Neale produced two such collections, *Hymns for the Sick* (1843), which contained hymns for various physical ailments, and *Hymns for the Sick-room* (1860).[56] Hymnals sold in huge quantities in Victorian England because they were bought by individuals for private devotional use as well as by churches for worship. As Bradley notes, 'They appeared at a time of rapidly rising literacy as a result of advances in education, and appealed to a public that had a seemingly insatiable appetite for reading, particularly devotional works.'[57] Thus the hymn collections not primarily (or not at all) intended for use at public worship witness to an expanded vision of the applicability of hymns: private devotion was considered a valid use for hymns along with their public function.

In his Preface to *Lyra Catholica* Caswall quotes the *Catholic*

[51] Many hymnals had two sections, one very successful example being the *Congregational Hymn Book*, published in 1836. Its editor, Josiah Conder, included 500 hymns for public worship and 120 for private devotion (Bradley, *Abide with Me*, p. 57).

[52] *The Book of Praise from the Best English Hymn Writers*, selected and arranged by Roundell Palmer (London: Macmillan & Co., 1867).

[53] Ibid., p. i.

[54] Bradley, *Abide with Me*, p. 57.

[55] E.g., 'Blest are the pure in heart', 'New every morning is the love'.

[56] Ibid., p. 56.

[57] Bradley, *Abide with Me*, p. 57.

Choralist's suggestion that the hymns and canticles of the Office 'might be frequently ... *recited by*' the laity,[58] yet he also refers to *Lyra Catholica* as a 'contribution to the existing store of Catholic vernacular hymns'.[59] Further, he feels it necessary to point out that 'the greater number [of the Latin hymns] appear to have been originally written, not with a view to private reading, but for the purpose of being sung [by monks and other religious in choir]'.[60] Thus Caswall indicates that he intended *Lyra Catholica* as a resource for private devotion, while also suggesting that its contents can add to the existing sung repertoire at services. Caswall, then, allows that a hymn can validly serve two purposes: the hymn's proper function of enhancing public worship, and the function that belongs to devotional poetry, that of aiding personal prayer. And even when serving the latter purpose, the hymn still must retain the essential character of a hymn.

How, actually, would nineteenth-century hymnologists have defined a 'hymn'? Based on the viewpoints of various prominent writers of the period,[61] a hymn can be defined as an aid to public devotion, sung by the people in worship services, and articulated in verse, but in simple, straightforward language, as distinct from artificial, affected language or the elevated language of poetry proper; the hymn serves to inculcate a devotional, theological, or

58 Caswall, *Lyra Catholica*, Preface, p. v. Italics added.

59 Ibid., p. vi.

60 Ibid., pp. vii–viii.

61 The Edinburgh minister W. L. Alexander ('Lectures on the Public Psalmody of the Church', *The Scottish Congregational Magazine*, August 1848, p. 254; quoted in Bradley, *Abide with Me*, p. 52) wrote that hymns embody 'some great principle or idea of a devotional kind', set forth in verse words that are sung to an attractive tune, thereby familiarizing the mind with the idea that is 'surrounded with agreeable associations, which tend to make us love it, and cling to it'. R.H. Baynes (*Lyra Anglicana* [1863], Preface, p. vi; quoted in Bradley, *Abide with Me*, p. 52) acknowledged the power of hymns 'to influence our views, and mould our theology', adding that hymns are a 'fitting ... expression for ... deep religious feeling'. In the Preface to his annotated edition of *Hymns Ancient and Modern* (1867) the Rev. L. C. Biggs stated that a hymn must be devotional, intelligible, earnest, and 'simple enough to allow its material to be immediately comprehensible' (quoted in Susan Drain, *The Anglican Church in Nineteenth Century Britain: Hymns Ancient and Modern [1860–1875]*, Texts and Studies in Religion 40 [Lewiston, Lampeter, and Queenston: Edwin Mellen Press, 1989], p. 40). A century earlier the Revd John Newton had said that hymns 'should be hymns, not odes, if designed for public worship'; Sir Roundell Palmer asserted, 'Affectation or visible artifice is worse than excess of homeliness'; while Dean Alford maintained that the lines of a hymn 'should be cunningly wrought, so that they may easily find their way to the ear of the simplest, and stay unbidden in his memory'. The last three are quoted in Josiah Miller, MA, *Singers and Songs of the Church: Being Biographical Sketches of the Hymn-Writers in All the Principal Collections*, 2nd edn (London: Longmans, Green, & Co., 1869), p. vii.

religious idea into the hearers'/singers' hearts and memories.

These characteristics of a hymn are intimately related to and dependent upon one another. A hymn's suitability for congregational singing depends on its 'simple, straightforward language'. Caswall, and others, would add that a hymn's suitability for public worship depends on whether it confines itself to inculcating devotional, theological, or religious ideas into people's hearts and memories, for if instead it crosses over into expressing feelings, which, by their nature, are individual rather than communal, the verse is no longer appropriate for public use – it has become devotional poetry. For Caswall objectivity was an essential characteristic of hymnody:

> An advantage [of the Latin hymns in *Lyra Catholica*] not to be despised in a sentimental age is the exceedingly plain and practical character of these Hymns. Written with a view to constant daily use, they aim at something more than merely exciting the feelings ... Their character is eminently objective. Their tendency is, to take the individual out of himself; to set before him, in turn, all the varied and sublime Objects of Faith; and to blend him with the universal family of the Faithful. In this respect they utterly differ from the hymn-books of modern heretical bodies, which, dwelling as they do, almost entirely on the state and emotions of the individual, tend to inculcate the worst of all egotisms.[62]

In her comprehensive section on The Theory and Function of Hymnody[63] Susan Drain terms Caswall's judgments 'somewhat extreme'; she admits, however, that 'his understanding of what is objective is valid, and is a useful standard, in that he never repudiates the human element: his objectivity is simply a larger concern, the common interest of the universal family of the faithful, as opposed to the individual and egotistic'.[64] Caswall would have shared Drain's view that no hymn can possibly be 100 per cent objective; we finite humans only know God through our own experience, and elements of that experience are bound inevitably to find their way into our hymns.[65] Nevertheless, objectivity was an impor-

[62] Caswall, *Lyra Catholica*, Preface, pp. viii–ix. Here Caswall surely had the Wesleys' and other Methodist hymns in mind. Edward Houghton, in *The Handmaid of Piety and Other Papers on Charles Wesley's Hymns* (The Wesley Fellowship, 1992), presents quite a different viewpoint on Wesley, but the scope of my work does not permit a detailed discussion of Houghton's research.

[63] Drain, *The Anglican Church in Nineteenth-Century Britain*, pp. 23–75.

[64] Ibid., p. 56.

[65] Drain maintains that 'there are hardly any hymns which are wholly objective ... Almost always, ... an element of human experience intrudes ... [A] hymn cannot objectively dwell on the infinite qualities of God which finite humans cannot know save through their own necessarily subjective experience of them. The two are inevitably and inextricably bound up.' (Ibid., p. 48.)

tant criterion in the selection of material for hymnals: many major hymnal compilers, as we will see, would not include hymn texts that contained subjective language, or they would alter words as necessary in order to eliminate personal elements and thereby make the text more suitable for communal worship. Objectivity is also eminently useful as a standard by which to answer the question, posed earlier, as to whether and how one can distinguish among Caswall's various types of religious verse. Further, the essential 'sung' nature of hymns yields still another criterion – singability – by which Caswall's translations compare favourably with those of most of his contemporaries.

Six of Caswall's 'Hymns and Meditative Pieces' are actually titled 'Hymn'. The Hymn to the Holy Ghost[66] ('Grace Increate! From whose vivific fire') apostrophizes the Holy Spirit as Lord and Giver of Life, source of all grace that undergirds virtuous human endeavours, and implores the Spirit's continued help for final perseverance. Although formulated in the first person singular,[67] this latter part of the prayer articulates a request shared in common by all believing Catholics.

The Hymn to the Precious Blood[68] ('O precious Life-Blood of the Lord') consists of thirteen stanzas. Nine of them constitute a litany of praise, the first two or the first and third lines of each of these stanzas beginning with 'I praise Thee'. The use of the plural in the first two stanzas[69] raises the question why Caswall switched to the singular for the praises; however, the hymn throughout presents solid christological doctrine in which the Precious Blood sometimes figures literally and sometimes as a metonym for Christ.

The Hymn for Christmas[70] – better known (and loved) as 'See, amid the winter's snow' – has a refrain exhorting the listener, '*Sing* through all Jerusalem, / Christ is born in Bethlehem'. In his study of the English hymn[71] J. R. Watson comments on this hymn as a model of Caswall's treasured objectivity:

> It develops into a dialogue between the singers and the shepherds . . ., and then into a reflection on the divine love. It eschews any reference to the individual: the singers are too busy taking part in the

[66] Caswall, *Masque of Mary*, p. 254.
[67] From grace to grace, /Oh, grant me to proceed;
[68] Caswall, *Hymns and Poems*, p. 276.
[69] We strive to estimate Thy worth . . . /And must we then to Angels leave /A task too high for mortal men
[70] Caswall, *Masque of Mary*, p. 259.
[71] J. R. Watson. *The English Hymn: A Critical and Historical Study* (Oxford: Clarendon Press, 1999),

> drama, asking the shepherds questions and exclaiming at the wonder of the Incarnation ... [T]he refrain provides the redemptive theology, leaving the verses to get on with the narrative and the reflection.[72]

Bishop William Ullathorne, who was Bishop of the Diocese of Birmingham during the early decades of the Oratory, apparently introduced in Coventry, for the first time in England, various devotions among which were May processions with the image of Mary.[73] Since Coventry is not far from Birmingham, it is not unreasonable to suppose that a devotion such as the May procession was soon adopted in the Oratory's home city and that Caswall, who was deeply devoted to the children under the Oratory's spiritual care, wrote his Children's Hymn before Our Lady's Image in the Month of May[74] to accompany such processions.[75] This hymn, well known by its first line, 'This is the image of the Queen', has a chorus to be sung by all, while the stanzas are apportioned among different children, the first four children each being assigned four-line stanzas and eight additional children each getting two lines.[76] The lines entrusted to the fifth to twelfth children are constructed so as to allow the omission of some (without any sense of incompleteness) depending on the number of children available. The text, very consciously Roman Catholic with its pointed opening reference to the *image* of the Queen,[77] encompasses a number of commonly held elements of Marian faith and devotion, including a reference to the Immaculate Conception[78] – defined as a dogma four years before the publication of Caswall's book – and each version of the chorus asks Mary's prayers;[79] but it is a far cry from Faber's emotional and exuberant Marian hymns: for Caswall, Mary is Queen and Lady, not Faber's sweet Mother. Given their very diverse family and religious backgrounds – Caswall came from a large, intact, staunchly Anglican family while Faber had lost his mother at the age of fifteen and always remained heavily influenced by Evangelicalism – it was

72 Ibid., pp. 370–1.
73 Heimann (*Catholic Devotion in Victorian England*, p. 61) quotes two biographers of Ullathorne who make this claim.
74 Caswall, *Masque of Mary*, p. 265.
75 Ullathorne, who was active in Coventry from 1846, became Bishop of Birmingham in 1850 and founded a convent in Coventry in 1853.
76 This suggests the practical consideration that the greater the number of lines, the more difficult it is to find children who can manage them.
77 Recall the significance of veneration of images for Caswall during his conversion journey.
78 O Virgin born without a stain.
79 Do thou remember me!

inevitable that they should differ widely in their respective approaches to Marian hymn texts.[80]

After he published *Lyra Catholica* Caswall received numerous requests to translate other Latin hymns. One request was for a set of hymns from the Office of Reparation to the Blessed Sacrament. Caswall may well have written his own Hymn of Reparation to the Most Holy Sacrament[81] as a complement to these. The opening two (of thirteen) stanzas express, on the one hand, a restrained – not an emotional – joy at being in Christ's sacramental presence, and, on the other, grief at the thought of those who either deny or profane this gift. At the same time, however, the hymn immediately establishes the doctrine of the Real Presence and also touches on Christ's Passion endured for humanity and on Caswall's favourite theme of the vanity and fleetingness of life.

The Hymn for Renewal of Baptismal Vows[82] has eleven stanzas, of which five of the first six[83] are followed by a refrain renouncing 'Satan and his pomps for ever'. Stanzas seven through eleven ask Jesus' protection and invoke the intercession of Mary, Joseph, and the other saints and angels.

Three of the above six pieces with a 'Hymn' title, then, have refrains, and all were written with specific liturgical or extra-liturgical applications in mind. They were very likely the only original texts Caswall consciously wrote as hymns, that is, to be sung at public worship. This is not to say, however, that Caswall never envisaged any of the other 'Hymns and Meditative Pieces' being sung or that he deliberately intended them not to be sung. His Prayer to Jesus in the Blessed Sacrament ('O Jesus Christ, remember when Thou shalt come again') is a prime instance of a text that achieved considerable popularity as a hymn.[84] It is not difficult to see why: the six brief stanzas are models of simplicity and straightforwardness; they ask Jesus' mercy at the time of judgment out of

80 Cf. my paper 'Family of Origin, Early Life Experience, and Two Nineteenth-Century English Catholic Hymn writers: Faber's and Caswall's Marian Hymns', delivered at the Conference on Christianity and Literature meeting in Santa Clara, Calif., May 1998. It was the prolific hymnal compiler Orby Shipley who drew attention to Caswall and Faber as complementing each other with respect to the types of hymns each wrote: 'The vigorous dogmatic hymns of Father Caswall ... are well supplemented ... by the more subjective, emotional and personal hymns from the large heart of Father Faber' (*Annus Sanctus: Hymns of the Church for the Ecclesiastical Year* (London & New York: Burns & Oates, 1884), Preface, p. 16.

81 Caswall, *Hymns and Poems*, p. 290.

82 Ibid., p. 296.

83 Stanzas one and two are sung consecutively.

84 I have yet to discover an instance of any of Caswall's 'Poems' being included in a hymnal.

consideration that the supplicant during his or her lifetime acknowledged and adored Jesus as present in the Sacrament of the Altar. Another intriguing example is 'I met the Good Shepherd', its dialogue interspersed with first-person narrative strongly echoing a traditional folk-ballad style. This piece, too, made its way into a number of nineteenth-century hymnals, set to various tunes.

It is notable that, while Caswall values objectivity highly as a quality of hymn texts, his definition of 'objective' appears to depart from others' – for example, the compilers and editors of hymnals, as we will see – in that he does not automatically regard use of the first person singular as subjective. Rather, the overall thrust of the text is the determining factor for objectivity. Thus, for example, in the Hymn to the Precious Blood he can repeat, over and over, 'I praise Thee', but always as a preface to some aspect of christocentric belief, not as an emotional expression of the individual soul's attitude toward God.

How do the 'Hymns' and 'Meditative Pieces' differ from one another? The 'Meditative Pieces' lack any formal features of hymns such as a refrain; but as a group their language is not consistently less suited for congregational singing than are the 'Hymns', as we have already noted with 'O Jesus Christ, remember'.

In her discussion of Hymnody and Hymnology Susan Drain makes a distinction between Religious Poetry and Poetry of Religion that can usefully illumine the essential difference between Caswall's Meditative Pieces and his Poems.[85] *Religious poetry* does not necessarily deal with an overtly religious subject; it is, however, written out of a religious commitment and informed by a religious as well as a poetic insight. *Poetry of religion*, on the other hand, is specifically about religion in its theological essence or in human experience. According to Samuel Johnson, poetry of religion falls into three categories: (1) Didactic verse, (2) Praise (the principal kind, this deals with creation or redemption, and (3) Devotional or pious, i.e., an aid to devotion or means to worship.

Caswall's categorization of some of his works as Meditative Pieces and others as Poems is thus not arbitrary – it broadly follows Drain's distinction between Poetry of Religion and Religious Poetry. The Meditative Pieces differ from the Poems in that they are overtly religious and intensely personal, and on the whole they eschew the 'exalted language' of poetry proper. Thus they can be regarded as prayers or at least as aids to prayer in a sense that the Poems cannot. Some of them invite the reader to identify with the

[85] Drain, *The Anglican Church in Nineteenth-Century Britain*, p. 35.

poet in the situation he sets before him or her and thereby to glean nourishment for one's own discourse with God or for meditation on certain religious themes that affect a person's dealing with the divine. Others provide the reader with objective religious ideas (for example, doctrines) to meditate on.

In contrast, the subject matter of the Poems is not necessarily overtly religious. Some of them, especially (but not exclusively) the Odes, come directly from the tradition of Romantic nature poetry; some have more than a hint of features of the topographical poetry in vogue in the eighteenth century. The difference between Caswall's Poems and his Meditative Pieces is best illustrated by comparing and contrasting one from each category, both written on the same subject. The poem 'Evening'[86] and the meditative piece 'The End of My Creation'[87] both deal with Caswall's favourite 'vanity' theme.

'Evening' consists of three stanzas of uneven length (six, twenty, and sixteen lines respectively). As the poem's title suggests, the first two stanzas describe the onset of the end of the day as evening descends on a rural scene: the clouds repose

> . . . round the Sunset's crimson close
> In variegated piles . . . (lines 5–6)

while

> From the cot beside the oak
> Mounts a slender thread of smoke. (lines 19–20)[88]

The last stanza, while continuing this description, also encases a moral, as the poet calls himself now at day's end to contemplate the ultimate vanity of earthly life.

> Now then the pensive task be mine,
> As into dusk the tints decline,
> In meditative mood to stray
> Along some brier-scented way;
> . . . . .
> There let me muse, all else forgot,
> On the strange tide of human lot;
> How brief the measure of our day;
> On death's approach, on life's decay;
> On former times, on future things;
> On all our vain imaginings; . . .

[86] Caswall, *Masque of Mary*, p. 134.
[87] Ibid., p. 206.
[88] 'Cot' was a favourite Coleridgean abbreviation for 'cottage'.

Thus in true Tractarian tradition this poem begins by describing a rural setting and then draws upon the parallel between the end of the day and 'life's decay' (line 36) to articulate the moral: earthly life is short and, ultimately, vanity.

'The End of My Creation' consists of five regular four-line stanzas. The apocalyptic/eschatological sense pervades the piece from the very beginning as the poet plunges in with an exhortation to his soul:

> Oft, my soul, thyself remind,
> Of the end thy God designed,
> When He sent thee here on earth,
> Heir of an immortal birth.

Each succeeding stanza is a new variation on the theme of the importance of focusing constantly on one's end, putting whatever belongs strictly to this world in its proper perspective, in order to attain to eternal life. Here, then, especially through the poet's technique of addressing his own soul, the reader can identify with the poet, making the moral his or her own.

The question of distinguishing among devotional texts with regard to their function as sung or spoken, public or private, has existed for over two thousand years, ever since 150 such texts were compiled into what is now the biblical book of Psalms. The flourishing of Victorian hymnal publishing was one of the more recent contexts in which it emerged as a significant issue. Whatever label one might choose to attach to each of Caswall's creations, the end result was his invaluable and lasting contribution to Christian hymnody in the Victorian era and beyond.

Caswall's hymns and Victorian hymn publishing

The compiling and publishing of hymnals was a favourite pastime of Victorian country clergy. Indeed, it ranked with butterfly collecting and fossil hunting, according to Bradley, who points out: 'The provision of a cheap and efficient postal system enabled material to be gathered, proofs circulated and hymn-books distributed on a nationwide basis and greatly helped what was in effect a cottage industry largely carried out by country clergymen in remote rectories.'[89]

[89] Bradley, *Abide with Me*, p. 53.

Alongside hymnals produced by local clergy for their own and sometimes neighbouring congregations, and eventually largely replacing them,[90] appeared the major collections with a more widespread distribution. *Hymns* by the SPCK (1852), Nelson's *Salisbury Hymn-Book* (1857), and E. H. Bickersteth's *Psalms and Hymns* (1858) were among those that started the ball rolling. The great hymnal achievement of the nineteenth century, *Hymns Ancient and Modern*, was first published in a words-only edition in December 1860 with 273 hymns; the music edition with words and tunes together followed in March 1861.

The publication of these hymnals inevitably entailed such matters as assignment of copyright and editorial emendations to hymn texts. The hymn writers' attitudes toward these issues varied widely.[91] At one extreme were those who considered that their texts, having been written for the honour and glory of God, should automatically be available to anyone who wished to use them and should also, within reason,[92] be subject to whatever alterations the hymnal editors deemed necessary. At the other extreme, some authors were very exacting about payments and about tightly controlling any editorial work on their texts, if they permitted it at all.

Caswall began receiving requests for permission to use *Lyra Catholica* hymns very shortly after the book's publication.[93] Some one hundred permission-request letters to him are preserved in the Birmingham Oratory archives: some for one hymn, some for several, and others for long lists of hymns, original and translated. Some letters have probably been lost, some permissions may have been orally requested and granted, and a number of hymnals,

[90] *Hymns Ancient & Modern* was born out of a wish to improve on the cottage-industry hymnals.

[91] As documented by Bradley and Drain, the authors' attitudes ranged from 'generous and self-effacing' (e.g., John Mason Neale and Horatius Bonar) to 'more proprietorial' (e.g., Bradley names Christopher Wordsworth as the 'most awkward of those with whom ... *A & M* had to deal'). Bradley, *Abide with Me*, pp. 102, 103; Drain describes *Hymns Ancient & Modern*'s dealings with Wordsworth in detail (*The Anglican Church in Nineteenth-Century Britain*, pp. 169–77).

[92] John Mason Neale objected to *Hymns Ancient & Modern*'s proposal to change 'roseate' to 'crimson' in the line 'and tasting of his roseate Blood' in his translation of *Ad coenam Agni providi* ('The Lamb's high banquet called to share') on the grounds that the last drops of one's life-blood are not crimson but a far paler colour – i.e., roseate (Bradley, *Abide with Me*, pp. 103–4).

[93] Caswall told Bellasis that 'Mr Oldknow, for instance, the incumbent of Trinity Chapel, Birmingham, introduced, with my permission, nearly fifty of them, in his parochial hymn book, within a year of their publication'. Quoted in Bellasis, 'Biographical Preface', p. 10. The book edited by Joseph Oldknow was *Hymns for the Service of the Church, arranged according to the Seasons and Holy-days of the Christian Year* (London: J. Masters; Birmingham: B. H. Leather, 1854).

impossible to estimate, undoubtedly included his hymns without having sought his explicit permission. Caswall disclosed that '[f]rom the first I never refused any application for the hymns from whatever quarter it came, wishing that if there was anything good in them, it should be the common property of all'.[94] Regarding the terms, he appears generally to have asked for some outright fee in the case of profit-making ventures and simply accepted whatever offering was forthcoming in other cases.

Twice Caswall embarked on ambitious and potentially costly projects designed to protect his copyright. In October 1857 he wrote a circular letter to several 'Catholics of influence',[95] sending proof copies of the book and expressing his 'great desire to retain the copyright, in order to be able to let compilers of devotional works make extracts from it at their pleasure'. To this end he had printed the book at his own expense[96] and now hoped that the addressees might help with a subscription. He was not out for any personal profit, but rather would use the money to assist the Oratory's poor schools.[97]

Again in July 1869 Caswall formulated a proposal to publish a complete edition of all his hymns 'and other religious pieces whether original or translated'.[98] During the previous ten or fifteen years various hymnal compilers throughout the country had been using his hymns, and he wanted to keep them from becoming booksellers' property 'in order that he may still be at liberty to allow their use freely to all applicants', even going so far as to publish the collection at his own expense.[99]

It was indeed the expense that presented the major obstacle: Caswall estimated it at £150. He reckoned that some of the hymns

94 Quoted in Bellasis, 'Biographical Preface', p. 11.

95 Edward Caswall, letter 14 October 1857.

96 He estimated that the cost would be between £80 and £90; before the letter could be sent out he received the printer's bill, which amounted to £125, and added this information in a postscript.

97 Caswall's appeal seems to have had good results. A personal memorandum (undated but written ca. 1869–70: the last date on the income list is 1869, and as no mention is made of the *Hymns and Poems* edition of 1872 it was obviously from before that) enumerating the expenses and income for his first three published volumes of hymns and poems lists the 'generous subscriptions' (totalling £85) received from various persons, to judge from their names the 'Catholics of influence' to whom he sent the letter: they included Miss Farrant (noted in Chapter 6 as a major donor to the Oratory), Sir John Acton, and the Duke of Norfolk.

98 The extant copy is marked by him 'Copy'; thus this was intended to be, and was, circulated to those he wished to involve.

99 Caswall declared to Bellasis that 'it was with [the] view [that his work remain available to all and not be controlled by one publisher] I retained the copyright in my own possession' (Bellasis, 'Biographical Preface', p. 11).

had by then 'nearly a million copies printed of them by different publishers', yet the sum total he had realized either by sales of the hymns or from offerings received in return for their use[100] amounted to £19 less than the original expense of printing the three volumes in which they had appeared.[101]

Caswall thus planned to write to the compilers – insofar as he could identify the hymnal titles, which he reckoned to be over one hundred in number, and locate the editors – and suggest to them that 'if each of them would make him up a little contribution from friends or congregation or publishers or otherwise, he would be enabled to enter upon his proposed work with a good hope of carrying it through'. The response to this circulated memorandum, while apparently not systematically documented,[102] must have been sufficient to allow the project to be brought to fruition, since Caswall issued his *Hymns and Poems* in 1872.

Another incident illustrates Caswall's attitude toward the use of his verses in others' hymn compilations. It arose from the fact that many hymnals did not give the names of the various text authors.[103] An occasional consequence was that a compiler of a new hymnal, with one or more existing hymnals at his disposal as a resource from which to take material, would use some of those hymns in complete ignorance of the identity of the original author, who would then be in a position to claim for compensation only if he/she or a helpful

100 The largest sum Caswall received from the sale of his hymns was £50 from *Hymns Ancient and Modern* in 1867, as listed on his personal, undated memorandum. The story of how this donation came about is interesting. He had written to *A & M*'s proprietors requesting this donation toward the erection of a Calvary on Oratory property. (This was the mound referred to in chapter 5.) The reply from *A & M*'s chief compiler, Sir Henry Baker, dated 18 February 1867, informed Caswall that the committee had agreed to the donation, but they also wanted it on record that 'as a committee they feel that they cannot enter into any question as to *how* you may wish to dispose of any money'. It would appear that the Roman Catholic 'veneration of images' issue had even yet not ceased to dog him! Whatever the committee as such may have felt, however, Sir Henry closed the letter by stating that '*I* personally am very glad that you are going to use the money in the aforesaid way'.

101 According to the earlier memorandum, the exact loss was £19 15s 3d. In calculating this Caswall did not take into account the £85 received in subscriptions for *The Masque of Mary*.

102 Some responses to it have been preserved, including one from the famous Ritualist priest Alexander Mackonochie. Even those who could not afford to send anything – usually the compilers of modest 'cottage-industry' volumes with a limited circulation – sometimes replied apologizing for the fact and wishing him well.

103 Drain hypothesizes, 'Perhaps it was not considered consistent with the purpose of congregational worship to point out that in the act of common praise the Church was indebted to any individual' (*The Anglican Church in Nineteenth-Century Britain*, p. 164).

friend happened to come across the publication in question.[104] In 1858 the London-based publisher Joseph Masters produced a hymnal that included several pieces by Caswall for which he had not requested permission. Caswall's solicitor, George J. Durrant, ever vigilant on his client's behalf for copyright infringements,[105] discovered the publication and informed Caswall, who thereupon let Durrant deal with the matter. In reply Masters proposed and Durrant accepted a compromise arrangement.[106] A few weeks later, upon conclusion of the arrangements negotiated with Durrant, Masters wrote to Caswall voicing his regret that Caswall did not enter directly into correspondence with him to inform him that the hymns were his; instead his having left the matter in the hands of a solicitor involved Masters in considerable expense. He would have been glad to pay Caswall the fair price for the hymns and take his own letter of permission as sufficient. The solicitor's expenses amounted to more than Masters would normally have paid for use of the hymns; thus the publisher entreats Caswall to correspond with him directly if such a matter should arise again in future.

A deeply contrite Caswall replied to Masters[107] that he had no idea that the settlement would involve the publisher in 'an expense beyond that of a fair remuneration for the hymns themselves'; he expected, rather, that 'a *single* lawyers [*sic*] letter would have settled all'. Mr Durrant had made him aware of the hymnal and, because of his own lack of spare time and his ignorance of the law, he had left the matter in the hands of a lawyer on the advice of friends. He hoped that at some future time it would be in his power 'in *some form or other* to make what has happened less annoying – and should you at any time wish to have any other of my pieces [*sic*] hymns – I can only say that whatever you have had to pay extra on the lawyers [*sic*] bill of expenses shall be considered as so much advanced'.[108]

104 See Drain, *The Anglican Church in Nineteenth-Century Britain*, pp. 164–5.
105 At the same time, Durrant advised Caswall that he should 'at once make a stand against' a 'Hymnal for Use in the services of the Church' just published by Rivington with 'five or six' of Caswall's hymns in it, or else Caswall's copyright would 'get frittered away'. Letter of Durrant to Caswall, 19 March 1858.
106 Ibid.
107 Letter Caswall to Masters, 8 May 1858.
108 Caswall's solicitor and publisher were less irenically disposed. In February 1859 Durrant sent Caswall a copy of a letter to him from his publisher, J. Burns, advising Durrant that a Revd Mr Carter, a 'great anti-Catholic Anglican', had asked permission for 'some half dozen' of Caswall's hymns. Burns had referred Carter to Durrant, suggesting that if he allowed Carter to use the hymns he should 'make him pay sweetly'. Burns attributed the situation to 'the original offence of Mr Masters whose Book has been used by Mr Carter to copy from'. Durrant wrote to Carter warning him that 'any infringement of Mr Caswall's Copyright will be followed by legal proceedings'.

This conclusion to the episode reveals Caswall to be concerned principally with justice, for others and for himself. He wanted no one to be deprived of the use of his hymns provided that they requested permission fairly – but he wanted to make the decision himself and not forfeit the copyright to others who might decide to restrict access to his works by refusing some permission requests. Nor was he greedy – he did not seek to profit financially from his literary endeavours, but from those who stood to earn money through the sale of the hymnals he did not hesitate to ask a fair payment that he would use in aid of the Oratory's pastoral outreach. Further, more than once he consented to special requests for new translations, and on at least one of these occasions he asked for payment in kind: to a plea from Downside Abbey for new translations of some hymns in honour of their patron, St Benedict, he replied by asking for two Masses to be said for his intention – which, they assured him, would 'be most cheerfully' done.[109]

The adoption of a hymn text in a new hymnal often entailed alterations to that text. Depending on an author's basic attitude toward his or her work, alterations to hymn texts could be regarded either as an inevitable fact of their life or as the bane of one's existence. Sometimes, indeed, they could be both, depending on the nature of the alteration. A change could affect one or two words in an entire text, or it could involve so extensive a revision that one might indeed question why the compiler had wanted to use that hymn at all. Alterations could be made for a variety of reasons – including doctrinal grounds, considerations of objectivity vs. subjectivity, intelligibility, and musicality[110] – but the overall rationale behind them is, as Drain points out, that the hymnal compiler's primary responsibility is not to the integrity of the text but 'to the purpose that the text will serve. That purpose is primarily the worship of God in its various aspects: adoration, praise, and thanksgiving'.[111]

Concerning Caswall's attitude toward alterations to his hymn texts, we can only conjecture from such evidence as letters he received and changes effected after his permission was sought. The Anglican vicar and devotional compiler Orby Shipley, who stood greatly in Caswall's debt for the latter's generous permission to include his pieces in Shipley's several ambitious collections,[112]

[109] Letter to Caswall from a Fr Sweeney, 19 November 1852.

[110] Drain discusses alterations at length (*The Anglican Church in Nineteenth-Century Britain*, chap. 4).

[111] Ibid., p. 298.

[112] See, e.g., *Lyra Messianica: Hymns and Verses on the Life of Christ, Ancient and modern; with Other Poems* (London: Longman, Green, Longman, Roberts, & Green, 1864); *Lyra Eucharistica: Hymns and Verses on the Holy Communion, Ancient*

expressed regret that Caswall 'sh[d] have cause to complain of unwarrantable alterations in [his] hymns'[113] and assures Caswall that he has not intentionally made any alterations except one or two minor ones for which he had the author's sanction. Later, when requesting further permission to include some of Caswall's texts in a new volume, Shipley wrote: 'I do not forget the stipulation you make of acknowledgment & non-alteration.'[114]

Although Caswall may not have entirely approved of alterations to his texts, he seems to have preferred tolerating them – in some cases perhaps grudgingly permitting them? – in order to make the hymn accessible to a wider audience, over prohibiting them altogether.[115] To judge from the correspondence with Shipley, he was prepared to stipulate that alterations be avoided or at least kept to a minimum if he felt certain that the editor would comply.[116]

Caswall the poet at work

Despite his gifts as poet and hymn writer, then, and despite this partial revival of the once-desired career as man of letters, Caswall possessed 'no sort of literary vanity'.[117] His humility and his pastoral sense prevailed; the poet was always subsumed under the priest. Caswall's life as Oratorian reveals him as the most extraordinary combination of creative spirit and meticulous, methodical worker – a priest who celebrated Mass and ministered to the Birmingham poor, a composer of poetry in a variety of forms, and a most exacting businessman who kept track of his personal financial

and Modern; with Other Poems, 2nd edn (London: Longman, Green, Longman, Roberts, & Green, 1864); and *Annus Sanctus: Hymns of the Church for the Ecclesiastical Year*, vol. 1: *Seasons of the Church: Canonical Hours: and Hymns of Our Lord* (London and New York: Burns & Oates, 1884).

113 Letter from Shipley to Caswall, undated but written after 1861 since it mentions *A & M*.

114 Another undated letter from Shipley to Caswall. In the Preface to *Lyra Messianica* Shipley states his objection to the current practice of 'mangling hymns' and declares that the few changes he has made 'are either grammatical corrections or emendations which seemed to be imperatively demanded by the interests of truth, or were necessary in order to change the metre into such as could be sung' (p. viii).

115 Caswall did admit to Bellasis, '... it amuses me at times to see ... the difference of selections exhibited [in various hymnals], as well as the alterations made by various religious parties' (Bellasis, 'Biographical Preface', p. 11).

116 Possibly, too, Caswall considered that, since Shipley's volumes were devotional resources rather than 'singing' hymnals, there would be no excuse for alterations required by the demands of congregational singing.

117 Bellasis, 'Biographical Preface', p. 11.

matters as well as he negotiated with building contractors and other suppliers on the Oratory's behalf.[118]

Caswall brought to his composition of verse the same exacting meticulousness that characterized all of his more mundane undertakings. The gestation of his lengthier poems was preceded by painstaking preparations involving the gathering of copious notes based on research as well as on first-hand observation. Both his intellectual and his emotional and spiritual faculties were engaged in his creative process.[119]

Nor did this painstaking care cease once the verses had been committed to paper. Not only while still in manuscript, but also still at proof stage and even after already in print he was constantly revising. Copies of his books recently arrived from the printers bear pencilled marks, words, phrases, even entire lines crossed out, alternative suggestions noted in the margins.

More than one of Caswall's poems began its existence in a far more ambitious form than the final product turned out to be. *The Minster of Eld* was originally conceived as 'a religious drama' in several acts and scenes and featured speaking parts for various angels and an archangel. Caswall eventually whittled it down to three scenes with a brief prologue and epilogue, and reduced the characters to three: a Pilgrim, a Shepherd Boy, and a Hermit. 'The Easter Ship', which will be discussed in detail further on, was originally intended to be accompanied by explanatory notes of encyclopaedic proportions that, all in all, would have amounted to a comprehensive legal and cultural history of Roman Catholicism in England; in the end – who knows how an attack of practicality overtook him and he abandoned this project? – only the poem was published, first in *The Masque of Mary*. The odes also went through a complicated generative process (see below).

The 'Poet of the Oratory'[120]

What did the Father Superior of the Oratory think of Caswall's poetry? On the one hand, Newman seems to have had a long-stand-

[118] He once kept a chart of the weight he lost as a result of abstaining from such foods as butter and beer. And during the course of precisely one given year he kept a list of how many confessions he heard, and from how many *different* people.

[119] The gestation of 'A May Pageant' and 'The Easter Ship' is discussed in detail below.

[120] Thus was Edward referred to by Fr Matthew Russell, SJ, quoted in *The Hymns of the Breviary and Missal*, ed. Matthew Britt, OSB (New York: Benziger Brothers, 1924), p. 363.

ing suspicion of poetic activity as an end in itself, as evidenced, for example, by his attitude toward *Lyra Apostolica*. Concerning Caswall in particular this attitude would appear to be borne out by an anecdote related by Joyce Sugg. After dining in the London home of his convert Geraldine Fitzgerald and her mother and sister, he sent the mother a copy of his book of poems and the sister a volume of Caswall's poems: 'he had told them, laughing, that Father Caswall, who had since published more weighty works, had once written 'The Art of Pluck' and had never written anything so good since'.[121]

On the other hand, however, confronted with the fact of Caswall's poetic output, he was, in general, encouraging, as shown, for example, by the letter he wrote Caswall on the receipt of *Lyra Catholica*. His most touching reaction came in response to *The Masque of Mary*. Normally the duty of delivering the annual Oratory report fell to Caswall, but in September 1858 Newman insisted on giving the report himself – to seize the opportunity, as it turned out, to commend Caswall for his volume of poems published at the beginning of that year and have his remarks recorded in the Oratory official documents. The year on which he was reporting had brought considerable trials to the Oratory and, quoting a familiar proverb, Newman compared Caswall's volume, 'a beautiful New Year gift' made on 1 January to the rainbow that often precedes storms. As illustrations of 'one or two of the colours of our rainbow' Newman credited Caswall with the gift of being able to write with 'the force and sublimity of Milton' as well as with 'the tenderness and grace of Cowper'.[122] Newman wrote his poem 'To Edward Caswall', dated 1 January 1858, in response to Caswall's gift of that volume, and perhaps particularly to one poem contained therein, 'To the Hand of a Living Catholic Author'. The poem is clearly addressed to the Father Superior. Caswall pays tribute to Newman's pivotal role in his own conversion:

Thou, drawing back
The curtains of the night,
First on this guilty soul,
Shut up in heresy, didst open light

– and also prophetically anticipates Newman's impact on the future of Roman Catholicism:

[121] Joyce Sugg, *Ever Yours Affly: John Henry Newman and His Female Circle* (Leominster, England: Gracewing, 1996), p. 150.

[122] Oratory report 29 September 1858, A.51.5 /A.51.9.

Through thee have sped
Forth on their blazing way
Conceptions fiery-wing'd,
That shall the destinies of ages sway!

Newman, for his part, has succeeded in capturing the essence of Caswall's spirit in his poem, in which he addresses Caswall as 'my Brother and my Friend' and hails his poetry as 'the fresh upwelling of thy tranquil spirit'.

Caswall's favourite poetic themes

The Anglican poetic tradition, as explicated by William Countryman, 'has certain characteristic elements, including a high (but distinctive) regard for scripture, a sense of the spiritual value of nature, an investment in the life of the church, and a sense of the accessibility of the Holy in and through the ordinary and the child-like.'[123]

That the Tractarian poets, such as Keble and Isaac Williams, were carrying on a long-standing tradition in Anglican poetry while giving it their own unique focus becomes clear if one compares Countryman's list of characteristic elements with the features of Tractarian devotional poetry as enumerated by G. B. Tennyson:

> a concern for nature as a system of signs and a source of sacramental grace, a preference for rural persons and places over urban, a passion for holy places and holy structures, a sense of the Church as a mystical body and as an enduring institution in human history, an inclination toward verse related to an external religious plan or source like the Church year, and a love for early Church hymnody and devotional works.[124]

Two characteristic themes in Caswall's poetry will be considered here, on the one hand to demonstrate his place within this established tradition and, on the other, to illumine his uniquely Roman Catholic contribution to Victorian poetry.

[123] William Countryman, *The Poetic Imagination: An Anglican Spiritual Tradition* (Maryknoll, N.Y.: Orbis Books, 1999), p. 37.
[124] Tennyson, *Victorian Devotional Poetry*, pp. 186–7.

Sacramental view of creation

The sacramental view of creation – that is, the notion that *visible* nature is an analogue of or manifests its *invisible* Creator – is a touchstone of Tractarian poetics,[125] and was firmly established by Keble in *The Christian Year*. Keble's scriptural basis for this idea comes from Romans 1:20: 'The invisible things of [God] from the creation of the world are clearly seen, being understood by the things that are made'.[126] It heads his poem 'Septuagesima Sunday',[127] which Geoffrey Rowell calls the *locus classicus* expressing the notion of creation as a 'sacramental universe, speaking to those who read it with the eye of faith of the pattern of God's being and activity'[128] – in other words, Butler's doctrine of analogy. Here Keble speaks of creation as a book in which one may read of God's truth:

> The works of God above, below,
> Within us and around,
> Are pages in that book, to show
> How God Himself is found. (lines 4–8)

It was inevitable that Caswall's penchant for exploring the relationship between the visible and the invisible worlds would inform much of his poetry. In discussing the sacramental view of creation as a theme in Caswall's poetry I will focus on two areas: his contribution to the science–vs–religion debate and the idea of sacred space. In particular the first of these areas will be seen as significant in view of Caswall's pastoral orientation and his perception of the importance of religious formation.

Caswall's contribution to the science–vs–religion debate

The questions raised by science concerning creation's relationship with a divine Creator were by no means new by the time Edward Caswall had grown to young adulthood, but the debate about the relative truth of science and religion had been intensified due to the increased pace of scientific discoveries in the nineteenth century, particularly in geology. People of faith regarded this as a factor

125 Tennyson discusses this in depth in ibid., e.g. on pp. 93–101.

126 Quoted in ibid., p. 67.

127 John Keble, *The Christian Year* (New York: E.P. Dutton & Co., 1869), pp. 66–8.

128 Geoffrey Rowell, 'John Keble: A Speaking Life', in *A Speaking Life: The Legacy of John Keble*, ed. Charles R. Henery (Leominster, England: Gracewing/Fowler Wright Books, 1995), p. 52.

contributing to the crisis of unbelief then on the rise in Victorian Britain. Caswall believed that 'insatiable scientific curiosity'[129] was undermining religious faith, yet he rightly saw that science and religion could coexist. Typically, Caswall the pastor and educator sought to convey this message to ordinary Christians: How could he fashion a work whose purpose was to affirm all of creation as a 'work of the Lord' while yet maintaining the validity of the scientific view of creation? The Canticle of the Three Children from the Book of Daniel (Dan. 3:57–88) – 'Benedicite' after the first word of the Latin text – provided him with a framework.

The Masque of Mary contains a cycle of sixteen odes based on the 'Benedicite' canticle, each ode being prefaced by one of the canticle's Latin verses (e.g., *Benedicite, fontes, Domino*), which thus announces the topic of the ode.[130] We noted above that a few of Caswall's works began life in a far more extensive form than their final, definitive one, and the cycle of odes was among them. Consistent throughout all of Caswall's workings of the 'Benedicite' material is his attempt to forge an acceptable balance between science and religion.

Some time in the early 1840s[131] Caswall sketched three prose works based on the 'Benedicite' canticle,[132] none of which he completed. By far the most interesting and most extensively developed of these was the *Young Churchman's Book of All Creation* (*YCB*). While the *YCB* is a remarkable combination of forms, including meditation and poetry, its backbone is a series of questions and answers suggesting a catechism,[133] by means of which Caswall hoped to prevent a mechanistic view of creation from stamping itself on the minds of young people, who require instead to be

129 Edward Caswall, 'Mountains and hills', in *Benedicite or the Young Churchman's Book of all Creation* (hereafter cited as *YCB*).

130 In Caswall's 1872 collection the cycle was augmented to seventeen by the addition of a poem, 'Ajalon', that had appeared in *The Masque* but not among the odes.

131 Attempting to date this material precisely is a challenge. The ink and the way the paper has been used suggested that the sketches were all being worked on at approximately the same time. The quotations from the *Bridgewater Treatises* point to a date not earlier than 1840, when the *Treatises* were completed, and Caswall's reproduction of the prayer 'For Clergy and People' from the Book of Common Prayer indicates as the latest date 1846, his last full year as an Anglican.

132 These are preserved in a small bundle of blue manuscript sheets in the Birmingham Oratory archives.

133 In the Preface, in fact, Caswall refers rather critically to 'popular juvenile scientific catechisms', thereby implying that he intends his book to counteract these catechisms' 'worldly spirit' that regards creation as 'simply some vast machine'.

imbued with a deeper reverence toward God as author of creation.[134] He does not seek to refute or disregard science but strives to integrate it with religion.

Each section of the *YCB* is headed by and devoted to the creature addressed in one verse of the 'Benedicite' canticle. The basic outline of each section is:

1. the heading (= canticle verse);
2. a definition and scientific explanation of the creature or natural phenomenon addressed in the canticle verse;
3. explanations of how that specific creature glorifies God:
   by way of Nature
   by way of Miracle
   by way of Emblem.
   These sections are conceived in the form of a question-and-answer dialogue in which a Priest quizzes the young Churchman of the title and elicits from him responses that contain this information.
4. a meditation 'intended to serve as interludes between the drier portions of the work'.
   Occasionally poetry illustrates or expands upon a point being made.

The scientific explanations are derived from the *Bridgewater Treatises*, the same papers Caswall satirized in his *Sketches of Young Ladies*.[135]

Caswall's explanations of how the creature glorifies God by way of nature are based on scientific information, but are seen through a lens of religious faith that reveals the Creator as no mere 'master mechanic' but as a loving, caring provider who has ordained creation to serve the divine purpose, which is ordered to the good of all things. The descriptions of how the creature glorifies God by way of miracle rely on scriptural accounts of the role played by the specific natural phenomenon in God's apparently miraculous interventions in history.[136]

For the creature's glorification of God by way of emblem Caswall

134 It will be recalled that the meditation on Creation in *The Child's Manual*, written when Caswall was an Anglican, was influenced by the 'Benedicite' canticle.

135 Caswall makes use of the treatises by William Prout, William Whewell, and William Buckland, and has especially profited from Whewell's information on winds and on frost and cold, Prout's theories on fire and heat, and Buckland's geological discoveries about mountains.

136 E.g., when the Egyptians began crossing the Red Sea in pursuit of the fleeing Hebrews, God caused the winds to blow so that the sea covered the Egyptians and drowned them.

has appropriated patristic typology as described by John Keble in his Tract *On the Mysticism Attributed to the Early Fathers of the Church*.[137] Caswall regards the word *emblem* as synonymous with *type* and the two words refer to something that makes visible an invisible reality: another word for this is *sacrament*. The air and winds, for example, are a 'natural type of the power of the Holy Ghost, the Lord and giver of life'. He even uses sacramental language in the context of purely natural explanations of certain phenomena: snow and fire are defined as the visible manifestations respectively of cold and heat, which in themselves are invisible.[138]

It was from the poetic fragments in the *YCB* that Caswall developed the odes. What ultimately was published in his poetry collections as a cycle of odes was not, however, originally conceived as a self-contained entity. In his 1852 manuscript of poems the odes do not appear in their final order and in fact have some other poems interspersed among them. Moreover, in this two-volume manuscript two of the odes are in volume 2 and the others all in volume 1.[139] Caswall obviously conceived each poem individually as inspired by and based on a line of the 'Benedicite' canticle; what started as fragments of poetry in an ambitious prose work first became a collection of poems loosely related by their 'Benedicite' basis and was finally organized into a coherent cycle.

While Caswall uses the 'Benedicite' as an underpinning structure for the odes cycle, then, he does not slavishly follow the canticle text as it stands but adapts it for his own purposes. He sometimes combines two or more canticle verses in one ode. Heat and cold, each of which has a special verse in the canticle, are combined in the ode 'To the Heat and Cold'. This allows the poet to exploit their obvious contrast as well as to point out their commonalities: each is invisible in itself yet has visible manifestations that warn us of their existence. Similarly, mountains and hills form the main topic in the ode 'To the Earth', in which Caswall can stress the geological interpretation of 'earth'[140] and point out that, whether it took a few days or millions of years, the creation of the earth was indeed God's work.

[137] *Tracts for the Times* no. 89 (Oxford, 1868).
[138] Here is yet another example of Caswall's interest in the relationship between the visible and the invisible.
[139] Interestingly, 'Ajalon', one of the poems to appear among the odes in 1872 but not in 1858 (although it is elsewhere in the book), is grouped with the odes in the 1852 manuscript.
[140] Here the influence of Buckland is seen.

Caswall also reorders the canticle verses, omitting some, and interpreting them in ways that sometimes vary from what the scriptural context might suggest. Omitting *Benedicite omnia opera Domini Domino*, with which the canticle begins, he starts with the fifth verse, *Benedicite omnes virtutes Domini Domino*. The ode apostrophizes the various 'powers' (= *virtutes*), which Caswall interprets broadly as including rational, intelligent creatures as well as natural forces that all perform God's works 'in the natural or spiritual worlds'. Among them are the nine choirs of angels and the saints; ecclesiastical and secular rulers and such 'movers and shakers' of humanity as artists, poets, and inventors; the powers and faculties of the mind; and the natural forces of instinct and gravity. These greetings serve to establish the overall theme of the cycle: (1) the visible world is a 'book of Nature' that reveals God; (2) all creation carries out God's purposes. Thus the Odes maintain the thrust of the *YCB* by confirming the absolute sovereignty of the Creator over all of creation: however awesome, however sublime, however powerful the creatures – among which may be numbered the loftiest capabilities of human intelligence – it is still and always God who rules.

In the Ode to the Seasons, headed by the verse *Benedicite sol et luna Domino*, Caswall actually treats not the sun and the moon but the four seasons. The joys and sorrows, ups and downs of the natural cycle of seasons are tempered by the events in salvation history celebrated by the liturgical year: Christ's birth shines in the dark of winter, the shadow of the 'dread Cross' of Calvary falls across the rejoicing of spring.[141] Each season is an oracle of the Lord that reminds us of divine truths.

An ode based on *filii hominum* (usually 'sons of men') is actually devoted to 'the world', which here assumes the Johannine connotation of opposition to Christ, whom the world did not accept. The poet looks down from a height on what the eighteenth-century topographical poets would have called a 'prospect', except that for Caswall distance does not lend enchantment, as it did with Campbell,[142] but rather the contrary: it imparts the wisdom and insight that can come from detachment as the poet surveys the

[141] Compare the sestet of Wordsworth's 'Regrets' from the *Ecclesiastical Sonnets*:

Go, seek, when Christmas snows discomfort bring,
The counter Spirit found in some gay church
Green with fresh holly, every pew a perch
In which the linnet or the thrush might sing,
Merry and loud and safe from prying search,
Strains offered only to the genial Spring.

[142] Thomas Campbell, *The Pleasures of Hope* (1799); quoted in Lascelles Abercrombie, *Romanticism* (New York, 1963), p. 36.

'Tis distance lends enchantment to the view, And robes the mountain in its azure hue. — Thomas Campbell 'vanities' of history, from ancient pagan empires up to the present day, and takes to task those people who set all their store by the 'Fata Morgana of this fleeting world'.[143]

The last ode in the cycle, to 'The Sanctuary of the Church', is headed by the verse *Benedicite Israel Domino*. Caswall 'christologizes' the epigraphic text by using the patristic interpretation of Israel as a type of the church. In contrast to the 'pomps and vanities of this false world' the church is a rock and a haven, a place of peace, the culmination of creation, as the place of this ode as last in the cycle would suggest. By 'church' the poet most definitely means the Roman Catholic Church, the church 'of ancient days', built on Peter.

The engagement of the science–vs–religion question was not without precedent in the English poetic tradition. William Cowper's (1731–1800) lengthy poem *The Task* embraces the major unitive theme of nature as revelatory of God. In 'The Time-Piece' Cowper exposes the fallacy of philosophers who overlook God in their conception of the world.[144] Only the mind enlightened by God's grace can see God in nature, he maintains; this is not within the reach of purely scientific means.[145] But it was Caswall who worked within Tractarian poetics to engage the science–vs–religion debate.

To arrange a cycle of poems according to a pre-existing structure, as Caswall did, had precedents in the Tractarian poetic tradition, such as Keble's *The Christian Year*. Unlike Keble, for whom the liturgical year with its assigned readings was *per se* intrinsic to his purpose, Caswall does not follow his chosen structure exactly, but instead adapts it in such a way as to enhance its power to convey his message. The 'Benedicite' canticle, unlike the liturgical year, is not an entity unto itself but a text that exists within a much larger context – the Book of Daniel – and its own structure, the order of its verses, is determined by its function within that context. That original context is irrelevant to Caswall's purposes, and thus he feels free to rearrange the verses, paradoxically departing from strict adherence to Tractarian procedure in order to express what was originally a Tractarian concept: the apostolic church as culmination of God's creation.

[143] Is it mere coincidence that the American artist Thomas Cole (1801–1849) was painting his series *The Course of Empire* around this very time?

[144] See, e.g., lines 161–206.

[145] Cf. 'The Garden', lines 221–60.

Sacred space

As part of their program to revive Catholic tradition in England the Tractarians sought to restore the reverence for holy shrines and wells to which the Reformation officially put an end. As Tennyson points out, 'In [Tractarian] poetry the actual places often remain vague; they honour some holy well, some roadside shrine. Isaac Williams went farthest toward identifying particular places in *Thoughts in Past Years*, and Keble in his later poetry moved in this direction with poems about such things as the well at Ampfield near Hursley.'[146]

Two 'sacred space' poems by Caswall offer a dose of Roman Catholic polemic in the course of honouring the places named in their titles. When the body of the murdered boy-king St Kenelm was discovered and enshrined at Winchcombe in Gloucestershire all sorts of miracles began to occur at the site.[147] 'St Kenelm's Well' offers a straightforward narrative of the eleventh-century legend, with a Roman Catholic slant: the location of Kenelm's grave is revealed, by a dove bearing 'a golden scroll of mystic import', to the Pope, who is 'chanting solemn mass' in St Peter's Basilica

When God to him the spot reveal'd,
So long from British eye conceal'd.

'St Clement's Tomb', about the first-century pope martyred by being thrown into the sea with an anchor around his neck, builds on a legend about angels miraculously constructing a marble tomb for Clement's watery grave. The poem contains themes dear to the Tractarians – references to relics and a description of the anchor as

So late his instrument of martyrdom,
But emblem now of better things to come.[148]

A reference to mighty Rome satisfyingly rounds the poem off: as it began by recalling Clement's martyrdom by decree of the Roman emperor Trajan, so it ends by telling how in time 'mighty Rome' claimed his relics,

And she, who cast thee to a doom unjust,
Now worships every remnant of thy dust!

146 Tennyson, *Victorian Devotional Poetry*, pp. 178–9.
147 Cf. John J. Delaney, *Pocket Dictionary of the Saints*, abridged edn (New York: Doubleday Image, 1983), p. 294.
148 The last line is virtually a literal translation of *futurae gloriae pignus* from the ancient Latin eucharistic hymn *O sacrum convivium*.

A consequence of the Tractarian sacramental worldview was that Tractarian poetry expanded the concept of 'sacred space' to include any place that offered an encounter with the numinous. Thus Caswall can declare, in 'Associations with Places', that 'All earth is consecrated ground', for any place, whether the 'grot, the glen, the old grey tower', may be to some unknown person a 'memento dear of grief or mirth'; thus its sacredness consists in its association with a memory or event of significance to some person. But a meeting with the divine may also take the form of absorbing truth or wisdom bestowed by the Deity; and so 'Nature's Oratories'[149] salutes the 'private cells within [Nature's] shrine' – the 'mountain-height', the 'forest's dim recesses', and the 'natural cave hid far from sight' – to which the great sages of old, such as Socrates, Confucius, and Virgil, repaired 'to meditate ... on truths sublime'.[150] In these set-apart places God partially lifted 'the veil that hid their gaze from Thee'.[151] Thus they are sites where these wise 'true souls unspoilt by pride' found truth – an important commodity in Caswall's own conversion journey and those of so many of his contemporaries.

The literary forebear of the 'sacred space' poem is eighteenth-century topographical poetry. Such a poem might typically begin by describing the elements of nature in a scene and conclude by drawing a moral or 'higher meaning' from the nature observed.[152] Beyond topographical poetry, however, came the Romantic nature poets. An outstanding prototype of the 'sacred space' poem, by an author deeply revered by the Tractarians, and one of crucial significance for Caswall, was Wordsworth's 'Lines Written above Tintern Abbey', which provided much inspiration for his lengthy verse drama *A May Pageant*.

As in 'Tintern Abbey', so too in *A May Pageant* is the protagonist blessed by the presence of a dear childhood friend. In Wordsworth's

149 Surely the title must have had at least unconscious significance for the author.

150 In 'A Forest Hymn' (1825) William Cullen Bryant hailed the groves as 'God's first temples', where man opened his heart to 'the sacred influences' that /stole over him, and bowed /His spirit with the thought of boundless power /And inaccessible majesty (lines 14–16).

151 The veil was significant in Tractarian thought in connection with the doctrine of Reserve. As Tennyson explains, 'since God is ultimately incomprehensible, we can know Him only indirectly; His truth is hidden and given to us only in a manner suited to our capacities for apprehending it ... Both the sacredness and the complexity of the subject of religious truth are such that they require a holding back and a gradual revelation as the disposition and understanding of the recipient mature'. *Victorian Devotional Poetry*, p. 45.

152 See Robert Arnold Aubin, *Topographical Poetry in XVIII-Century England* (New York: The Modern Language Association of America, 1936; repr. 1966).

case the 'dear, dear Friend' is his own sister; for Caswall's protagonist[153] it is a visitor from the invisible world, a long-dead friend who, in their childhood, was like a brother to him because they were raised together after the death of the friend's mother. But the most salient point of commonality between Wordsworth's and Caswall's poems is the role of Tintern as the site of encounter with transcendent reality.[154] In *A May Pageant* this encounter assumes a specifically Roman Catholic form, as the protagonist experiences a ceremony of homage to our Lady held by denizens of the invisible world (saints and angels), who come to this hallowed spot each May for this purpose. The vision of this celebration is vouchsafed to the protagonist – a holy and aged Franciscan priest[155] named Euthanase (= 'happy death') – through the ministrations of his long-deceased boyhood friend Theodore (= 'gift of God'). Theodore appears to Euthanase while the latter is rapt in prayer in the depths of an ancient wood known as 'Our Lady's Wood'[156] and ferries him to Tintern along the River Severn, on a journey that takes them past several ruins of pre-Reformation abbeys that lie in the Severn Valley. Thus the River Severn assumes a sacral aspect of its own as a means of this holy journey that is facilitated by the friend from the realm of saints.[157]

If ever Caswall undertook a poetic labour of love, it must have been *A May Pageant*. He prepared for its composition by keeping a notebook in which dense factual pages copied out of historical tomes[158] are juxtaposed with phrases obviously jotted down in the course of lengthy walks through the countryside – picturesque observations, some of which have been transposed verbatim into the poem, or spontaneous ideas of things to do – e.g., 'Read Virgil's description of the Tiber's ascent', 'Read Wordsworth on rivers for epithets'. He was thus absorbing and processing information on several levels – intellectual, sensory, emotional – simultaneously and, since his family were originally West Country people, must have felt some affinity with the geographical region he was describing. More than the wells and shrines, then, this region was sacred ground for the poet on a deeply personal level.

153 Whereas 'Tintern Abbey' is written in the first person, Caswall's is written in the third.

154 Even Caswall's full title for the poem, *A May Pageant, or A Tale of Tintern*, reflects the poet's Wordsworthian roots.

155 Undoubtedly Caswall made him a Franciscan because of that order's tradition of promoting belief in the Immaculate Conception.

156 Coincidentally (or not), the area of Birmingham immediately to the north of Edgbaston is called Ladywood.

157 Note Wordsworth's invocation 'O sylvan Wye!' in 'Tintern Abbey'.

158 E.g., material on Bildas Abbey from a *History of Shropshire*.

Roman Catholic polemics

While the Church of England as the 'default' form of religion in post-Reformation England required no further definition, the Roman Catholics, on the other hand, found it necessary to stress their distinctiveness. Roman Catholic poetry, then, from the later poems of Crashaw to Newman's *Dream of Gerontius*, was 'dedicated largely to the emphasizing of boundary issues distinguishing Roman from Anglican Christianity'.[159]

Thus Roman Catholic polemical poetry can be defined as poetry emphasizing Roman Catholic distinctiveness over against the Established Church. If the Tractarian poet had sought to revitalize his own church, the Roman Catholic poet coming from the Tractarian tradition strove to establish the truth claims of his church in opposition to the claims of the Church of England. Given Roman Catholic belief in itself as the 'one true faith', such polemics in mid nineteenth-century England included a sense of destiny about the inevitable re-establishment of the Roman religion on English soil as well as a conviction concerning the rightness of certain disputed doctrines, especially those concerning the eucharist, Mary, and papal supremacy.

Of Caswall's entire published output some twenty pieces could be termed polemical according to the above definition. Four were written in 1846 and thus reveal the strength of his 'bias' toward Roman Catholicism already at that juncture; each of these treats major issues in his conversion process – the Real Presence ('Belief of Anglicans in the Real Presence Tested', 'Unreality') and the Communion of Saints ('The Two Mothers', 'St Stephen's Day'). A good proportion of the early polemical poems display a pronounced autobiographical element, having been composed in reaction to events surrounding Caswall's conversion. 'Belief of Anglicans ...' deplores the inconsistency of the 'unreal men' who profess belief in the Real Presence yet refuse to 'bow down' before the Sacrament, while 'Unreality' laments his betrayal by those[160] who misled him about the Real Presence. 'Remonstrance', sketched in his journal while family and friends began to express their reactions to his and Louisa's conversions, addresses those from whom he is now estranged, voicing the hope that they, too, will see the light before it is too late.[161]

159 Countryman, *The Anglican Poetic Tradition*, p. 195, n. 17.

160 In one prepublication manuscript Caswall titled the poem 'Tractarian Unreality', and in the 1872 edition he called it 'Unreality of Anglicanism'.

161 Here I take issue with J. R. Watson's evaluation of Caswall's mindset when he wrote this poem (*The English Hymn*, p. 368). His correspondence with loved ones at this period consistently maintains a firm but loving and gentle tone, and he expresses remorse over the pain he may be causing them. He may be exasperated at their persistent misconceptions about Roman Catholicism, but he is never 'patronizing' or 'far from benign'.

The extended poem afforded Caswall the scope to combine several polemical themes in one piece. *A May Pageant*, as we have seen, features Marian veneration, the Communion of Saints, and mourning for the ruined abbeys of England's Roman Catholic past. It also anticipates the eventual restoration of the Roman Catholic Church to its former high place in England and allows Caswall to resolve a matter he first noted during the early days of keeping his conversion journal. Citing an author named Bennet[162] who criticized a Roman Cardinal for applying the psalms to the Virgin Mary, Caswall counters that Anglicans do the same in their service for the accession of Queen Victoria. He quotes the relevant prayer and then retorts, 'Here we apply various prophecies of Christ as King to Queen Victoria, how then can we blame an individual in the Roman Church for applying the same to Christ's own Mother ...?'[163] The frontispiece to *A May Pageant and Other Poems* features a line drawing of Mary as a young woman wearing a crown, and the accompanying text reads, 'Regina Coeli, accipe coronam, quam tibi Dominus praeparavit in aeternum'. Clearly Caswall was taking advantage of the devotion of the English to their Queen, making a subtle identification of Victoria with Mary in order to foster devotion to the latter. Springing from an authentic place in the poet's inmost being, *A May Pageant* is superior to 'A Masque of Angels' which, more contrived and triumphalistic, can hardly be credited as a 'fresh upwelling of [his] tranquil spirit'.

Another extended polemical poem, 'The Easter Ship', underwent an extraordinary process of gestation. Tracing the genesis of this poem will illumine Caswall's sometimes involved, always methodical working methods as well as the significance of the poem's polemical themes.

'The Easter Ship' was conceived as a grandiose work that would have featured the poem supplemented by immensely detailed explanatory notes and by illustrations.[164] Caswall consulted history books,[165] religious works,[166] poetry collections,[167] and miscellaneous sources,[168] intending to reproduce relevant excerpts from

162 Caswall alludes only to Bennet's writing 'on the errors of Romanism' and gives no further information.

163 Caswall, 'Journal', p. 64.

164 Caswall's extant material includes his own sketches along with several signed 'MRG' – Newman's good friend Maria Giberne, an accomplished artist.

165 E.g., John Lingard's *History of England* and Cobbett's *History of the Protestant Reformation*.

166 E.g., the works of Bernard of Clairvaux, Newman's *Lectures on the Difficulties Felt by Anglicans on Submitting to the Catholic Church*, and Perrone *de Immaculato BV Mariae Conceptu*.

167 E.g., *Percy's Reliques of Ancient Poetry* and various books of carols.

168 E.g., John Mason Neale's *Hierologus; or, the church tourists*.

these works, along with his own comments, as notes illuminating selected verses in his poem. He envisioned the work as demonstrating the antiquity of Roman Catholicism in the British Isles and thereby showing it to be deeply rooted in British culture. This would have implicitly refuted claims that Roman Catholicism was a foreign element and thus only the Church of England could be the true Catholic Church on English soil. Yet the tone of the work, which was aimed at Protestants and Catholics alike, was educational rather than argumentative, Caswall apparently assuming an open-minded readership.

The material he intended to include in the notes falls roughly into three categories: *historical* – e.g., the dissolution of the monasteries in the Reformation; *cultural* – e.g., the importance of saints in English place and personal names, showing why England once earned the epithet 'Isle of the Saints'; *religious* – this largest category is chiefly devoted to the history of Marian devotion in England. Caswall demonstrates how vestiges of the intense devotion to Mary that gave England the name 'Mary's Dowry' survive as folk customs and culture, most strikingly in old ballad poetry and carols, provides a theological explanation of and history of belief in the dogma of the Immaculate Conception then recently proclaimed by Pius IX, and explains how the eventual reclamation of England for Roman Catholicism to which the current 'Catholic movement' was surely leading had been anticipated and predicted for two centuries.

In the end, however, Caswall abandoned the idea of a 'shilling book' including the vast historical apparatus and illustrations and instead published the poem alone in his collected works.[169]

Caswall originally titled this project 'The Vision and Prophecy of the Hermit of Finisterre'. In the manuscript prepared in 1852, by which time he had apparently decided against the book project, he had shortened the title simply to 'The Hermit of Finisterre' before giving it its definitive title 'The Easter Ship', which highlights the rich ecclesiastical symbolism of the ship as the church[170] in conjunction with the resurrection motif pertaining to England's rescue from

169 In *The Masque of Mary* (1858) it appears between 'A Masque of Angels' and 'St Kenelm's Well', all three before any categories; in *Hymns and Poems* (1872) 'The Easter Ship', now subtitled 'A Legend', and 'St Kenelm's Well' are included under 'Poems'.

170 Caswall's notes include source material on the ship as symbol of the church; he indicates that in this context it is to be interpreted as the Catholic Church in England. Margaret Johnson refers to Tractarian use of the ship 'as an image of spiritual journeying' (*Gerard Manley Hopkins and Tractarian Poetry*, p. 209).

The black Satanic deep
Of heresy's awful flood.

The Hermit is not an unfamiliar figure in writings of this period and is probably a manifestation of the then current fascination with things medieval. One of Wordsworth's 'Inscriptions' commemorates St Herbert, the friend of St Cuthbert who lived out his days as a hermit on an island in Derwentwater that now bears his name,[171] and a Hermit plays a key role in Part VII of Coleridge's *Rime of the Ancient Mariner*. *The Minster of Eld* is another Caswall poem with a hermit as a key person. The mysterious Stranger from the Middle Ages who appears in Faber's *Sights and Thoughts in Foreign Churches*[172] is probably a version of this personage.

The Hermit of 'The Easter Ship' is, significantly, the 'last of Tintern's exil'd sons' – a Cistercian monk forced, along with his fellows, to flee from England when Henry VIII dissolved the monasteries. 'In the reign of Queen Elizabeth' he has a vision 'concerning the Immaculate Conception and the Restoration of England to the Catholic Faith', and it is this vision that supplies the main theme of Caswall's poem. One Easter morning the Hermit sees

. . . a Ship in the misty dawn
Becalm'd on the silent sea;
Her sails all drooping – her helm unwatch'd –
As though no crew had she!

A deadly storm 'from Satan's breath' quickly blows up and sinks the ship. Soon nothing of it is visible except

The topmost spar! – whence gallantly still,
In the face of the storm unfurl'd,
Old England's Catholic ensign wav'd, –
The Cross that rules the world!

Scarcely has the cross touched the waters than the ship begins gradually to rise again, whereupon it steers 'for England's shore'. The Hermit now sees that the ship's crew consists of England's native saints and that Mary, once beloved in the British Isles, is at the helm.

171 The poem's full title is 'Inscription for the Spot Where the Hermitage Stood on St Herbert's Island, Derwent-Water'.

172 Frederick William Faber, *Sights and Thoughts in Foreign Churches and among Foreign Peoples* (London: J.G.F. & J. Rivington, 1842).

The vision inspires the Hermit to utter a prophecy: For three centuries the Catholic Church will languish in England, reduced to virtual lifelessness. In the following fourth century, however, a Pope (clearly meant to be Pius IX) will formally define the dogma of the Immaculate Conception and Our Lady, in gratitude, will 'restore … the Isle of the Saints' to the true faith.

In crafting this poem Caswall drew on and synthesized an impressive variety of sources. The image of a ship apparently doomed yet miraculously and triumphantly restored is reminiscent of the 'Ancient Mariner';[173] his depiction of the ship rising from the watery depths also owes something to Coleridge's poem:

CASWALL	COLERIDGE
And after the spar, the three tall masts, With sails of glistening white; And after the masts, the Ship herself, With all her armoury bright.	At first it seemed a little speck, And then it seemed a mist; It moved and moved, and took at last A certain shape, I wist. (87)

as does the glass simile to describe the calm sea after the ship is redeemed:

CASWALL	COLERIDGE
… soothing the waves, Till they lay as molten glass. (59)	The harbour-bay was clean as glass, So smoothly it was strewn. (99)

and the description of the interplay between the ship and the sun.

Borrowing from Scripture for his image of the risen ship beginning 'To walk the waters o'er', Caswall also appropriates trinitarian symbolism: when the ship starts to emerge from the watery depths the first things visible after the spar are

The *three* tall masts,
With sails of glistering white

and the Hermit sees his vision not once, but on *three* successive Easter Sunday mornings.

'The Easter Ship' stands squarely in the tradition of a prophecy, expectation, or yearning that England would one day be restored to

[173] Is it possible that Newman's Coleridgean experience of being 'becalm'd on the silent sea' off the Italian coast in 1833, which inspired 'The Pillar of the Cloud', may have given the Tractarian and Roman Catholic poets additional impetus for such use of ship imagery?

the Roman Catholic faith.[174] Never did the time for the fulfilment of this expectation appear so ripe as it did in the middle of the nineteenth century, after the restoration of the hierarchy and the appointment of Dr Nicholas Wiseman, former Rector of the English College in Rome, as Archbishop. The realization of the prophecy appears at times to have been associated with belief in the Immaculate Conception, possibly because of the country's historic devotion to Mary, and because, as Caswall had pointed out in his notes for 'The Easter Ship', English and Spanish monks had been particularly diligent in promoting this belief. It is, at any rate, undoubtedly England's historic reputation as 'Our Lady's dowry' that caused expectation of the country's return to the 'true faith' to be fairly consistently associated with Marian devotion. Faber's classic hymn 'Faith of Our Fathers' anticipates that 'Mary's prayers / Shall win our country back to thee', while a song penned by Newman in 1849, 'The Pilgrim Queen', has Mary promise:

> I am coming to rescue
> my home and my reign
> And Peter and Philip
> are close in my train.[175]

Conclusion

As a writer of verse Caswall started as a poet in the Anglican and Tractarian traditions who began composing and occasionally publishing his verses while an undergraduate at Oxford in the 1830s. His early poems follow the convention of using nature as a springboard from which to draw a moral, often on the typically Victorian theme (and one of Caswall's personal favourite themes) of

[174] Caswall recounts in some detail a vision experienced by the Ven. Marina de Escobar (1554–1633) in which England would lie in the grip of 'heresy' for three centuries, after which a pope would proclaim the dogma of the Immaculate Conception and Mary, in gratitude, would restore England to the 'true faith'. Marina de Escobar was a Spanish mystic whose visions fill many volumes and were written down by her spiritual guide, Ven. Luis de Ponte (1554–1624). They were translated into German in 1861. Caswall mentions a translation by Wordsworth of the vision in question, but I have not been able to trace this. (He does not specify which Wordsworth he meant.)

[175] Philip is, of course, St Philip Neri. Newman regarded the Oratorian mission to be a key instrument in the (re)evangelizing of England for Roman Catholicism. Interestingly, Caswall's short poems on this subject – 'Catholic Ruins', 'England's Future Conversion', and 'A Prophecy' – do not draw the connection with Mary.

the transience of earthly life. Aside from the sketches of a few polemical and very personal poems that he entered in his journal shortly after his conversion, his first consciously Roman Catholic poetry was the *Lyra Catholica* translations of the ancient Latin hymns. The verses he composed following his conversion tend to be, more than previously, of an overtly religious or devotional nature.

Caswall's more ambitious poetry – the odes, the lengthy verse dramas, and *The Minster of Eld* – date from his Roman Catholic years. The odes are nature poetry cast in a Miltonian mode and firmly anchored in the theological conviction that nature is a sacrament revealing not only the creative but also the redemptive aspects of God; specifically, Caswall celebrates the (Roman Catholic) Church as locus of God's continuing work of redemption.[176] Proceeding from this notion, the theme of valorizing the church becomes the *raison d'être* for the extended verse dramas and other lengthy poems.

Typically, pastoral concerns informed the way Caswall negotiated the maze that was the Victorian hymnal publishing industry. His motivation for taking all possible steps to retain the copyrights to his hymn texts was his wish that the hymns continue to be available to anyone – of whatever denomination – who wanted to use them. Even the business considerations were ultimately subordinated to the pastoral: while not concerned about income for his own sake, Caswall knew well that the Oratory could use the proceeds, both during and after his lifetime.

When he came to publish his first collection of original verse, after eleven years as a Roman Catholic, he did not hesitate to include the poetry of his Anglican days, some of which, as we have seen, dated from as much as twenty-five years earlier. Thus, one cannot simply label Caswall a 'Roman Catholic poet'.[177] His verse, like his life, spans a continuum of concerns that affected all who experienced the religious upheavals and revivals of mid nineteenth-century England. It was Caswall's peculiar vocation to minister to countless souls along that continuum not only by carrying out a clergyman's normal pastoral duties, but also through his eloquent expression of their issues, their spirituality, their religious devotion, in verse.

[176] Cf. the ode 'The Sanctuary of the Church', in *Masque of Mary*, pp. 129–32.

[177] Thus Tennyson's assessment of Caswall's poetry is misleading, as it is based not only on a wrong date for Caswall's conversion (1850, which leads Tennyson to regard *Lyra Catholica* as a Tractarian work), but also on the assumption that the poems in *The Masque of Mary* had been composed not long before the 1858 publication of this volume (*Victorian Devotional Poetry*, pp. 183–4).

Chapter Seven

Later Prose Works and Final Years

The middle and later years of the nineteenth century opened the floodtides of Catholic devotions that poured into England from the Continent. Due to Wiseman's and Faber's love-affairs with all things Italian many of the new devotions were imported more or less unchanged from that country, but by no means all, for Catholic devotional life in France was also undergoing a renewal.

In addition to applications for permission to use his already published works, Caswall occasionally received requests for new translations, for example of hymns from the office of a particular local saint. In a letter to Caswall requesting such translations the Bishop of Plymouth acknowledged that 'Poetry cannot be forced in the midst of sick calls & other parochial duty'.[1] Indeed, when the increasing pressure of pastoral responsibilities at the Oratory did not permit the leisure for Caswall's poetic muse to flow, he occasionally managed to find time to produce devotional works in prose, a number of which originated in France. This chapter will describe Caswall's later prose works, review his relations with his family in later years as well as his own final illness and death, and offer a brief evaluation of his life and work.

Later prose works

Several of Caswall's prose Catholic devotionals were translations or compilations by others, which he edited and prepared for publica-

[1] Letter from Bishop William Vaughan to Edward Caswall, 5 February 1861.

tion. The earliest translation is *The Altar Manual*, from volume 2 of a French work entitled *Les Délices des Ames pieuses*, a work that Caswall claimed was 'highly popular' in France.[2] Caswall edited and eventually[3] revised the work. Originally the English version appeared 'contemporaneously with the *Lyra*',[4] thus around 1849. For the most part, the translation was done not by Edward but 'in the first instance, by a lady very nearly and dearly connected with the Editor, since gone to her rest' – that is, by Louisa Caswall, and it speaks for Edward's lasting devotion to her that he could describe her thus in the Preface to the 1870 edition.

The contents of *The Altar Manual* include exercises for confession as preparation for Communion, Meditations and Prayers for Communion, and prayers for use at 'visits to the most Holy Sacrament', a devotion then coming into vogue.[5] Caswall added a number of prayers not in the original: for example, a selection of psalms that might be recited before or after Communion, the Benedicite canticle, and various Hymns on the Blessed Eucharist with Others; among the latter are several of his translations of Latin hymns, such as *Pange lingua*,[6] *Lauda Sion*,[7] *Adoro te devote*,[8] *Jesu dulcis memoria*,[9] *Veni Creator Spiritus*,[10] and *O Deus ego amo te*,[11] and some original hymns by himself and others, including 'O Jesu Christ, remember when thou shalt come again'.[12] It very likely was this additional material that secured the continued popularity of this manual, for otherwise it is rather dated in language and in concept.

Another book devoted to the Eucharist and edited by Caswall also began as a collaboration: *Hours at the Altar: or, Meditations on the Holy Eucharist*.[13] An 'accomplished lady' – Miss Dorothea Smith, a peni-

2 Edward Caswall, *The Altar Manual or, Devotions for Confession and Communion*, 5th edn (Dublin, 1870), Preface.

3 For the fifth edition.

4 Edward Bellasis, 'Biographical Preface', in Edward Caswall, *Hymns and Poems Original and Translated*, new edn (London: Burns & Oates, 1908), p. 12.

5 Cf. Mary Heimann, *Catholic Devotion in Victorian England* (Oxford: Clarendon Press, 1995), p. 36.

6 'Sing, my tongue, the Saviour's glory', in Edward Caswall, *Lyra Catholica: Containing All the Breviary and Missal Hymns with Others from Various Sources* (London: James Burns, 1849), p. 91.

7 'Sion, lift thy voice, and sing', in ibid., p. 236.

8 'O Godhead hid, devoutly I adore Thee', in ibid., p. 247.

9 'Jesu, the very thought of Thee', in ibid., p. 56.

10 'My God, I love Thee, not because', in ibid., p. 295.

12 Prayer to Jesus in the Blessed Sacrament, in Edward Caswall, *The Masque of Mary and Other Poems* (London: Burns & Oates Ltd., 1858), p. 270.

13 Edward Caswall, *Hours at the Altar: or, Meditations on the Holy Eucharist* (Dublin: James Duffy, 1855).

tent of Caswall's – had introduced him to the work and 'had ... [a] large share in its translation'.[14] The original, *Méditations sur l'Eucharistie* by M. l'Abbé de la Bouillerie, Vicar General of Paris, had 'been received with ... extraordinary favour in France' because of its association with a 'grand devotional movement' started by the author, what would now be known as a Nocturnal Adoration Society of the Blessed Sacrament.

Hours at the Altar consists of twelve meditations, each beginning with a Scripture quotation (given in Latin and English) that is used as a starting point for the meditation. Its echoing of the patristic typological interpretation of the Hebrew Bible possibly explains its appeal for Caswall; nine of the meditations begin with a quotation from the Hebrew Bible, yet all lead to the Eucharist.

For example, Meditation 2, 'The Divine Field of the Eucharist', based on Ruth 2:8, expounds the story of Ruth and Boaz. Boaz, as husbandman (tiller of fields), is a type of Jesus, while Ruth represents the Gentiles abandoning their false gods and thus also the 'holy soul renouncing the world and its vain pleasures' for the sake of union with Christ alone. The field of benediction where Ruth comes to glean is the Blessed Sacrament or 'wheat of the elect' that feeds the spiritually hungry, and the marriage of Ruth and Boaz represents union with Jesus.

Meditation 9, 'First and Last Communion', uses Psalm 64:9 (Septuagint numbering) as a starting point for meditating on the Christian life as bounded by these two events. Our first Communion is an event 'sweet to dwell upon', a time of innocence, while our last Communion brings a complete detachment from the world and an anticipation of attaining the bliss of heaven.

Another translation was of a popular French devotional manual, *Love for Holy Church*,[15] which formed part of a series, the other two parts having been *Amour à la Sainte Eucharistie* and *Amour à la Sainte Vierge*. Quite possibly Caswall chose this particular one to translate because he saw it filling a gap: nothing of the kind existed in English, whereas books of devotion to the Eucharist and to Mary were readily available. There are seven chapters, each with four to ten meditations. The chapter titles include 'Origin and Titles of the Church', 'Foundation and Preservation of the Church', 'Distinctive

14 Ibid., Preface, viii.

15 Edward Caswall, *Love for Holy Church*, from the French of M. l'Abbé Petit (London: Richardson & Son, 1862). The original was *Amour à la Sainte Église ou Élevations sur l'Église Catholique* (1856), one of 'a large number which the gifted Author has contributed to the religious movement in France' (*Love for Holy Church*, Preface, p. vii). Caswall must have done the entire translation himself, as he credits no one else.

Marks of the Church', two on 'Services Rendered by the Church to Mankind in the Spiritual Order' and a similar on the temporal order, and 'Our Duties to Holy Church, and How to Do Her Service'. One can understand why such a book might have appealed to English Catholics, who felt themselves to be members of a beleaguered church in their own country; however, there are no indications as to the level of popularity it achieved.

Given his passion for the spiritual formation of children, it is not surprising that Caswall should have edited a book titled *The Children's Bread: A Manual of Devotions for First Communicants Followed by Devotions for Confirmation.*[16] This was yet another joint effort, this time with an anonymous collaborator who compiled the book 'as a tribute of devotion to ... St Philip Neri' during her residence in France. Caswall published the book 'in the hope that it will supply a want long experienced by several priests, in presenting them with a little book to place in the hands of the more educated portion of the younger members of their flock, when they are preparing for First Communion and Confirmation'.[17]

The Children's Bread consists of daily exercises for the month preceding First Communion Day, each devoted to a topic such as 'The great love our Blessed Lord shows to children in inviting them to come to Him', 'Sorrow for sin', and 'The necessity of prayer'. For each meditation there is a Scripture reading, reflection, resolution, prayer, and ejaculatory prayer to Mary. To this are added further exercises for the nine days before First Communion, an exercise for confession, and a section to help the child prepare for the Sacrament of Confirmation. The fact that a new edition of *The Children's Bread* was published as late as 1900 gives some indication of its continued success.

The one original devotional book that Caswall published was *Verba Verbi: The Words of Jesus, arranged in Order of Time, as a Daily Companion Epitome of the Gospel, and Treasury of Mental Prayer.*[18] Bearing a motto from Aquinas's eucharistic poem *Adoro te devote* – 'Credo quidquid dixit Dei Filius'[19] – this book may have been compiled for the Oratorium Parvum or Little Oratory, a confraternity attached to the Oratory, for it is dedicated to 'the devout

16 Edward Caswall, *The Children's Bread: A Manual of Devotions for First Communicants Followed by Devotions for Confirmation* (London and Leamington: Art & Book Co., 1900).

17 Ibid., Preface, pp. vii–viii.

18 Edward Caswall, *Verba Verbi: The Words of Jesus, arranged in Order of Time, as a Daily Companion Epitome of the Gospel, and Treasury of Mental Prayer* (London: Burns & Lambert, 1855).

19 In Caswall's translation, 'Firmly I believe whatever God's Son has spoken'.

children of St. Philip' and thus counts as one more of his efforts at aiding the spiritual development of younger Catholics. Caswall envisioned it as an aid to meditation, a small pocket book convenient for those 'brief intervals [in the course of a day] in which the mind is free to pursue some religious line of thought', rather than a substitute for the use, at regular times of day, of books written expressly for the purposes of meditation.[20]

Verba Verbi appears to have been inspired by an earlier concordance that had 'exhibited in one connection all those passages of the Old Testament which are quoted by our Lord Jesus Christ and His Apostles in the New'.[21] What Caswall attempts to do is to arrange the words of Jesus chronologically. First he provides a 'Chronological Index to the Life of Our Blessed Lord' (from the Douay version) in which the events in Jesus' life are listed according to years (A.D. 1 = Jesus' birth) and, after each event, the scriptural source (Gospel and chapter number) indicated. Then the actual words of Jesus are presented in the body of the text. The heading at the top of each page announces the context or topic (e.g., 'Sermon of Jesus to his disciples', 'The deaf and dumb spirit cast out – The Son of Man to be delivered up'), followed by Jesus' words. Footnotes in the text refer to Notes from the Douay Testament given at the back of the book.

In later years Caswall wrote two other books not of a devotional nature but aimed at educating reasonably intelligent Catholics about pertinent matters connected with their religion. His ongoing concern about the average Catholic's inability to understand the Latin services bore fruit, thirty years after he first committed such concerns to paper, in *The Catholic's Latin Instructor in the Principal Church Offices and Devotions*.[22] The book was specifically intended to benefit 'those whose education admits of ... an acquaintance with those portions of the Latin Liturgy which are in most frequent public use'. The existence of interest in becoming acquainted with Latin in such a context was shown, he believed, 'by the multiplication ... of Missals and Prayer-books containing the Latin and Vernacular side by side'.[23] Among those whom Caswall envisaged as likely to benefit from the book were choir singers, persons using the 'bilingual' missals and prayer books who, with the right guidance,

[20] *Verba Verbi*, Preface, pp. vi–vii.

[21] Caswall describes *Verba Verbi* as 'little more than the *Verba a Christo prolata* of the Scripturae Sacrae Cursus Completus, harmonized agreeably with the *Concordia Evangelica*' (Preface, p. v).

[22] Edward Caswall, *The Catholic's Latin Instructor in the Principal Church Offices and Devotions* (London: Burns & Oates, 1876).

[23] Ibid., Preface, p. iii.

might derive more advantages from them at present, devout persons who 'might greatly profit by the occasional use of Latin prayers' but are restrained by the misconception that they would require a thorough knowledge of Latin, and 'most especially, ... the increasing multitude of children now in course of education in our Catholic mission schools'.[24] Here the voice of Caswall the educator is clearly discernible:

> It is to be hoped that, as Latin is one of the extra subjects now proposed by the Education Department, the study of it will soon find a settled place in our elementary school course; in which case Catholics will enjoy ... a great and singular advantage ... [I]f from the dogmatic character of such a selection [as contained in this book] ... it is inadmissible within the school-time proper, as fixed for schools in connection with Government; it would none the less be found serviceable in the time set apart for religious instruction, or as a Catholic supplement to secular Latin.[25]

Caswall arranges the chapters according to the main church services (Benediction, the Mass, a chapter for altar servers on 'Serving at Mass', and, finally, one on 'Various Prayers and Offices'). Rather than attempting a systematic instruction in grammar he provides exercises aimed chiefly at helping the reader to understand frequently-used texts from, for example, church services and private prayers. Thus he breaks up the given texts according to certain grammatical constructions (e.g., 'Preposition and Noun', 'Genitive Case after Noun') and, in part 1 of the exercise, gives examples from the texts. He then refers to a corresponding section a few pages later in which those texts are repeated, broken up into words with their English translation (e.g.: ostium *the gate* coeli *of heaven*). The reader is supposed to commit to memory the meanings of the phrases 'until [he or she] feels quite at home in it'.[26]

Caswall's booklet *A Brief Account of Catholicism in Norway*[27] may appear to be a departure from his usual output; however, Norway, like England, was a country in which Roman Catholics were only

[24] Ibid., Preface, p. iv.
[25] Ibid., Preface, pp. iv–v.
[26] Ibid., p. 2.
[27] Edward Caswall, *A Brief Account of Catholicism in Norway* (London: Burns, Lambert, & Oates, 1867). The inside title page gives the lengthy subtitle 'The Catholic Mission Lately Commenced at Bergen in Norway; including a Brief History of Religion in That Country, with Some Account of the Present Civil Status of Catholics There'.

just beginning to regain the rights of which they had been deprived at the Reformation, and as a consequence Roman Catholicism was experiencing something of a resurgence there. Caswall hoped and assumed that his English co-religionists would be eager to learn about, pray for, and possibly contribute financially to their fellow Roman Catholics in that Nordic land.

A clue to what may have sparked Caswall's interest in Norway is found in a brown hardcover notebook that he kept up to the end of his life. An entry for 12 August 1866 refers to a Miss Lucie Dahl from Bergen, Norway, received into the church on 8 July by a Fr Trappes in Hull and now staying with her uncle, a Mr Wingaard, in Edgbaston Lane. One can surmise that Caswall made the acquaintance of Lucie Dahl on that day and that his interest in the revival of Roman Catholicism in Scandinavia dates from that encounter.

Immediately under the 12 August entry comes 'Herr Komner Dahl, Bergen, Norway, the Father of Miss Lucie Dahl above', and under that, dated 12 September 1866 (perhaps the date Caswall sent or received correspondence with him?), 'Rev. Houen Hoelfeldt, Katholsk Prost, Bergen'.[28] The presence of three travel guides to Norway on a list of books he had purchased in October 1866[29] points to an impending trip, and indeed his little booklet was ready for publication by spring 1867.[30] In all likelihood the visit to Norway was facilitated through personal contact with Fr Hoelfeldt; as a convert who was at the Propaganda College in Rome at the same time as Newman, and an author who had 'published several works in the Norwegian language well adapted to their present phase of religious thought',[31] he and Caswall would have found they had much in common.

The little twelve-page booklet starts with a history of Christianity in Norway, beginning with the evangelization of the country in the tenth century under the English King Athelstan and continuing through the Protestant Reformation and the consequent persecution of Catholics. Caswall then describes in detail the current efforts to reintroduce Catholicism into Norway, which had begun in the 1840s after the passage of laws that released all 'dissenters' from control of the Lutheran state church. Not unexpectedly, he is most knowledgeable about relevant events and the status of Catholics in

[28] I.e., 'Catholic priest'. His name is given in *Catholicism in Norway* as Holfeldt Houen, and he was then the pastor of the Bergen mission (p. 7).

[29] *Handbook of Sweden, Denmark & Norway*, *Knapsack Guide for Norway*, and *A Month in Norway*.

[30] A notebook entry for 24 March 1867 mentions an advertisement for the book just placed in the *Tablet*.

[31] *Catholicism in Norway*, p. 8.

Bergen and devotes some space to Norwegians' attitude toward converts: converts to Catholicism were 'looked upon with dislike, and in some classes with a kind of horror, as something monstrous and unaccountable'.[32] Nonetheless, the situation in this respect had improved since ten years before, when Catholics had been 'almost confounded in the public mind with Mormonism. It is now no longer so'.[33]

Caswall concludes with the hope that his account will have sparked the interest of 'some good souls in the work of the Norway Mission'. Commending to the prayers of English Catholics the 'noble effort now making at Bergen', he 'will be happy to answer communications on the subject, and to forward contributions in money, books, vestments, paintings, or other articles, agreeably with the authorisation which ... he has received from the Rev. Director of the Norwegian Mission'.[34]

Remarkably, *Catholicism in Norway* was also published and sold in Spanish translation. Perhaps there is a parallel to be drawn between nineteenth-century Spaniards' interest in Norway's return to Roman Catholicism and their seventeenth-century counterparts' interest in England's reconversion as illustrated by the prophecy of Ven. Marina de Escobar. Caswall retained his contacts with his Catholic friends in Norway; the same notebook referred to above contains an entry, 'May 1874 Mrs. H.H. Krohn, Strandgaden, Bergen' – perhaps the married name of Lucie Dahl, now returned to her native land. He did return to Norway that year[35] and visited again, for the last time, in the summer of 1876; it was there that he suffered a heart attack from which he never fully recovered.

Caswall and his family in later years

On the family scene Caswall's later years brought a poignant blend of joy and sorrow – joy over the frequent contact with his American niece and nephew, and sorrow at the chronic misfortunes that dogged his brother Fred, and at the deaths, in America, of his brothers Tom and Henry.

Although a family history reports that Edward had 'had to suffer

[32] Ibid., p. 10.
[33] Ibid. Considering his brother Henry's experiences with the Mormons, it is not surprising that this should have made an impression on Edward.
[34] Ibid., p. 12.
[35] In June 1874 his sister Emma had written to Fred and Kate that Edward was coming to visit her and proposed 'soon after' to go to Norway.

ostracism for [his conversion to Roman Catholicism] and died almost unknown to the various branches of the rising generation of his family',[36] Henry's son and daughter were a happy exception. Much affectionate correspondence and exchange of photographs and gifts crossed the Atlantic. Mary Elizabeth Caswall, known in the family as Lipsie, had married David Grant of Pennsylvania, and after the birth of their son, David Caswall Grant,[37] Edward sent them a letter and picture. Lipsie replied thanking him, assuring him that he 'would receive a most hearty welcome' if he were to visit them and quoting from a letter that devoted grandfather Henry had written the baby: 'Don't cry too much, but be always very good, and Grandpapa will like you much, and so will Uncle Edward'.[38] Some months later Lipsie sent Edward a photograph of her son.[39]

From Henry's son Robert Clarke Caswall, who became a clergyman and eventually Canon of Christ Church in Hamilton, Canada, there also survive a number of letters to Edward signed 'Your affectionate nephew', and in later years it was to Edward that Robert wrote concerning Tom's grave: having learned that the cemetery in which Tom was buried had been sold, the family wished to assure themselves that it would remain a cemetery and not be sold to developers.

The end of Tom's sad life came in 1862. From the time of his confinement in an asylum in the 1840s to the end of his life, Tom's mental health remained a fairly constant source of worry to his siblings. He apparently suffered from depression sufficiently debilitating to have prevented him from ever following a profession.[40] Henry regularly expressed concern, fearing the consequences if Tom did not receive treatment. He appeared to suffer from hallucinations and possibly paranoia as well, since he tended to live under assumed names and at one point wanted his money sent not to his proper address via the 'cheap and safe' method of one bill of exchange but to another location, divided among six post-office orders. 'Tom's strange precautions must render him an object of

[36] *Memoirs of the Caswall Family*, p. 17.

[37] It was the custom in the Grant family – which was related to the family of the President, Ulysses Simpson Grant – to name the eldest son David and append the mother's maiden name, as Lipsie explained in a letter to Edward (15 November 1869).

[38] Ibid.

[39] Letter to Edward from M. E. Grant, 7 June 1870.

[40] In 1852 Alfred wrote to Edward asking, 'Is Tom with you? If so, do urge him to ... do something, and not always sleep this life in such a dull lethargy as of late years. He might have been a barrister or a physician long ere this ...' (letter dated 15 July 1852).

suspicion everywhere,' Henry remarked.[41] Tom had followed his brothers to America, stayed a while with Fred, and then went to Canada, where he met up with Henry's son Robert. Robert suspected that there was something wrong with Tom without having previously known anything of his malady. Eventually Tom ended up in New York City. The Civil War had broken out, and in 1862, fearful of danger lest hostilities reach that city, Tom bought a pistol, and accidentally shot himself in the stomach with it. He died three days later, on 5 March 1862, a few weeks short of his forty-sixth birthday, and was buried in the Evergreen Cemetery in Brooklyn.

Apparently there must have been some suspicion of suicide, for a few weeks after Tom's death Henry wrote to Edward asking if he could spare time to 'run over to New York' to 'settle everything at once' with the help of 'the most powerful man in America', Archbishop John Hughes. 'The coroner might be made to sign a paper to the effect that the verdict was grounded on insufficient evidence, & that it would have been different if the testimony of the two doctors had been received', wrote Henry.[42] Henry was also concerned that Tom's personal effects be retrieved, such as a watch – presumably the watch given him by his father shortly before the latter's death – and clothes.[43] Fortunately Mary Burgess Caswall had not lived to witness these events: the mother of the clan had died in July 1861.[44] Tom did die fortified by the sacraments, however, so that the Catholic Church authorities must have been satisfied that his self-inflicted wounds were not intentional.[45]

As intimated by Henry's reference to 'Uncle Edward' in his letter to Lipsie's infant son, the bonds of affection between Henry and Edward were too strong to have been irrevocably sundered by Edward's submission to the Roman Catholic Church. Henry enjoyed a personal acquaintance with Newman before Edward had

41 Cf. several undated letters from Henry to Edward in the Birmingham Oratory archives.

42 Letter of Henry Caswall to Edward Caswall, 30 April 1862.

43 There is no evidence in Newman's letters or diaries, or anywhere else, that Edward ever made such a trip.

44 *Memoirs*, p. 26.

45 Edward's friend Benjamin Wilson, on sending condolences, wrote, 'The consolations of the Church and the kind attendance of a Catholic landlady who relates the last moments of dear Thomas must . . . be a source of happy reflections to his surviving relatives, especially to yourself' (11 June 1862), and a sketch of a proposed tombstone in Edward's possession describes Tom as 'fortified by the holy sacraments of the Church'. By ironic coincidence, the priest who attended Tom at the end was another convert, a Fr Neligan, who as an Anglican had been curate to the Caswalls' brother-in-law Benjamin Dowding (Maria Caswall's husband) at Devizes in Wiltshire (*Memoirs*, 17).

ever known him, and a mutual respect had developed between the two men that, at least on an unconscious level, must have mitigated Henry's negative reaction when Edward followed his mentor to Rome. In November 1869 Lipsie reported to Edward that '[o]ur dear Pater continues in the same state of health, but we are afraid he will never be much better than he is at present'.[46] In October 1870 Henry's wife wrote that Henry was suffering from diabetes, and on 18 December 1870 Lipsie conveyed the sad news from Franklin, Pennsylvania that 'our dear Father' had died.[47] The last word Henry had spoken, except for his wife's name, was Edward's name, three times: 'You were the brother and friend', Lipsie wrote, 'to whom he was the most tenderly attached in life'.

Journey to the invisible world

An entry in Newman's diary for Wednesday 23 August 1876 read: 'Edward returned [from Norway] – with gout'.[48]

The problem turned out not to be gout at all but a heart complaint. Toward the end of his trip to Norway he had suffered a sudden attack of breathlessness, which may have been a heart attack or the beginning of congestive heart failure.[49] It distinctly marked the beginning of a lingering illness and of the end of Caswall's life of extraordinary devotion and service to the Oratory. By the end of September Newman realized this clearly. As he wrote to his niece:

> We have had a shock here since I saw you. There were three men, two of them strangers to me, who in past years gave themselves up to me generously and unreservedly – Ambrose St John, John Gordon, and Edward Caswall. These three have been the life and centre of the Oratory, since we came to Birmingham. Gordon ... died more than 23 years ago, Ambrose last year. There remained and remains Caswall, who ... within this few weeks, has shown distinct signs of a heart complaint, which of course is the beginning of the end. He was travelling in Norway, and had a sudden attack which might have proved fatal.[50]

[46] Letter to Edward from M. E. Grant, 15 November 1869.
[47] Henry died on 17 December 1870.
[48] *Letters and Diaries* (*LD*) XXVIII, ed. Charles Stephen Dessain and Thomas Gornall, SJ (Oxford: Clarendon Press, 1975), p. 101.
[49] On 15 September 1876 Newman recorded that 'Edward had a fit of asthma, or rather from the heart'.
[50] Letter of Newman to Anne Mozley, 1 October 1876; (*LD*) XXVIII, p. 118.

A few weeks later he wrote to Maria Giberne: 'I don't expect Edward will ever be well again – How long God will let him stay here, He alone knows – but he will always be an invalid.'[51]

Edward's sisters arrived for a week's visit on 12 December.[52] Although he was well enough to visit the Botanical Garden with them,[53] he must quickly have taken a turn for the worse, for he was anointed on the day they left.[54] He deteriorated markedly over the next few weeks; Newman informed their mutual friend Copeland that 'the doctor thinks the change *great* during the last three weeks or month' and lamented that, whereas Caswall had been able to go out with his sisters only a fortnight earlier, he was now unable to leave his room.[55]

The turn of the year brought Newman melancholy thoughts about the way friends were being unexpectedly and suddenly struck down and about the serious loss the Oratory would suffer with Caswall gone.[56] He remarked on the parallel between Caswall's situation and that of the Oratory's staunch supporter Mrs Wootten, who had died on 9 January 1876. Caswall, then in the best of health, had diligently attended her in her last illness, which was virtually identical to that which he now suffered, and had complied with her last wishes and executed her will. In his grief at his impending loss Newman formed the conviction that Mrs Wootten was calling Edward home. To Mrs Wilberforce he wrote:

> Father Caswall's illness is ... a great trouble to us. To the Congregation he is even a greater loss than Ambrose. And he seemed so vigorous, doing no end of work. He had just carried through all the business connected with Ambrose's and Mrs Wootten's wills. She died a year since next Tuesday. He took all her instructions and was her Priest on her deathbed, instead of Ambrose. It is as if Ambrose called her, and she called Fr Caswall.[57]

51 Letter of Newman to Maria Giberne, 21 October 1876; ibid., p. 127.
52 Diary entry; ibid., p. 144.
53 Letter of Newman to W. J. Copeland, 26 December 1876; ibid., p. 150.
54 Newman wrote to John Hungerford Pollen that 'there is no chance, humanly speaking of his living' (18 December 1876; ibid., p. 147) and to Catherine Anne Bathurst asking her prayers for Fr Caswall: 'His life is a matter of days or weeks. It is a complaint the heart suddenly developed, and he might go off any moment suddenly' (ibid.).
55 Letter of Newman to W. J. Copeland, 26 December 1876; ibid., p. 150.
56 Cf. letters of Newman to Lord Emly, 26 December 1876 (ibid., p. 151), Emily Bowles, 29 December (ibid.), Sr. Mary Gabriel du Boulay, 29 December (ibid., p. 152), Robert Ornsby, 29 December (ibid., p. 153), Mother Mary Imelda Poole, 29 December (ibid., p. 154), Mrs. Henry Wilberforce, 3 January 1877 (ibid., p. 155), and Mrs. William Froude, 9 Jan (ibid., p. 158).
57 Letter of Newman to Mrs Henry Wilberforce, 3 January 1877; ibid., p. 155.

To Mrs William Maskell, Newman posed a rhetorical question: 'Which is the worse, to lose dear friends suddenly or to have them slowly die under your eyes?'[58] With Caswall it was fated to be the latter, though Newman could not know this at the time: there ensued a year-long ride on an emotional roller coaster, with Caswall occasionally appearing to rally only to relapse after a short time. Newman's letters suggest that he was experiencing a good deal of anticipatory grieving during these months.

By the third week in February 1877 it became apparent that Caswall's death was not so imminent,[59] although he was not expected ever again to 'be other than an invalid'.[60] Newman feared that he would 'go off suddenly' rather than slowly decline;[61] by Holy Week Caswall himself, despite feeling better, was 'uncertain ... whether he shall ever say Mass again'.[62]

April and May brought considerable improvement in Caswall's condition: Newman could report that he was 'wonderfully better. He promises to be as well as an invalid can be'[63] and rejoice that 'after six months of confinement in his room, [he] is now walking about'.[64] '[T]he change is wonderful', wrote Newman, 'and to see him down stairs is like seeing the dead revive'.[65] The possibility of a sudden relapse, or worse, preyed constantly on Newman's mind, however, so that in June he urged Copeland to 'come and see him, *while* he is well'.[66]

In July Caswall was well enough to spend a month at Reading with his sisters.[67] By the beginning of October, however, his condition had worsened again[68] and a gradual decline set in, so that by early December his state of health gave considerable cause for alarm and he received the last sacraments.[69] He lingered for

[58] Letter of Newman to Mrs William Maskell, 6 January 1877; ibid., p. 156.

[59] Cf. letters of Newman to W. J. Copeland, 21 February (ibid., p. 169); and Mrs Henry Wilberforce, 22 February (ibid., p. 171).

[60] Letter of Newman to Mrs J. W. Bowden, 7 March (ibid., p. 174); cf. also letter to Henry Bedford, 10 March (ibid., p. 177).

[61] Letter of Newman to Maria Giberne, 8 March (ibid., p. 175; cf. also letter to W. J. Copeland, Easter Day (1 April) (ibid., p. 186).

[62] Letter of Newman to Catherine Anne Bathurst, Good Friday (30 March) (ibid., p. 185).

[63] Letter of Newman to Anne Mozley, 26 May (ibid., p. 200).

[64] Letter of Newman to John Thomas Walford, SJ, 26 May (ibid.).

[65] Letter of Newman to Sr Mary Gabriel du Boulay, 28 May (ibid., p. 201).

[66] Letter of Newman to W. J. Copeland, 20 June (ibid., p. 209).

[67] Newman's diary records that Edward left Birmingham on 12 July and returned 16 August in the company of his cousin 'Mr Burgess': probably John James Burgess, from whom a letter to Caswall survives, written at the time of Tom Caswall's death.

[68] Letter of Newman to Anne Mozley, 4 October (ibid., p. 243).

[69] Letters of Newman to Anne Mozley, 3 December (ibid., p. 273) and Baron Friedrich von Hügel, 3 December (ibid.).

another month, his physical health rapidly declining, his mind 'as clear and as active, as ever it was – no weakening of memory, observation, or reflection'.[70]

The new year 1878 dawned 'wet warm foggy'.[71] On 2 January Newman recorded simply: 'Fr. Edward Caswall died.'[72]

Newman gave the details in a flurry of letters to various friends over the next few days. He immediately wrote to one of Edward's sisters:

> . . . I cannot doubt, so long an illness has prepared you for what I have to tell you about your dear Brother.
>
> He suddenly fell off about seven this evening, and was taken from us, in a quarter of an hour, so peacefully, that we could not fix the time when he went. Nor did we pronounce that he was no more, though he had gone for some minutes, till the medical man Dr Jordan, who has been unremitting in his attentions, came and assured us that we are not mistaken.
>
> He seems to have felt that he was drawing to his end, for in the middle of the day he began to express his sense of God's mercies in having been so tender and careful of him all through his life, and having kept him from pain during his last illness.
>
> He was one of my dearest friends, and is a great loss to us all, for he was loved far and wide round about the Oratory.[73]

To some friends Newman confided that Caswall's death, though long anticipated, was nonetheless sudden. A letter to Mrs F. R. Ward poignantly contrasted this suddenness with the gradual process by which Caswall had been coming to terms with the invisible world:

> His end after all was sudden. One evening he said 'I think I will go to bed' – and made for his bed – but fainted before he got to it. They got him to it . . . He lay as if sleeping, and died we could not tell when. His death was as tranquil as his life. I think that for the last three days he knew that death was at hand. He did not suffer much, except from weakness and weariness. He had been looking death and the unseen world in the face, and its prospective revelations, for seventeen months. He had his mind clear and vigorous to the last.[74]

[70] Letter of Newman to Mrs. Edward Bellasis, 22 December (ibid., p. 286).
[71] Diary entry, Tuesday 1 January 1878 (ibid., p. 291).
[72] Ibid.
[73] Letter of Newman to Miss Caswall, 2 January 1878 (ibid., p. 292). It is unclear whether the addressee was Emma or Olivia; both of Caswall's unmarried sisters were still alive.
[74] Letter of Newman to Mrs F. R. Ward, 13 January (ibid., p. 301).

Perhaps three letters most eloquently sum up Caswall's life and death. One was from Newman to a former pupil of the Oratory School who used to accompany Caswall on his visits to the sick: 'Father Caswall died as he lived – tranquil, kind, full of faith, and of gratitude for a calm happy life'.[75]

Another letter came from Bishop Ullathorne in reply to Newman's notification of Caswall's death: 'He was one whom every one loved, and could not but love. If he is a great loss to you in the human sense, he is a great loss to us all, for he was an ornament and benediction to the Diocese'.[76]

The third letter was written to Newman from Edward's sister in reply to news of his will: 'It is just like himself, always so full of love and gentleness for us, and he has ever been most generous to my youngest Brother Fredk throughout all his difficulties'.[77]

Caswall's brother Oratorian, Fr Ignatius Ryder, officiated at the Solemn Requiem Mass on 7 January and Frs Austin Mills and Bellasis[78] were the deacon and subdeacon respectively. Other priests present, some seventeen in number, came from the Oratory community and beyond; they included the Canons of Birmingham's Roman Catholic Cathedral and, of course, Newman himself. It was Newman who read the burial service and absolution at the Oratory cemetery in Rednal in the presence of Caswall's relatives and fellow priests.

The funeral 'naturally brought together a very large congregation'.[79] Obituaries pointed out Caswall's unstinting pastoral work and his immense popularity with those blessed to receive his care:

> ... he was an untiring worker [who] threw himself heartily into the parochial duties assigned him ... Among the poor and sick, into whose sorrows he freely entered, he was a welcome and frequent visitor. His gentle genial ways won the hearts of all, and his charity was limited only by his means. Nothing could exceed his fondness for little children, unless it were the delight they found in his company

[75] Letter of Newman to Robert J. Blake, 10 January (ibid., p. 299), in reply to a letter of condolence enclosing an obituary notice.

[76] Letter of Bishop Ullathorne to Newman, 4 January (ibid., p. 294).

[77] Letter of Miss Caswall to Newman, 9 January (ibid., p. 297). Caswall had appointed Frs Austin Mills, William Neville, and Newman as executors, to whom he left the bulk of his estate. He also left £400 to Frederick, £25 to each of his three sisters, £20 to each of Henry's five children, £100 to his friend Benjamin Wilson, and £25 to his cousin Mr Burgess.

[78] The obituary does not give first names of the priests; thus it is not known whether the Fr Bellasis involved was Richard or Lewis.

[79] Obituary in *The Weekly Register and Catholic Standard*, 19 January 1878, from which this account of the funeral is taken.

> ... If he had a fault it was that of optimism. He looked at everything from its best side, discovered virtues invisible to people of weaker faith, and was always slow to believe in the wickedness of human nature.[80]

Not surprisingly, then, a huge crowd of people came out on a grey winter day to pay their last respects to this beloved priest.[81] But no one could have been more deeply bereaved than Newman himself, to whom Caswall's death brought the acute awareness that the first generation of Oratorians was passing away. The sorrowing Father Superior wrote to Mrs. Henry Wilberforce, 'Three great and loyal friends of mine, Frs Joseph Gordon, Ambrose St John and Edward Caswall now lie side by side at Rednal, and I put them there.'[82]

Conclusion

Pastor and poet

Caswall's pastoral work and his authorship of devotional poetry (including hymns) and prose were the constants in his life; we have seen how they constituted the points of continuity between the Anglican vicar and the Roman Catholic priest. Indeed, the creative activity can in some sense be regarded as one form that Caswall's pastoral work took. For example, his love for and commitment to the faith formation of children bore fruit in two books, one written as an Anglican and the other as a Roman Catholic, designed to prepare children for the sacraments. And while we have suggested that his hymns and poems may to some extent have represented a means of fulfilling his youthful literary ambitions, the chief impulse behind their creation was decidedly the wish to provide laypersons with texts with which to pray or to meditate upon divine mysteries. Caswall the priest was incarnating the Word not only in the eucharistic elements in the Mass but also in the poetic word, disseminated through the medium of print.

In crafting translations with poetic worth in their own right, Caswall made available to English-speaking Christianity not only a

[80] From an otherwise unidentified newspaper obituary, filed in the Oratory Letters in the Birmingham Oratory archives immediately after Newman's letter of 2 January 1878 to Miss Caswall.

[81] The *Weekly Register* obituary reported that Caswall's funeral 'naturally brought together a very large congregation'.

[82] Letter of Newman to Mrs Henry Wilberforce, 18 January 1878, *Letters and Diaries* XXVIII, p. 303.

devotional but also a worship resource from the timeless treasures of the church. By underlining the importance of objectivity in hymns and embodying this quality in his own translations and original texts, he helped to prevent the developing art of Roman Catholic hymnody from domination by emotional excess; and by his understanding of Mary as having significance only within the context of the Incarnation, he balanced the tendency, from other quarters, for hymns to degenerate into Mariolatry.

The early decades of the Birmingham Oratory have customarily been viewed through the lens of Newman's life and thought which, because of his lengthy absence in Dublin and his preoccupation with issues on a wider scale, means 'from a distance' and therefore tends to leave one with the impression that the Oratory was an adjunct to Newman's work. Viewed from the vantage point of Newman's trusted administrator, however, there emerges a picture of the Oratory that takes within its scope the Oratory's everyday practical workings and the effects of these on its immediate environs: through this lens we clearly see the concerns and activities of the priests and laity within the Oratory community as they dealt with pastoral challenges and their practical ramifications.

Caswall's story typifies the educated convert of personal financial means who enriched and influenced the face of Roman Catholicism in England. Living out the Oratory's charism, as Newman envisioned it, of using one's personal wealth to build up the apostolate and reaching out to the well-off, educated Catholics in and around Birmingham, Caswall succeeded in moving in that milieu and influencing them to support the Oratory's outreach; yet, at the same time he ministered tirelessly to the ordinary, less fortunate laity, developing education that met their needs, providing pastoral and spiritual resources for them as well as a Catholic presence in such places as the local prison and workhouse. In the process he and the other Oratorians encouraged and empowered the laity to become involved in the apostolate through such organizations as the Pious Union and the Little Oratory.

Caswall's story, then, was typical in one way. Yet, his Oxford education notwithstanding, his life journey, while sharing much in common with many other Roman Catholic converts in mid-nineteenth-century England, did not replicate the pattern of the convert intellectuals explored by Allitt.[83] He did not engage himself in the theological or ecclesiastical controversies of the day, and to

[83] Patrick Allitt, *Catholic Converts: British and American Intellectuals Turn to Rome* (Ithaca and London: Cornell University Press, 1997). See esp. chapter V.

the extent that he indulged in polemics he did so not in order to 'devote [his] energy to converting more Protestant intellectuals'[84] but in order, first, to justify his own conversion before his family and friends, and, second, to strengthen the faith of his fellow Catholics. Caswall's contributions to the Roman Catholic Church were not those of an intellectual: rather, as an anonymous author observed after his death, 'the time which he could spare from his clerical and parochial labours was devoted chiefly to the composition of hymns and poems'.[85] He was an extraordinary administrator, an indefatigable priest, and one of the great hymnologists of the nineteenth century.

The visible and invisible worlds

The continuity between Caswall's Anglican and Roman Catholic lives also manifested itself in the consistency with which the relationship between the visible and the invisible worlds occupied his thoughts and played itself out in his life and writings. As early as *The Elements of the World* and the *Sermons on the Seen and Unseen* he equated the seen with the transitory and ephemeral and the unseen with the eternal and posited a connection as well as a tension between the two. On the one hand, the visible world is subservient to the invisible, yet tries to supplant it in the human soul. Here the 'vanity' theme is also operative inasmuch as people may act or think with no consideration of God or of transcendent meaning. On the other hand the visible world is also a sacrament of the invisible world: the seen (creation, especially nature) makes visible that which is unseen (the Creator). In the *Sermons on the Seen and Unseen* 2 Corinthians 4:18 provided a theological framework for this theme, with its opposition between faith (relating to the invisible and eternal) and sight (relating to the worldly).[86]

In the course of his conversion journey Caswall's fascination with the visible vs. the invisible enfleshed itself in two principal ways. First, doctrinally and devotionally: his deep attraction to the communion of saints and related issues, particularly prayers for the dead and the invocation of the saints. For Caswall this was not,

[84] Ibid., p. 87.
[85] Unidentified obituary of Edward Caswall.
[86] An investigation of Caswall's treatment of faith (= the invisible, eternal) vs sight (= worldly) in terms of Wordsworth's opposition, in *The Prelude*, between 'genuine freedom' and the state of 'mastery exerted by the physical eye and its material objects, which hold in servitude the perceiving mind' would prove a fruitful study; cf. M.H. Abrams, *Natural Supernaturalism: Tradition and Revolution in Romantic Literature* (London: W.W. Norton & Company, 1971), p. 357.

however, a mere valorization of doctrines but rather a commitment to a way of living. Second, Caswall's assignment of priority to the invisible or eternal over the visible or ephemeral world, as demonstrated by his readiness to forsake ties of family and friendship should his search for the truth lead him to where relatives and friends could not or would not follow. Here the scriptural basis was provided by Matthew 10:37, the words of Jesus that 'He who loves father or mother more than me is not worthy of me'.

Finally, Tractarian poetics combined with an established English poetic tradition afforded Caswall a means of expressing the sacramentality of creation in his poetry: visible nature is a manifestation of its invisible Creator. In engaging the science–vs–religion debate Caswall insisted that the visible *must* be referred back to the invisible. Science alone is inadequate to explain the mysteries of creation; the eyes of faith are required that we not only recognize and appreciate God behind these mysteries but also that we see God as loving, caring provider and not simply as 'master mechanic'. Further, sacred spaces are those places in the world of nature in which communion or contact between the visible and invisible worlds takes place, whether it be a matter of the pagan sages of antiquity drinking in wisdom and truth or blessed sites where the saints – the Church Triumphant – communicate with members of the Church Militant.

Relevance to Christianity in our time

Although Caswall would have been far too humble to see himself as a prophet, certain aspects of his life and work speak with eloquent relevance to issues significant in our own time.

Search for the truth as priority

Caswall was keenly aware of the pain that their respective families would suffer if he and Louisa became Roman Catholics and conscious too of the ostracization that they would suffer.[87] Despite this, and despite the remorse he felt at being the catalyst for such circumstances, he constantly set before himself something higher: the priority of commitment to one's religious convictions in the search for the truth. Thus Caswall's conversion journey provides a model – and lives out a scriptural basis – for challenging the notion of the 'family' as an absolute value. As a recent author has observed:

[87] The author of the *Memoirs of the Caswall Family* ventures the opinion that the elder Caswall would certainly have disinherited Edward and Thomas had he lived to witness their conversions.

'Jesus claimed "those who do the will of my Father in heaven" as his family, called his disciples away from their families, and declared the gospel a sword that would divide families. Traditional-family-values groups would have crucified Jesus.'[88]

Caswall's experience was far from unique, as we know, but in his journal he has left a detailed record of his thought processes on this subject as well as copies of his communications to others. Consistently it was Jesus' words as recorded in the Gospel that undergirded Caswall's conviction that submission to truth takes precedence over family considerations; and just as he trusted in divine providence to provide for him if he should take this great leap of faith, so too he believed that the same divine providence would supply the needs of his family through the likely crisis to come.

Prophetic aspects of Caswall's devotional works

In various ways Caswall's work as author of hymns, poems, and prose devotional books anticipates aspects of post-Vatican II Roman Catholicism.

We saw in chapter 6 that the original author's or translator's crafting of a hymn text was only the first in a series of steps in the process of putting a finished product in the hands of the praying and worshipping faithful. The original text frequently underwent alterations, either with the author's complicity or by the author at an editor's suggestion, and may then have been set to music as well, either matched with or adapted to an existing tune or given a newly composed tune of its own. The entire process amounted, in effect, to a 'priesthood of all believers' in which various people – lay/cleric, poet/nonpoet/ musician – collaborated to bring forth and preach the Word that would be an aid to worship or devotion. Caswall's prose devotional works also anticipated post-Vatican II collaborative ministry in that he edited the translations and compilations of lay people, and indeed of women. *The Altar Manual* must be the only example of a devotional manual in the nineteenth century that resulted from collaboration between a Roman Catholic priest and his wife. And *Verba Verbi* was prophetic in another sense; though innocent of any knowledge (or at least any application) of the historical–critical method, it is remarkable for its attempt to use Scripture as the foundation for a devotional work, and thereby to

[88] Chris Glaser, 'The Love That Dare Not Pray Its Name: The Gay and Lesbian Movement in America's Churches', in *Homosexuality in the Church: Both Sides of the Debate*, ed. Jeffrey S. Siker (Louisville, KY: Westminster John Knox Press, 1994), p. 154.

inculcate a large amount of Scripture into the minds of young Catholics, in an era when Catholics still considered Bible reading a 'Protestant' activity and no significant popular devotions were scripturally based.

Liturgy

Caswall's reflections on public worship, occasioned by his comparisons between the Roman Catholic services he witnessed in Ireland and the Church of England services to which he was accustomed, speak to liturgical concerns today. So, too, does the high value he placed on objectivity in hymn texts, which he would have defined as focus on the majesty and mercy of God.[89] In his journal he wrote of his disillusionment with the Anglican over-reliance on the verbal dimension of worship and the difficulty of many parishioners in keeping up with the printed word; he wrote, too, of the sense of mystery he experienced at Roman Catholic worship, and of the revelation that the visual element and symbolic gestures played an important role in supplementing, indeed complementing the verbal aspect. One hundred and fifty years later, when Roman Catholic liturgy has come to resemble more closely the Anglican worship Caswall rejected than the Roman Catholic worship he came to appreciate, his experience has much to say about the recovery of the sense of mystery; the recovery of the importance of visual symbolism; and the realization that there are times when silence is golden and that 'participation' in a communal venture need not always focus on and be synonymous with everyone together *doing* the identical thing at all times.[90] Further, Caswall's valorization of objectivity in hymn texts can serve as model for hymn writers of any era and certainly as corrective to the narcissistic 'self-praise' hymns current today.

Caswall, then, was for the recovery of beauty. He anticipated the sentiments of a younger poet-priest whom he must surely have met during the latter's brief stint as a lay teacher at the Oratory School in 1867: it was Gerard Manley Hopkins who wrote:

[89] Cf. his Preface to *Lyra Catholica*, in which he writes of the Latin hymns: 'Their tendency is, to take the individual out of himself; to set before him, in turn, all the varied and sublime Objects of Faith; and to blend him with the universal family of the Faithful' (pp. viii–ix).

[90] Writings on this have been numerous, and include Thomas Day, *Why Catholics Can't Sing: The Culture of Catholicism and the Triumph of Bad Taste* (New York: Crossroad, 1990), and chapter 9 in Eugene Pascal, *Jung to Live By* (New York: Warner Books, 1992). Caswall's prophetic voice in this regard can well serve as a topic for investigation in its own right.

> Give beauty back, beauty, beauty, beauty, back to God, beauty's
> self and beauty's giver.[91]

It was Edward Caswall who gave God's beauty to the children he nurtured into an adult faith life, the adults to whom he ministered, the Oratorian community to whom he brought a gentle and genial presence and an awesome talent for organization – and to God, to whose praise and glory he offered the eloquent poetic word.

[91] Gerard Manley Hopkins, 'The Leaden Echo and the Golden Echo', in *Gerard Manley Hopkins: A Selection of His Poems and Prose*, ed. W.H. Gardner (Harmondsworth, England: Penguin Books, 1953).

Bibliography

Archives

Archives of the Oratory of St Philip Neri, Birmingham, England:
Edward Caswall, papers.
Oratory Letters.
Brasenose College Archives, Oxford, England:
Brasenose College Register 1509–1909, 2 vols. Oxford: B.H. Blackwell, 1909.
Collections 1835–1848. ('Collections' was the term for oral examinations.)
Degrees 1807–1849.
Record of terms kept 1825–1901.
Room Book 1818–1867.
Trowbridge Record Office, Trowbridge, Wiltshire, England:
1837. Register. [Archbishop] Denison.
Last will and testament of Louisa Stuart Caswall, a copy, 5 May, 1847.

Works by Edward Caswall

Unpublished (Housed at the Oratory archives, Birmingham: see above)
'Benedicite or the Young Churchman's Book of all Creation'.
'The Elements of the World considered in themselves and as aids towards ascertaining the true Church'. Also titled 'An Essay on The

Empire of the World in the Soul of Man'. 'Journal 1846–7'.
'Travels to Castles in the Air'. Also titled 'A Visit to Cloudland' and 'Modern Sinbad, or, The Castle Builder'.

Published

The Altar Manual or, Devotions for Confession and Communion, 5th edn, Dublin, 1870.
A Brief Account of Catholicism in Norway, London: Burns, Lambert, & Oates, 1867.
The Catholic's Latin Instructor in the Principal Church Offices and Devotions, London: Burns & Oates, 1876.
The Child's Manual: Forty Days' Meditations on the Chief Truths of Religion, as Contained in the Church Catechism, London: James Burns, 1846.
The Children's Bread: A Manual of Devotions for First Communicants Followed by Devotions for Confirmation, London and Leamington: Art & Book Co., 1900.
Hours at the Altar: or, Meditations on the Holy Eucharist, Dublin: James Duffy, 1855.
Hymns and Poems Original and Translated, 2nd edn, London: Printed by Spottiswoode & Co., 1872.
Hymns and Poems Original and Translated, new edn with Biographical Preface by Edward Bellasis, London: Burns & Oates, 1908.
Letter to 'George,' 15 March 1847, reprinted in *The Oratory Parish Magazine*, n.d.
Love for Holy Church, from the French of M. l'Abbé Petit. London: Richardson & Son, 1862.
Lyra Catholica: Containing All the Breviary and Missal Hymns with Others from Various Sources, London: James Burns, 1849.
A May Pageant and Other Poems, London: Burns, Lambert, & Co., 1865.
The Masque of Mary and Other Poems, London: Burns & Oates Ltd., 1858.
Morals from the Churchyard in a Series of Cheerful Fables, with illustrations by H. K. Browne, London: Chapman & Hall, 1838.
[Scriblerus Redivivus.] *A New Art teaching how to be Plucked, being a Treatise after the fashion of Aristotle; writ for the use of Students in the Universities. To which is added a Synopsis of Drinking*, 11th edn, Oxford: J. Vincent, 1864.
'The Oxonian', Various articles published in *The New Casket*, Oxford, 1833.
Poems, London: Thomas Richardson & Son, 1861.
Sermons on the Seen and Unseen, London: James Burns, 1846.

[Quiz.] *Sketches of Young Gentlemen*, London: Chapman & Hall, 1838.

[Quiz.] *Sketches of Young Ladies in which These Interesting Members of the Animal Kingdom Are Classified according to Their Several Instincts, Habits, and General Characteristics*, London: Chapman & Hall, 1837.

Verba Verbi: The Words of Jesus, arranged in Order of Time, as a Daily Companion Epitome of the Gospel, and Treasury of Mental Prayer, London: Burns & Lambert, 1855.

Other Hymn Collections

Appendix to the Hymnal Noted, revised and greatly enlarged. 3rd edn, London: G.J. Palmer, 1867.

Bickersteth, E. H., ed. *The Hymnal Companion to the Book of Common Prayer*. Annotated edition, with introduction and notes. London: Sampson Low, Son, & Marston, 1870.

The Catholic Hymnal. Hymns selected for public and private use, 1st edn, London: Burns & Lambert, 1860.

Chandler, John. *Hymns of the Primitive Church: Now first collected, translated, and arranged*. London: John W. Parker, 1837.

Choix de Cantiques sur des airs nouveaux pour toutes les fêtes de l'année. À 3 et 4 voix, avec accompagnement d'orgue ou de piano par le Père L. Lambillotte, Paris: Libraire de Mme Ve Poussielque-Rusaud, 1855.

Chope, Revd R. R. *The Congregational Hymn and Tune Book, containing three hundred different four-part tunes, with their hymns, ancient and modern*, London: Mackenzie, ca. 1862 (First edition 1857).

Copeland, William John. *Hymns for the Week, and Hymns for the Seasons translated from the Latin*, London: W. J. Cleaver & John Henry Parker, 1848.

Faber, Frederick William. *Hymns*. New York: E. P. Dutton, 1882.

Formby, Revd H., and J. Lambert, eds. *Collection of Catholic Hymns for the use of Choirs and Congregations*, London: Burns & Lambert, 1853.

Hymns Ancient and Modern for Use in the Services of the Church with Accompanying Tunes, Compiled and Arranged under the Musical Editorship of William Henry Monk. London: Novello; Philadelphia: Lippincott, 1861.

Mant, Richard, DD *Ancient Hymns from the Roman Breviary for Domestic Use, to which are added original hymns*, new edn, London: Rivingtons, 1871.

Neale, Revd John Mason. *Mediaeval Hymns and Sequences*, London: Joseph Masters, 1851.

Nelson, Earl [Horatio], ed. *The Salisbury Hymn-Book*. Salisbury: Brown & Co.; London: Simpkin, Marshall, & Co., 1857.

Oldknow, Dr Joseph, ed. *Hymns for the Service of the Church, arranged according to the Seasons and Holy-days of the Christian Year*, Second thousand, London: J. Masters; Birmingham, B.H. Leather, 1854. (First edn, 1850.)

Palmer, Roundell, ed. *The Book of Praise from the Best English Hymn Writers*, selected and arranged by Roundell Palmer, London: Macmillan & Co., 1867.

Shipley, Orby. *Lyra Messianica: Hymns and Verses on the Life of Christ, Ancient and Modern; with Other Poems*, London: Longman, Green, Longman, Roberts, & Green, 1864.

——. *Lyra Eucharistica: Hymns and Verses on the Holy Communion, Ancient and Modern; with Other Poems*, 2nd edn London: Longman, Green, Longman, Roberts, & Green, 1864.

——. *Annus Sanctus: Hymns of the Church for the Ecclesiastical Year*. vol. 1, *Seasons of the Church: Canonical Hours: and Hymns of Our Lord*, London and New York: Burns & Oates, 1884.

Spurgeon, Charles Haddon, compiler. *Our Own Hymn Book. A Collection of Psalms and Hymns for Public, Social, and Private Worship*, 2nd edn London: Passmore & Alabaster, 1867.

Walker, Henry Ashton, mus. edn *Music of the Appendix to the Hymnal Noted*, London: Novello, Ewer & Co., ca. 1867.

Williams, Isaac. *Hymns Translated from the Paris Breviary*, London: J.G.F. & J. Rivington, 1839.

Young, Revd Alfred, *Catholic Hymns and Canticles, together with A Complete Sodality Manual*, 3rd edn New York: D. & J. Sadlier & Co., 1866.

Young, William, ed. *The Catholic Choralist. For the Use of the Choir, Drawing Room, Cloister, and Cottage, harmonized and arranged for voice, band, piano forte, organ*. Dublin: Catholic Choralist Office, 1842.

Other Works

Abercrombie, Lascelles. *Romanticism*, New York, 1963.

Abrams, M.H. *Natural Supernaturalism: Tradition and Revolution in Romantic Literature*, London: W.W. Norton & Company, 1971.

Adamson, John William. *English Education 1789–1902*, Cambridge: At the University Press, 1930.

Allies, Thomas William. *A Life's Decision*. 2nd edn, London: Burns & Oates Ltd., 1894, originally published 1880.

Allitt, Patrick. *Catholic Converts: British and American Intellectuals Turn to Rome*, Ithaca and London: Cornell University Press, 1997.

Alumni Oxonienses: The Members of the University of Oxford, 1715–1886. Being the Matriculation Register of the University. Alphabetically arranged, revised, and annotated by Joseph Foster, vol. 1, *Later Series*. Oxford: James Parker & Co., 1891.

Aubin, Robert Arnold. *Topographical Poetry in XVIII-Century England*. New York: The Modern Language Association of America, 1936, Reprint, 1966.

Bellasis, Edward. 'Biographical Preface' in Edward Caswall, *Hymns and Poems Original and Translated*, London: Burns & Oates, 1908.

Best, Geoffrey. *Mid-Victorian Britain 1851–1875*, New York: Schocken Books, 1972.

Book of Common Prayer. London: R. and A. Suttaby, *c.* 1868.

The Book of Common Prayer, New York: The Church Hymnal Corporation and The Seabury Press, 1977.

Bowden, John Edward. *Life and Letters of Frederick William Faber, DD,* London: Burns & Oates Ltd.; New York: Benziger Bros., 1869.

Bradley, Ian. *Abide with Me: The World of Victorian Hymns*, London: SCM Press, 1997.

Briggs, Asa. *The Making of Modern England 1783–1867: The Age of Improvement*, New York: Harper Torchbooks, 1965.

Britt, Matthew, OSB, ed. *The Hymns of the Breviary and Missal*, New York: Benziger Brothers, 1924.

Burgess, Thomas. *Tracts on the Divinity of Christ, and on the Repeal of the Statute against Blasphemy*, London: Printed for J. Hatchard & Son, 1820.

——. *Tracts on the Origin and Independence of the Ancient British Church; on the Supremacy of the Pope, and the Inconsistency of All Foreign Jurisdiction with the British Constitution; and on the Differences between the Churches of England and of Rome*, 2nd edn, with additions. London: Printed for F.C. & J. Rivington, 1815.

Byrne, Maurice. 'The Church Band at Swalcliffe,' *Oxoniensia* 28 (1963): p. 79.

Chadwick, Owen. *The Victorian Church*, London: Adam & Charles Black, 1970.

Chapman, Ronald. *Father Faber*, Westminster, Md.: The Newman Press, 1961.

Church of St Philip Neri Smethwick: Souvenir Booklet of Consecration Day (June 25, 1936).

Collinson, Patrick. *The Religion of Protestants: The Church in English Society 1559–1625*, Oxford: Clarendon, 1982.

Countryman, William. *The Poetic Imagination: An Anglican Spiritual Tradition*, Maryknoll, N.Y.: Orbis Books, 1999.

Cox, G. V. *Recollections of Oxford*, London: Macmillan & Co., 1868.

Crittall, Elizabeth. ed. *A History of Wiltshire*, vol. 6, London: Published for the Institute of Historical Research by Oxford University Press, 1962.

Crowley, D.A., ed. *History of the County of Wiltshire*, vol. 15, *Amesbury Hundred and Part of Branch and Dale Hundred*, Oxford: Oxford University Press, 1995.

Crossley, Alan, ed. *A History of the County of Oxford*, vol. 10, *Banbury Hundred*, London: Published for the Institute of Historical Research by Oxford University Press, 1962.

Delaney, John J. *Pocket Dictionary of Saints*, abridged edition, New York: Doubleday Image, 1983.

Dictionary of National Biography, edited by Sir Leslie Stephen and Sir Sidney Lee, Oxford and New York: Oxford University Press, 1908–1909, reprinted 1959–60.

Drain, Susan. *The Anglican Church in Nineteenth-Century Britain: Hymns Ancient and Modern (1860–1875)*, Texts and Studies in Religion 40, Lewiston, Lampeter, and Queenston: Edwin Mellen Press, 1989.

Faber, Frederick William. *Sights and Thoughts in Foreign Churches and among Foreign Peoples,* London: J.G.F. & J. Rivington, 1842.

Fairchild, Hoxie Neale. *Religious Trends in English Poetry,* vol. 4, *1830–1880, Christianity and Romanticism in the Victorian Era*, New York and London: Columbia University Press, 1964.

Frost, Maurice. *Historical Companion to Hymns Ancient and Modern*, London: Printed for the Proprietors by William Clowes & Sons, Ltd., 1962.

Gill, Conrad. *History of Birmingham.* vol. 1, *Manor and Borough to 1865*, London and New York: Oxford University Press, 1952.

Gilley, Sheridan. *Newman and His Age*, Westminster, Md.: Christian Classics, 1990.

Harford, John S., Esq., DCL, FRS. *The Life of Thomas Burgess, D.D., F.R.S., F.A.S. &c. &c. &c., Late Lord Bishop of Salisbury*, 2nd edn London: Printed for Longman, Orme, Brown, Green, & Longmans, 1841.

The HarperCollins Study Bible. New York: HarperCollins, 1993.

Heimann, Mary. *Catholic Devotion in Victorian England*, Oxford: Clarendon Press, 1995.

Hicks, Charles. *A Walk through Smethwick: A Sketch of Its General*

Aspects and Its Prospects. A Lecture delivered April 1850 in the British School Rooms, Smethwick, Birmingham: Guest, Allen, n.d.

Houghton, Edward. *The Handmaid of Piety and Other Papers on Charles Wesley's Hymns*, The Wesley Fellowship, 1992.

Johnson, Margaret. *Gerard Manley Hopkins and Tractarian Poetry*, Aldershot, England, and Brookfield, VT: Ashgate, 1997.

Keble, John. *The Christian Year*, New York: E.P. Dutton & Co., 1869.

———. *On the Mysticism Attributed to the Early Fathers of the Church, Tracts for the Times* no. 89. Oxford, 1868.

Ker, Ian. *John Henry Newman: A Biography*, Oxford and New York: Oxford University Press, 1988.

Lyra Apostolica. London: Rivingtons, 1879.

Maclure, J. Stuart. *Educational Documents: England and Wales 1816–1968.* London: Methuen Educational Ltd., 1965. 2nd edn, 1968, reprint, 1969, 1971.

McClelland, V. Alan. '"The Most Turbulent Priest of the Oxford Diocese": Thomas William Allies and the Quest for Authority 1837–1850' in *By Whose Authority? Newman, Manning and the Magisterium*, ed. V. Alan McClelland, Bath: Downside Abbey, 1996.

Memoirs of the Caswall Family, privately printed, n.d.

Miller, Josiah, MA. *Singers and Songs of the Church: Being Biographical Sketches of the Hymn-Writers in All the Principal Collections*, 2nd edn, London: Longmans, Green, & Co., 1869.

Milner, John. *The End of Religious Controversy in a Friendly Correspondence between a* Religious Society of Protestants and a Roman Catholic Divine. *Addressed to the Rt. Rev. Dr. Burgess, Lord Bishop of St. David's, in answer to His Lordship's PROTESTANT'S CATECHISM*, New York: D. & J. Sadlier, 1844.

Mozley, Dorothea, ed. *Newman Family Letters*, London: SPCK, 1962.

Mozley, Tom. *Reminiscences, Chiefly of Oriel College and the Oxford Movement*, 2 vols. London: Longmans, Green, 1882.

Murray, Placid. *Newman the Oratorian*, Dublin: Gill and MacMillan, 1969.

Newman, John Henry. *The Letters and Diaries of John Henry Newman*, vol. xii, edited by Charles Stephen Dessain, London and New York: Thomas Nelson & Sons, 1962; vol. xiii, edited by Charles Stephen Dessain. London & New York: Thomas Nelson & Sons, 1963; vol. xiv, edited by Charles Stephen Dessain and Vincent Ferrer Blehl, SJ, London and New York: Thomas Nelson & Sons, 1963; vol. xvi, edited by Charles Stephen Dessain, London: Thomas Nelson & Sons Ltd., 1965; vol. xxviii, edited by Charles

Stephen Dessain and Thomas Gornall, SJ, Oxford: Clarendon Press, 1975. Referred to in Notes as LD.

——. *Meditations and Devotions of the late Cardinal Newman*, London: Longmans, Green & Co., 1893.

———. 'On the Roman Breviary as Embodying the Substance of the Devotional Services of the Church Catholic,' Tract 75 in *Tracts for the Times by Members of the University of Oxford*, vol. 3, *For 1835–6*, new edn, London: Printed for J.G.F. & J. Rivington, 1840.

Newsome, David. *The Convert Cardinals: Newman and Manning*, London: John Murray Ltd., 1993.

———. *The Parting of Friends: The Wilberforces and Henry Manning*, Grand Rapids, Mich.: William B. Eerdmans; Leominster, Gracewing, 1966.

Nockles, Peter. 'Sources of English Conversions to Roman Catholicism in the Era of the Oxford Movement' in V.A. McClelland, ed., *By Whose Authority? Newman, Manning and the Magisterium*, Bath: Downside Abbey, 1996.

Pugh, R.B. 'Stratford-sub-Castle' in Elizabeth Crittall, ed., *A History of Wiltshire*, vol. 6, London: Published for the Institute of Historical Research by Oxford University Press, 1962.

Routley, Eric. *The Music of Christian Hymns*, Chicago, IL: G.I.A. Publications, 1981.

Rowell, Geoffrey. *Hell and the Victorians*, Oxford: Clarendon Press, 1974.

——. 'John Keble: A Speaking Life' in Charles R. Henery, ed., *A Speaking Life: The Legacy of John Keble*, Leominster, England: Gracewing/Fowler Wright Books, 1995.

Russell, Dr. Review of Caswall's *Lyra Catholica*, *Dublin Review* 26, no. 52 (June 1849): pp. 300–315.

[St John, Ambrose.] *The Raccolta: or, Collection of Indulgenced Prayers*, Authorized translation by Ambrose St John, London: Burns & Lambert, 1857.

Sturt, Mary. *The Education of the People: A History of Primary Education in England and Wales in the Nineteenth Century*, London: Routledge & Kegan Paul, 1967, reprint, 1970.

Sugg, Joyce. *Ever Yours Affly: John Henry Newman and His Female Circle,* Leominster, England: Gracewing, 1996.

Tennyson, G B. *Victorian Devotional Poetry: The Tractarian Mode*, Cambridge, Mass., and London: Harvard University Press, 1981.

Trevor, Meriol. *Newman: The Pillar of the Cloud* [to 1853]. Garden City, New York: Doubleday, 1962.

——. *Newman: Light in Winter*, London: Macmillan, 1962.

Watson, J.R. *The English Hymn: A Critical and Historical Study*. Oxford: Clarendon Press, 1999.

Windle, Bertram C.A. *Who's Who of the Oxford Movement*, New York and London: The Century Company, 1926.

Index